Modern Chinese Complex Sentences II

This book is the second volume of a four-volume set on modern Chinese complex sentences, with a focus on coordinate complex sentences and their relevant forms.

Complex sentences in modern Chinese are unique in formation and meaning. The author proposes a tripartite classification of Chinese complex sentences according to the semantic relationships between the clauses, that is, coordinate, causal, and adversative. This volume analyzes the coordinate type in the broad sense and the relevant forms, including the representative form in which the clauses are juxtaposed with each other, paired and single occurrences of the connective *yībiān*, and various forms of successive, progressive, and alternative complex sentences, as well as the compound forms.

The book will be a useful reference for scholars and learners interested in Chinese grammar and language information processing.

XING Fuyi is a renowned Chinese linguist and a senior professor at Central China Normal University. He has been devoted to the studies of modern Chinese grammar and has initiated the clause-pivotal approach to modern Chinese grammar studies. His other major publications include *Modern Chinese Grammar: A Clause-Pivot Approach* and *Three Hundred Qs & As about Chinese Grammar*.

Chinese Linguistics

Chinese Linguistics series selects representative and frontier works in linguistic disciplines including lexicology, grammar, phonetics, dialectology, philology and rhetoric. Mostly published in Chinese before, the selection has had far-reaching influence on China's linguistics and offered inspiration and reference for the world's linguistics. The aim of this series is to reflect the general level and latest development of Chinese linguistics from an overall and objective view.

Titles in this series currently include:

Modern Chinese Complex Sentences II
Coordinate Type
XING Fuyi

A Brief History of the Chinese Language IV
Old Chinese Lexicon
Xi Xiang

A Brief History of the Chinese Language V
Middle Chinese Lexicon 1
Xi Xiang

A Brief History of the Chinese Language VI
Middle Chinese Lexicon 2
Xi Xiang

A Brief History of the Chinese Language VII
Modern Chinese Lexicon 1
Xi Xiang

A Brief History of the Chinese Language VIII
Modern Chinese Lexicon 2
Xi Xiang

For more information, please visit www.routledge.com/Chinese-Linguistics/book-series/CL

Modern Chinese Complex Sentences II
Coordinate Type

XING Fuyi

LONDON AND NEW YORK

This book is published with financial support from the Chinese Fund for Humanities and Social Sciences.

First published in English 2023
by Routledge
4 Park Square, Milton Park, Abingdon, Oxon OX14 4RN

and by Routledge
605 Third Avenue, New York, NY 10158

Routledge is an imprint of the Taylor & Francis Group, an informa business

© 2023 XING Fuyi

Translated by WANG Yuhong, YI Honggen

The right of XING Fuyi to be identified as author of this work has been asserted in accordance with sections 77 and 78 of the Copyright, Designs and Patents Act 1988.

All rights reserved. No part of this book may be reprinted or reproduced or utilised in any form or by any electronic, mechanical, or other means, now known or hereafter invented, including photocopying and recording, or in any information storage or retrieval system, without permission in writing from the publishers.

Trademark notice: Product or corporate names may be trademarks or registered trademarks, and are used only for identification and explanation without intent to infringe.

English version by permission of The Commercial Press

British Library Cataloguing-in-Publication Data
A catalogue record for this book is available from the British Library

ISBN: 978-1-032-42301-2 (hbk)
ISBN: 978-1-032-42303-6 (pbk)
ISBN: 978-1-003-36216-6 (ebk)

DOI: 10.4324/9781003362166

Typeset in Times New Roman
by Apex CoVantage, LLC

Contents

Tables		vi
Abbreviations		vii
1	"*jì p, yòu q*" and relevant forms	1
2	Paired and single occurrences of the connective *yībiān*	37
3	"*p, jiēzhe q*" and relevant forms	65
4	"*bùdàn p, érqiě q*" and relevant forms	84
5	"(*huòzhě*) *p, huòzhě q*" and relevant forms	117
6	"*yàome p, yàome q*" and relevant forms	130
7	Varieties of "*yī p, jiù q*"	152
Appendix		189
Index		191

Tables

2.1	Statistics of Group A	38
2.2	Statistics of Group B	39
2.3	Statistics of Group C	39

Abbreviations

BA	*bǎ*
CL	classifier (e.g., *gè, zhāng*)
COMP	comparative marker, *bǐ*
COP	copula (*shì*)
EXP	experiential aspect (e.g., *guò*)
LOC	localizer (e.g., *shàng, lǐ*)
MP	modal particle (e.g., *le, ma, ne, ba*)
NEG	negative element (e.g., *bù*)
NP	nominal phrase
PAP	para-aspect marker (e.g., *suǒ, gěi*)
PASSIVE	passive marker (e.g., *bèi*)
PEF	perfective marker (e.g., *le*)
PL	plural marker (e.g., *men*)
PRG	progressive aspect marker (e.g., *zhe*)
CM	complement marker (e.g., *dào*)
REDP	reduplication
SP	structural particle (e.g., *de*)
ONO	onomatopoeia
INJ	interjection
DC	directional complement (e.g., *lái*)

1 "*jì p, yòu q*" and relevant forms

In this chapter, "*jì p, yòu q*" is chosen as the representative form of complex sentences in which the clauses are juxtaposed with each other (hereafter referred to as coordinate complex sentences). Each of the first seven sections of this chapter is devoted to the discussion of a relevant form: (1) "*jì p, yòu q*"; (2) "*jì p, yě q*"; (3) "*yòu p, yòu q*"; (4) "*yě p, yě q*"; (5) "*yībiān p, yībiān q*"; (6) "*yīmiàn p, yīmiàn q*"; and (7) "*yī fāngmiàn p, lìng yī fāngmiàn q.*" The last section presents other forms of coordinate sentences.

1.1 "*jì p, yòu q*"

The form of "*jì p, yòu q*" is the representative of coordinate sentences, and the paired conjunction "*jì . . . yòu . . .*" is a typical marker for coordinate sentences.

1.1.1 Linguistic form

In sentences in the form of "*jì p, yòu q*," *p* and *q* usually have the same or similar numbers of syllables, and are consistent in form—both are affirmative or negative. In the following two examples, the anterior and posterior clauses are both in the affirmative form.

(1) 赵汉中<u>既</u>是严师，<u>又</u>是慈母。
    Zhào Hànzhōng <u>jì</u>. . . <u>yòu</u>. . . shì yánshī, <u>yòu</u> shì cí mǔ.
    ZHAO Hanzhong both . . . and . . . COP strict teacher COP loving mother
    {ZHAO Hanzhong is both a strict teacher and a loving mother.}

(2) 她的小说和散文的文采<u>既</u>融化了古典文学的神韵，<u>又</u>融合了欧美文学的乳汁，……
    Tā de xiǎoshuō hé sǎnwén de wéncǎi <u>jì</u>. . . <u>yòu</u>. . .
    she SP novel and literary prose SP literary style both . . . and . . .
    rónghuà-le gǔdiǎn wénxué de shényùn, <u>yòu</u> rónghé-le
    assimilate-PEF classical literature SP charm absorb -PEF
    ōuměi wénxué de rǔzhī, . . .
    European and American literature SP milk
    {The style of her novels and prose assimilated the charm of classical literature, and absorbed nutrients from European and American literature as well . . . }

DOI: 10.4324/9781003362166-1

2 *"jì p, yòu q" and relevant forms*

In the following two examples, the anterior and posterior clauses are both in the negative form:

(3) 那些人<u>既</u>不许他外出就诊，<u>又</u>不准医生登门。
Nàxiē rén <u>jì</u>... <u>yòu</u>... bù xǔ tā wàichū jiùzhěn, <u>yòu</u> bù
those person both...and... NEG allow him go out see a doctor NEG
zhǔn yīshēng dēngmén.
allow doctor call at someone's house
{Those people didn't allow him to visit a doctor, nor did they allow any doctors to visit him.}

(4) （干这一行，他手脚笨拙。）包出的饺子，<u>既</u>不漂亮，<u>又</u>不牢实。
(Gàn zhè yī háng, tā shǒujiǎo bènzhuō.) Bāo-chū de jiǎozi
do this one job his movement clumsy wrap SP dumpling
<u>jì</u>... <u>yòu</u>... bù piàoliang, <u>yòu</u> bù láoshi.
both...and... NEG pretty NEG firm
{[He is clumsy at this type of work.] The dumplings he makes are neither pretty nor firm.}

However, there are instances in which *jì* and *yòu* are followed by different numbers of syllables or one clause is affirmative in form and the other is negative, as in the following example:

(5) 她的服饰全部接近年龄的底线，<u>既</u>不到刺眼的程度，<u>又</u>显得年轻大方。
Tā de fúshì quánbù jiējìn niánlíng de dǐxiàn,
she SP clothing and accessories all be close to age SP lower limit
<u>jì</u>... <u>yòu</u>... bù dào cìyǎn de chéngdù, <u>yòu</u> xiǎn de niánqīng dàfang.
both...and... NEG reach flashy SP extent look SP young elegant
{As all her clothes and accessories are close to the lower age limit, she looks young and elegant but not flashy in them.}

Sentences in the form of "*jì p, yòu q*" often consist of two coordinate clauses, but they can be expanded to include three or more. In that case, *tóngshí* ('meanwhile') or *hái* ('besides') can be added to the sentence, such as "*jì ... yòu ... tóngshí ...*" or "*jì ... yòu ... hái ...*". The following are two examples:

(6) 郑国荃夫妇对于他，<u>既</u>敬重，<u>又</u>感恩，<u>同时</u>倾注羡慕之心。
Zhèng Guóquán fūfù duìyú tā, <u>jì</u>... <u>yòu</u>
ZHENG Guoquan husband and wife to him both...and...
jìngzhòng, <u>yòu</u> gǎn'ēn, <u>tóngshí</u> qīngzhù xiànmù zhī xīn.
respect feel grateful meanwhile be filled with envy SP feeling
{ZHENG Guoquan and his wife are respectful and grateful to him, and meanwhile full of envy.}

(7) 既门当户对，又才貌双全，还加上个专业对口——两人都是搞环保工作的。
 Jì...yòu... méndāng-hùduì, yòu cáimào-shuāngquán
 both...and... families are equal in social rank be talented and good looking
 hái jiāshàng gè zhuānyè duìkǒu —liǎng rén dōu shì gǎo
 besides furthermore CL specialty be the same field two person both COP do
 huánbǎo gōngzuò de.
 environment protection work SP
 {The two of them come from families equal in social rank, and both of them are talented and good-looking, and besides, they have the same specialty—they are both in the field of environmental protection.}

1.1.2 Logical basis

Sentences in the form of "*jì p, yòu q*" have two types of logical basis.

First, *p* and *q* are intrinsically coordinate. The conjunctions *jì* and *yòu* are used to explicate the coordination. The following are four examples:

(8) ……在那里既能得到理解，又能得到照顾。
 ...zài nàli jì...yòu... néng dédào lǐjiě, yòu néng
 at there both...and... can get understanding can
 dédào zhàogù.
 get look after
 {...There (someone) can be both understood and looked after.}

(9) 它分布广、材质好、用途多，既适合四旁绿化和成片造林，又是华北、中原广大地区实行农田林网化和农桐间作的好树种，……
 Tā fēnbù guǎng, cáizhì hǎo, yòngtú duō, jì...yòu... shìhé
 it be distributed widely texture good use many both...and... suit
 sìpáng lǜhuà hé chéngpiàn-zàolín, yòu shì
 environs of four different types of places green and afforest COP
 huáběi, zhōngyuán guǎngdà dìqū shíxíng nóngtián-línwǎnghuà hé
 North China Central Plains vast area practice agroforestry and
 nóngtóng-jiànzuò de hǎo shùzhǒng, ...
 interplanting of tung trees and crops SP good tree species
 {It (Paulownia) is widely distributed. Because of its fine texture, it can be used for a variety of purposes. It is not only suitable for the greening of land next to houses, villages, roads and waters, and afforestation, but also a good species for agroforestry and being interplanted with crops in the vast areas in northern and central China...}

(10) 当时她既不可能与工农结合，又缺乏先进思想的武装，（只能以自己"美满"的家庭中的"亲子之爱"作为灵药，推荐给当时患有时代病的青年，……）
 Dāngshí tā jì...yòu... bù kěnéng yǔ gōng nóng jiéhé, yòu quēfá
 tack then she both...and... NEG may into worker farmer integrate lack
 xiānjìn sīxiǎng de wǔzhuāng, (zhǐ néng yǐ zìjǐ "měimǎn" de
 advanced ideology SP equipment only can with oneself perfect SP
 jiātíng-zhōng de "qīnzǐ zhī ài" zuòwéi língyào, tuījiàn gěi
 in family SP parents and children SP love regard...as panacea recommend to

dāngshí   huànyǒu   shídàibìng
back then suffer from people's common problems characteristic of the time
de   qīngnián,...)
SP   youth
{Back then, it was impossible for her to be integrated into the working class, nor was she equipped with the advanced ideological weapons, [but could only recommend the "parents' love for their children" in the perfect family of hers, which she regarded as a panacea, to the youth who were suffering from the common "diseases" characteristic of that time...]}

(11) 食物就是一种能够构成躯体和供应能量的物质，……它们<u>既</u>能构成躯体，<u>又</u>能在呼吸时被氧化而放出能量。

Shíwù jiù shì yī zhǒng nénggòu gòuchéng qūtǐ hé gōngyìng néngliàng de
food just COP one type can make up body and provide energy SP
wùzhì,... tā-men <u>jì</u>...<u>yòu</u>... néng gòuchéng qūtǐ, <u>yòu</u> néng zài shí
substance they both...and... can make up body can when
hūxī shí bèi yǎnghuà ér fàngchū néngliàng.
breathe PASSIVE oxidize and release energy
{Food is a substance that can make up the body and provide energy... They (the substances) can both form the body and be oxidized to release energy during respiration.}

Second, *p* and *q* are inherently adversative. The conjunctions *jì* and *yòu* are used to transform the adversative relationship into a coordinate one; thus, a coordinate complex sentence is formed. In other words, the inherent adversative relationship is transformed with a coordinate marker under the speaker's subjective will; therefore, the relationship between the clauses is marked as coordinate. The following are five examples:

(12) 韩成贵心里很复杂，他<u>既</u>是望子成龙，<u>又</u>不想全家一古脑进城。

Hán Chéngguì xīn-li hěn fùzá, tā <u>jì</u>...<u>yòu</u>... shì
HAN Chenggui in heart very complicated he both...and... COP
wàngzǐ-chénglóng, <u>yòu</u> bù xiǎng quán jiā yīgǔnǎo
have high hopes for one's child NEG want whole family all at the same time
jìn chéng.
enter town
{HAN Chenggui has conflicting thoughts. He has high hopes for his child(ren), and meanwhile, he does not want everyone in his family to move into town at the same time.}

(13) 我荣升"大姐级"的同时，<u>既</u>为自己是公司的元老而自豪，<u>又</u>暗暗感慨时光不饶人。

Wǒ róngshēng "dàjiě jí" de tóngshí, <u>jì</u>...<u>yòu</u>... wèi zìjǐ shì
I promote big sister level SP at the same time both...and... for oneself COP
gōngsī de yuánlǎo ér zìháo, <u>yòu</u> àn-àn gǎnkǎi shíguāng bù
company SP senior staff therefore proud secretly sigh time NEG
ráo rén.
spare person

"jì p, yòu q" and relevant forms

{When I was promoted to the "Big Sister" Level, I not only felt proud of being a senior staff member in the company but also secretly lamented that time spares no one becoming old.}

(14) 这使我<u>既</u>感到欣慰，<u>又</u>体会到某种凄凉。
Zhè shǐ wǒ <u>jì</u> <u>yòu</u> gǎndào xīnwèi, <u>yòu</u> tǐhuì-dào mǒu zhǒng qīliáng.
this make me both...and... feel gratified realize certain type desolate
{It made me feel both relieved and somewhat desolate.}

(15) 我无意贬低我的生身母亲，因而我在20几年的曲折生活中，对母亲这一概念<u>既</u>熟悉，<u>又</u>陌生。
Wǒ wúyì biǎndī wǒ de shēngshēn mǔqīn, yīn'ér wǒ zài èrshí-jǐ nián de qūzhé shēnghuó-zhōng, duì mǔqīn zhè yī gàiniàn <u>jì</u> <u>yòu</u> shúxī, <u>yòu</u> mòshēng.
I have no intention belittle I SP biological mother therefore I during more than twenty year SP complicated in life with mother this one concept both...and... familiar unfamiliar
{I have no intention of belittling my biological mother ... so the concept of mother was both familiar and strange to me during my complicated life of more than 20 years.}

(16) 你真的疯狂就好了，红娣也会这样想的。可惜，你<u>既</u>疯狂，<u>又</u>不疯狂！
Nǐ zhēnde fēngkuáng jiù hǎo le, Hóngdì yě huì zhèyàng xiǎng de. kěxī, nǐ <u>jì</u> <u>yòu</u> fēngkuáng, <u>yòu</u> bù fēngkuáng!
you really crazy then good MP Hongdi also will so think MP unfortunately you both...and... crazy NEG crazy
{I wish you were really crazy, and so does Hongdi. Unfortunately, you are both crazy and sensible!}

All "*jì . . . yòu . . .*" sentences with an inherent adversative relationship between *p* and *q* allow the occurrence of adversative words, for example, *dàn*, that is, "*jì . . . dàn yòu . . .*" sentences. Detailed analysis can be found in Chapter 3, Volume III.

1.2 "*jì p, yě q*"

"*jì p, yě q*" is also a form of coordinate complex sentences in which the two clauses are coordinate.

1.2.1 Linguistic form

In sentences in the form of "*jì p, yě q*," *p* and *q* usually have the same or approximately the same number of syllables and are consistent in form; that is, both are affirmative or negative. The following are two examples:

(17) 小屋的光线<u>既</u>富于科学的时间性，<u>也</u>富于浪漫的文学性。
Xiǎo wū de guāngxiàn <u>jì</u> <u>yě</u> fùyú kēxué de
small room SP light both...and... be rich in science SP

6 *"jì p, yòu q" and relevant forms*

        shíjiānxìng,   yě   fùyú   làngmàn   de   wénxuéxìng.
        time-related characteristics be rich in romance SP literariness
        {The light in the cabin changes with time. This change is not only a scientific phenomenon but also adds a touch of romantic literature to the cabin.}

(18)   这些话<u>既</u>激怒了他，<u>也</u>提醒了他。
        Zhèxiē huà   <u>jì</u>...<u>yě</u>...   jīnù-le   tā,   yě   tíxǐng-le   tā.
        these   words both...and... infuriate-PEF him   remind-PEF him
        {These words both infuriated and reminded him.}

The anterior and posterior clauses in (17) and (18) are both in the positive form. The following are three more examples:

(19)   ……那匹白马仍孤零零地呆立在原先的位置上，<u>既</u>不吃草，<u>也</u>不挪动。
        ...Nà pǐ bái mǎ réng gūlínglíng de dāi lì zài yuánxiān de
        that CL white horse still alone SP dully stand at original SP
        wèizhì-shàng, <u>jì</u>...<u>yě</u>... bù chī cǎo, yě bù nuódòng.
        on spot both...and... NEG eat grass NEG move
        {The white horse remained alone on the same spot, neither eating grass nor moving.}

(20)   （听到这个消息，大家态度都很淡漠，）<u>既</u>说不上惋惜，<u>也</u>谈不上高兴。
        (Tīngdào zhè gè xiāoxi, dàjiā tàidù dōu hěn dànmò,) <u>jì</u>...<u>yě</u>...
        hear this CL news everyone attitude all very indifferent both...and...
        shuōbùshàng   wǎnxī, yě tánbùshàng   gāoxìng.
        not have reached the extent of sympathetic not have reached the extent of pleased
        {[After hearing the news, everyone was indifferent,] neither sympathetic nor pleased.}

(21)   她<u>既</u>没有到过水暖班，<u>也</u>没有见过管子钳工。
        Tā <u>jì</u>...<u>yě</u>... méiyǒu dào-guò shuǐnuǎn bān, yě méiyǒu jiàn-guò
        she both...and... NEG go to-EXP plumbing team NEG see-EXP
        guǎnzi qiángōng.
        pipe bench worker
        {She has never been to the plumbing team's place, nor has she seen any plumbers or bench workers.}

In each of the three examples above, the anterior and posterior clauses are both in the negative form.

However, there are instances where one clause is affirmative and the other is negative in form. The following are two examples:

(22)   她的回答和态度，都是鲜明的，<u>既</u>平和、礼貌，<u>也</u>不虚套、迁就。
        Tā de huídá hé tàidù, dōu shì xiānmíng de, <u>jì</u>...<u>yě</u>... pínghé,
        she SP reply and attitude both COP clear MP both...and... gentle
        lǐmào, yě bù xūtào, qiānjiù.
        polite NEG empty accommodating
        {Both her reply and attitude are clear: gentle but polite and not empty or accommodating.}

(23) 对于我的旅行，次仁旺堆<u>既</u>表示了理解，<u>也</u>没忘行使他的 "有权"。
Duìyú wǒ de lǚxíng, Cìrénwàngduī <u>jì</u>...<u>yě</u>... biǎoshì-le lǐjiě, <u>yě</u>
for I SP travel Cirenwangdui both...and... show-PEF understand
méi wàng xíngshǐ tā de "yǒu quán".
NEG forget exercise he SP Have right
{Cirenwangdui showed his understanding of my travel and did not forget to exercise his "rights."}

In the examples above, *tóngshí* can be present, that is, "*jì* ... *tóngshí yě* ... ," for example:

(24) 此行，<u>既</u>是为了走访新疆，<u>同时也</u>是为了挺进新藏路。
Cǐ xíng, <u>jì</u>...<u>yě</u>... shì wèile zǒufǎng Xīnjiāng, <u>tóngshí</u>
this trip both...and... COP for the purpose of visit Xinjiang meanwhile
<u>yě</u> shì wèile tǐngjìn Xīnzàng lù.
COP for the purpose of press on Xinjiang–Tibet Highway
{The purpose of this trip is to visit Xinjiang and to press on to the Xinjiang–Tibet Highway, too.}

Usually, the anterior and posterior clauses share the same subject. And in this case, the subject precedes *jì* in the anterior clause but is absent in the posterior clause. However, there are cases in which the two clauses each have their own subjects. If so, the two subjects respectively precede *jì* and *yě*, as in the following two examples:

(25) 房钱<u>既</u>拿不出来，饭钱<u>也</u>没着落。
Fángqián <u>jì</u>...<u>yě</u>... ná bù chūlái, ***fànqián*** <u>yě</u>
rent both...and... cannot get something out money for food
méi zháoluò.
there not be reliable source
{There is no money to pay the rent, nor has the money for food been secured.}

(26) 我<u>既</u>习惯别人这样来评论我，我<u>也</u>习惯这样看待生活。
Wǒ <u>jì</u>...<u>yě</u>... xíguàn biérén zhèyàng lái pínglùn wǒ, ***wǒ*** <u>yě</u>
I both...and... be used to other people this to comment me I
xíguàn zhèyàng kàndài shēnghuó.
be used to this treat life
{I'm used to others commenting on me like this, as well as treating life this way.}

In (25), the first and the second clauses have different subjects, whereas in (26) the two clauses have the same subject.

1.2.2 Logical basis

The form "*jì p, yě q*" also has two types of logical basis.

First, *p* and *q* are inherently coordinate. The conjunctions *jì* and *yě* are employed to highlight the coordination. The following are three examples:

(27) 剧本把青鸟作为一种象征，<u>既</u>体现人类精神上的幸福，<u>也</u>体现人类物质上的幸福。

Jùběn bǎ qīngniǎo zuòwéi yī zhǒng xiàngzhēng, <u>jì</u>...<u>yě</u>... tǐxiàn rénlèi
script BA bluebird use...as one type symbol both...and... reflect humans
jīngshén-shàng de xìngfú, <u>yě</u> tǐxiàn rénlèi wùzhì-shàng de xìngfú.
in spirit SP happiness reflect humans in material SP happiness
{In the script, the bluebird is used as a symbol, which embodies both spiritual happiness and material satisfaction of human beings.}

(28) 蔡老师说得平平静静，自自然然，<u>既</u>没有激昂的词句，<u>也</u>没有深奥的道理，……

Cài lǎoshī shuō de píngpíng-jìngjìng, zìzì-ránrán, <u>jì</u>...<u>yě</u>... méiyǒu
CAI teacher say SP calm natural both...and... there not be
jī'áng de cíjù, <u>yě</u> méiyǒu shēn'ào de dàolǐ,...
passionate SP language there not be profound SP truth
{Teacher CAI spoke calmly and naturally, with no impassioned language or profound truths...}

(29) 大约几十万万年以前，当地球还是非常年轻的时候，地面上尽是高山和岩石，<u>既</u>没有平地，<u>也</u>没有泥土。

Dàyuē jǐshí wànwàn nián yǐqián, dāng...shíhou dìqiú hái shì fēicháng
about several billion year before when the earth still COP very
niánqīng de shíhou, dìmiàn-shàng jìn shì gāo shān hé yánshí,
young SP on ground all COP high mountain and rock
<u>jì</u>...<u>yě</u>... méiyǒu píngdì, <u>yě</u> méiyǒu nítǔ.
both...and... there not be flat land there not be soil
{About several billion years ago, when the earth was very young, the ground was covered with high mountains and rocks, with neither flat land nor soil.}

Second, the relationship between *p* and *q* is essentially adversative, but "*jì...yě...*" transforms the adversative relationship into a coordinate one, thus a coordinate complex sentence is formed. The use of "*jì...yě...*" highlights the coexistence of the adversative and coordinate relationships. The following are three examples:

(30) 对面前的这人<u>既</u>产生同情，<u>也</u>感到惋惜。

Duì miànqián de zhè rén <u>jì</u>...<u>yě</u>... chǎnshēng tóngqíng, <u>yě</u>
to/for before SP this person both...and... start to have sympathy
gǎndào wǎnxī.
feel regret
{(Someone) has felt both sympathetic to and sorry for the person in front of (them).}

(31) 你这个人就是责任感太强，这<u>既</u>是你的优点，<u>也</u>是你致命的缺点。

Nǐ zhè gè rén jiù shì zérèngǎn tài qiáng, zhè <u>jì</u>...<u>yě</u>...
you this CL person just COP sense of responsibility too strong this both...and...

"jì p, yòu q" and relevant forms 9

shì   nǐ   de   yōudiǎn,   yě   shì   nǐ   zhìmìng   de   quēdiǎn.
COP   you   SP   strength   COP   you   cause death   SP   weakness
{You have such a strong sense of responsibility, which is your strength but your fatal weakness as well.}

(32) （饺子）吃得一个不剩，<u>既</u>没人叫太饱，<u>也</u>没人说不够。
*(Jiǎozi)   chī   de   yī   gè   bù   shèng,   jì . . . yě . . .   méi   rén   jiào
dumpling   eat   SP   one   CL   NEG   be left   both . . . and . . .   there not be   person   say
tài   bǎo,   yě   méi   rén   shuō   bù   gòu.
too   full   there not be   person   say   NEG   enough*
{[The dumplings] had all been finished. No one said that they were too full or didn't have enough to eat.}

In (30) and (31), "*jì . . . yě . . .*" links two affirmative clauses, and in (32) it connects two negative clauses. If *jì* and *yě* were absent in these sentences, only a contrastive or adversative relationship would remain between *p* and *q*, namely, between "*chǎnshēng tóngqíng*" ('felt sympathetic') and "*gǎndào wǎnxī*" ('felt sorry'), between "*shì nǐ de yōudiǎn*" ('is your strength') and "*shì nǐ zhìmìng de quēdiǎn*" ('is your fatal weakness'), and between "*méi rén jiào tài bǎo*" ('no one said they were too full') and "*méi rén shuō bùgòu*" ('no one said they didn't have enough to eat').

All "*jì . . . yě . . .*" sentences with an inherent adversative relationship between *p* and *q* allow the occurrence of adversative words, such as *dàn* ('but') and the like, hence "*jì . . . yě . . .*" can turn into "*jì . . . dàn yòu . . .*" Detailed analyses can be found in Chapter 3, Volume III.

1.2.3 Differences between "*jì p, yòu q*" and "*jì p, yě q*"

Both "*jì . . . yòu . . .*" and "*jì . . . yě . . .*" can link *p* and *q* that are coordinate, but *p* in "*jì p, yě q*" is usually the emphasis, and *q* is usually supplementary to *p*, while in "*jì p, yòu q,*" *p* and *q* are equally emphasized. Compare the following two examples:

(33) 他<u>既</u>没有大学的文凭，经济状况<u>也</u>不好，我不干！
*Tā   jì . . . yě . . .   méiyǒu   dàxué   de   wénpíng,   jīngjì   zhuàngkuàng   yě   bù
he   both . . . and . . .   not have   college   SP   diploma   financial   situation   NEG
hǎo,   wǒ   bù   gàn!
good   I   NEG   do*
{He doesn't have a university diploma, plus he is in a poor financial position. I'm not keen on him!}

(34) 他<u>既</u>没有大学的文凭，经济状况<u>又</u>不好，我不干！
*Tā   jì . . . yòu . . .   méiyǒu   dàxué   de   wénpíng,   jīngjì   zhuàngkuàng   yòu   bù
he   both . . . and . . .   have not   college   SP   diploma   financial   situation   NEG
hǎo,   wǒ   bù   gàn!
good   I   NEG   do*
{He doesn't have a university diploma; neither is he in a sound financial position. I'm not keen on him!}

In (33), "*jì . . . yě . . .*" indicates that the speaker is mainly concerned with "*méiyǒu dàxué de wénpíng*" ('does not have a university diploma'), and "*jīngjì zhuàngkuàng bù hǎo*" ('is in a poor financial situation') is supplementary. In (34), "*jì . . . yòu . . .*" indicates that the speaker regards "*méiyǒu dàxué de wénpíng*" and "*jīngjì zhuàngkuàng bù hǎo*" as equally important.

If *p* and *q* are in opposition and both of them need to be emphasized, then only "*jì . . . yòu . . .*" can be used, for example:

(35) （苦三儿的心跳得更厉害了！……）<u>既</u>怕她说，<u>又</u>愿意她说。
    (*Kǔsānr de xīn tiào de gèng lìhài le!* . . .) <u>jì</u> . . . <u>yòu</u> . . . pà tā
    Kusanr SP heart beat SP more wild MP   both . . . and . . . fear she
    shuō, yòu yuànyì tā shuō.
    say   prefer   she say
    {[Kusanr's heart was beating even more wildly! . . .] On one hand, Kusanr feared that she was going to say it, but, on the other hand, would rather she said it.}

In the above example, "*jì . . . yòu . . .*" cannot be replaced by "*jì . . . yě . . .*"

1.3 "*yòu p, yòu q*"

Another coordinate form is "*yòu p, yòu q*," which indicates the two clauses are coordinate.

1.3.1 Linguistic form

Normally, "*yòu . . . yòu . . .*" links two affirmative clauses, but sometimes two negative clauses can also be linked, as in the following two examples:

(36) 两间一套的房子，<u>又</u>简单，<u>又</u>杂乱。
    Liǎng jiān yī tào de fángzi, <u>yòu</u> . . . <u>yòu</u> . . . *jiǎndān, yòu záluàn.*
    two   room one set SP apartment both . . . and . . . simple   messy
    {The two-bedroom apartment is simple and messy.}

(37) 这人真是祖传的爱多管闲事，<u>又</u>不是个工程师，<u>又</u>不多挣工资加班费，厂里改革不改革与你有什么相干呀？！
    Zhè rén zhēn shì zǔchuán   de ài
    this person really COP passed down from ancestors SP like
    duōguǎn-xiánshì,   <u>yòu</u> . . . <u>yòu</u> . . . *bù shì gè gōngchéngshī,*
    be fond of meddling in other's business both . . . and . . . NEG COP CL engineer
    <u>*yòu*</u> *bù duō zhèng gōngzī jiābānfèi, chǎng-li gǎigé bù gǎigé*
         NEG more earn salary overtime pay in factory reform NEG reform
    yǔ nǐ yǒu shénme xiānggān ya?!
    with you have what relationship MP
    {This person comes from a long line of busybodies. You are not an engineer, nor would you earn higher wages or get paid for working overtime. What does it have to do with you whether the factory will be reformed or not?!}

If there are more than two coordinate clauses, there can be more occurrences of *yòu* hence "*yòu* . . . *yòu* . . . *yòu* . . . ." The following is an example:

(38) 乘康<u>又</u>能干，<u>又</u>勤快，对你<u>又</u>那么好……
Chéngkāng <u>yòu</u> . . . <u>yòu</u> . . . <u>yòu</u> . . . nénggàn, <u>yòu</u> qínkuai, duì nǐ <u>yòu</u> nàme hǎo . . .
Chengkang . . . and . . . and . . . capable   diligent to you   that nice
{Chengkang is capable as well as diligent, and very nice to you . . . }

In some sentences with three coordinate clauses, "*yòu* . . . *yòu* . . . ." occurs to link the second and third clauses, and *yòu* can be present or absent in the first clause, for example:

(39) 老崔是党员，<u>又</u>是书记，<u>又</u>是校长……
Lǎo Cuī shì dǎngyuán, <u>yòu</u> . . . <u>yòu</u> . . . shì shūjì, <u>yòu</u> shì xiàozhǎng . . .
old CUI COP party member both . . . and . . . COP secretary   COP headmaster
{Old CUI is a (Communist) Party member, a Party secretary, and a headmaster . . . }

By the same token, in sentences with four coordinate clauses, *yòu* occurs in each of the last three clauses, and the presence of *yòu* is optional in the first one, for example:

(40) 她是老婆，<u>又</u>是老妈子，<u>又</u>是厨子，<u>又</u>是护士。
Tā shì lǎopo, <u>yòu</u> . . . <u>yòu</u> . . . <u>yòu</u> . . . shì lǎomāzi, <u>yòu</u> shì chúzi, <u>yòu</u>
she COP wife   . . . and . . . and . . . and . . . COP maid   COP cook
shì   hùshi.
COP nurse
{She is not only (his) wife but also (his) maid, cook, and nurse.}

Sometimes, "*yòu* . . . *yòu* . . ." can be replaced by "*yòu shì* . . . *yòu shì* . . ."; therefore, if a sentence contains three coordinate clauses, the sentence can be structured with "*yòu shì* . . . *yòu shì* . . . *yòu shì* . . . ," and in that case, "*yòu shì*" needs to be present in the first clause, for example:

(41) 上午他叫小阮、小冯两个年轻人，<u>又</u>是和泥，<u>又</u>是搭墩，<u>又</u>是拣漏，<u>又</u>是粉墙，整整一天忙得不亦乐乎。
Shàngwǔ tā   jiào   Xiǎo Ruǎn,   Xiǎo Féng   liǎng   gè   niánqīngrén,
morning   he   ask   little RUAN   little FENG   two   CL   youth
<u>yòu shì</u> . . . <u>yòu shì</u> . . . <u>yòu shì</u> . . . <u>yòu shì</u> . . . huó ní, <u>yòu shì</u> dā dūn, <u>yòu shì</u>
. . . and . . . and . . . and . . .   mix mortar   build scaffold
jiǎnlòu,   <u>yòu shì</u> fěn   qiáng,
look for cracks in the wall and fill them out with mortar even wall surface
zhěng-zhěng yī tiān máng de bùyì-lèhū
whole   one day busy   SP very much
{As he requested, Little RUAN and Little FENG started to work in the morning. For a whole day, the two young men busied themselves mixing mortar, building the scaffold, looking for cracks in the wall and filling them in, and evening the wall surfaces.}

1.3.2 Logical basis

Sentences in the form of "*yòu p, yòu q*" have three types of logical basis.

First, the intrinsic relationship between *p* and *q* is coordinate, and "*yòu . . . yòu . . .*" explicates this relationship. The following are two examples:

(42) 鼎足式的，式样<u>又</u>新颖，<u>又</u>匀称。
   Dǐngzú shì de, shìyàng <u>yòu</u> . . . <u>yòu</u> . . . xīnyǐng, <u>yòu</u> yúnchèn.
   tripod style MP style   both . . . and . . . novel   well-proportioned
   {(It's) the tripod style, novel and well-proportioned.}

(43) （吴菲拉开椅子请我坐。……）她<u>又</u>熟悉，<u>又</u>随便。
   (*Wú Fēi lā-kāi yǐzi qǐng wǒ zuò. . . .*) *Tā <u>yòu</u> . . . <u>yòu</u> . . . shúxī, <u>yòu</u> suíbiàn.*
   WU Fei pull back chair ask me sit   she both . . . and . . . familiar   casual
   {[WU Fei pulled back the chair and asked me to sit down . . .] She was both familiar and casual.}

Second, the relationship between *p* and *q* is inherently adversative, but "*yòu . . . yòu . . .*" transforms this adversative relationship into a coordinate one; thus, a coordinate complex sentence is formed. The use of "*yòu . . . yòu . . .*" highlights the coexistence of the adversative and coordinate relationships. The following are two examples:

(44) 你呀！<u>又</u>想吃，<u>又</u>怕烫。
   Nǐ ya! <u>yòu</u> . . . <u>yòu</u> . . . xiǎng chī, <u>yòu</u> pà tàng.
   you MP both . . . and . . . want to eat   fear be burned
   {Ah! You want to eat (it) but are afraid of burning (your mouth).}

(45) 宝全<u>又</u>恨他，<u>又</u>巴不得他来，酸溜溜儿的说不上啥滋味。
   Bǎoquán <u>yòu</u> . . . <u>yòu</u> . . . hèn tā, <u>yòu</u> bābùde tā lái,
   Baoquan both . . . and . . . hate him eagerly look forward to he come
   suānliūliūr de shuōbùshàng shá zīwèi.
   sour   SP unable to tell what feeling
   {Baoquan hated him but couldn't wait for him to come, with a feeling of jealousy or something that he couldn't tell.}

Third, the occurrences of the actions in the clauses follow a chronological order, and "*yòu . . . yòu . . .*" transforms the successive actions into concurrent ones so that the actions that occur one after another seem to take place concurrently, and thus, a tense and exciting atmosphere is created. In such sentences, "*yòu p, yòu q*" is usually in the form of "*yòu shì p, yòu shì q.*" The following are two examples:

(46) 他<u>又是</u>扳我的肩膀，<u>又是</u>捶我的胸。
   Tā <u>yòu shì</u> . . . <u>yòu shì</u> . . . bān wǒ de jiānbǎng, <u>yòu shì</u> chuí wǒ de xiōng.
   he both . . . and . . .   pull I SP shoulder   pound I SP chest
   {He pulled my shoulders and hit my chest.}

(47) 我们去后，他<u>又是</u>倒茶，<u>又是</u>拿糖，<u>又是</u>留饭。
Wǒ-men qù hòu, tā <u>yòu shì</u>...<u>yòu shì</u>...<u>yòu shì</u>... dào chá, <u>yòu shì</u> ná
we   go after he both...and...   pour tea <u>yòu shì</u> get
táng, <u>yòu shì</u> liú fàn.
candy   invite meal
{When we arrived, he poured us tea, offered us candies, and invited us to have dinner with him.}

1.3.3 Differences between "yòu p, yòu q" and "jì p, yòu q"

There are four differences between "yòu p, yòu q" and "jì p, yòu q."

First, for clauses that are logically coordinate, the items in "yòu...yòu..." sentences appear to be more compact than in "jì...yòu..." sentences. Compare the following two examples:

(48) 他呀，<u>又</u>喝酒，<u>又</u>抽烟，<u>又</u>喜欢玩牌，坏习惯多着呢！
Tā ya, <u>yòu</u>...<u>yòu</u>...<u>yòu</u>... hējiǔ, yòu chōuyān, yòu xǐhuān wán pái, huài
he MP ...and...and...   drink smoke   and like   play card bad
xíguàn duō zhe'ne!
habit many MP
{He has a lot of bad habits: drinking, smoking, and playing cards (for gambling)!}

(49) 他呀，<u>既</u>喝酒，<u>又</u>抽烟，<u>又</u>喜欢玩牌，坏习惯多着呢！
Tā ya, <u>jì</u>...<u>yòu</u>...<u>yòu</u>... hējiǔ, yòu chōuyān, yòu xǐhuān wán pái, huài
he MP ...and...and...   drink smoke   and like   play cards bad
xíguàn duō zhe'ne!
habit many MP
{He not only drinks, but also smokes and plays cards (for gambling). Lots of bad habits!}

The three bad habits are listed all at once in (48), while they are pointed out one by one in (49).

Second, in sentences in the form of "jì p, yòu q," the clauses are logically adversative, thus adversative connectives, such as dàn or què, can occur before yòu, whereas not all sentences in the form of "yòu p, yòu q" allow adversative connectives to occur before the second yòu. Compare the following examples:

(50) a 宝全<u>又</u>恨他，<u>又</u>巴不得他来。
Bǎoquán <u>yòu</u>...<u>yòu</u>... hèn tā, <u>yòu</u> bābùdé   tā lái.
Baoquan both...and...   hate him   eagerly look forward to he come
{Baoquan hated him but couldn't wait for him to come.}

→b *宝全又恨他，却又巴不得他来！

Bǎoquán yòu... yòu... hèn tā, què yòu bābùdé tā lái!
Baoquan both...and... hate him however and eagerly look forward to he come

→c 宝全既恨他，却又巴不得他来！

Bǎoquán jì... yòu... hèn tā, què yòu bābùdé tā lái!
Baoquan both...and... hate him however eagerly look forward to he come
{Baoquan hated him but, on the other hand, couldn't wait for him to come.}

(51) a 你呀！又想吃，又怕烫。

Nǐ ya! Yòu... yòu... xiǎng chī, yòu pà tàng.
you MP both...and... want to eat fear be burned
{Ah! You want to eat (it) but are afraid of burning (your mouth).}

→b 你呀！又想吃，却又怕烫，真是个窝囊废！

Nǐ ya! Yòu... yòu... xiǎng chī, què yòu pà tàng, zhēn shì
you MP both...and... want to eat but fear be burned really COP
gè wōnangfèi!
CL wimp
{Ah! You want to eat (it), but meanwhile, you are afraid of burning (your mouth). What a wimp!}

As can be seen, "yòu . . . yòu . . ." sentences are less tolerant to the occurrence of adversative connectives before the second yòu than "jì . . . yòu . . ." sentences if "yòu . . . yòu . . ." closely follows the subject; however, if the sentence does not have a subject, the tolerance increases.

Third, "yòu (shì) . . . yòu (shì) . . ." can occur in a coordinate complex sentence if the clauses are logically successive, but "jì . . . yòu . . ." cannot. The following is an example:

(52) 我妈呢，在一边又是骂，又是笑，又是打，又是拉，又是出点子，总算把我爸那榆木脑袋瓜说开窍了。

Wǒ mā ne, zài yībiān yòu shì... yòu shì... yòu shì... yòu shì... yòu shì...
my mother MP on side ...and...and...and...and...
mà, yòu shì xiào, yòu shì dǎ, yòu shì lā, yòu shì chū diǎnzi,
scold laugh hit coax offer suggestion
zǒngsuàn bǎ wǒ bà nà yúmù nǎodàiguā shuō kāiqiào le.
eventually BA my father that diehard say be enlightened MP
{My mother was scolding, laughing, hitting, coaxing, and making suggestions and eventually brought my father—the diehard—around.}

In the above example, "yòu shì" occurs five times in a row but cannot be replaced by "jì . . . yòu . . ." Even if there are only two occurrences of "yòu shì," they still cannot be replaced by "jì . . . yòu . . ."

Fourth, the position of "yòu . . . yòu . . ." in a complex sentence is more flexible than "jì . . . yòu . . ." in the sense that the first yòu and the second yòu can precede the complement in their own clauses, but "*jì . . . yòu . . .*" does not have this capability. The following is an example:

(53) 他一头钻了进去，领会得<u>又</u>深刻，记得<u>又</u>牢固。
Tā yītóu zuān-<u>jìnqù</u>, le <u>jìnqù</u> lǐnghuì de <u>yòu</u> . . . <u>yòu</u> . . .
he enthusiastically get in PEF understand SP both . . . and . . .
shēnkè, jì de yòu láogù.
profound remember SP firm
{He threw himself into it, understanding and remembering it really well.}

In the above example, "*yòu . . . yòu . . .*" emphasizes the coordination of the two features of "being profound" and "being firm," and the sentence would be an ill-formed one if "*jì . . . yòu . . .*" was replaced by "*yòu . . . yòu . . .*"

1.4 "*yě p, yě q*"

The form of "*yě p, yě q*" is also a form of coordinate sentences, which indicate that the two clauses are coordinate.

1.4.1 Linguistic form and logical basis

In "*yě p, yě q*" sentences, "*yě . . . yě . . .*" links two clauses about similar or related matters. The following are two examples:

(54) 孟蓓呢，眼角<u>也</u>像在笑，嘴角<u>也</u>像在笑，还是轻轻的声音："谁让你用的是圆筷子……"
Mèng Bèi ne, yǎnjiǎo <u>yě</u> . . <u>yě</u> . . . xiàng zài xiào,
MENG Bei MP corner of the eye both . . . and . . . as if in progress smile
zuǐjiǎo <u>yě</u> xiàng zài xiào, háishì qīng-qīng de shēngyīn:
corner of the mouth as if in progress smile still gentle SP voice
"Shuí ràng nǐ yòng de shì yuán kuàizi . . ."
who tell you use SP COP round chopsticks
{"Who told you to use the round chopsticks . . ." MENG Bei asked gently as usual, with a smile at the corners of her eyes and mouth.}

(55) 说话嗓门<u>也</u>高了，脸色<u>也</u>好看了。
Shuōhuà sǎngmén <u>yě</u> . . <u>yě</u> . . . gāo le, liǎnsè <u>yě</u> hǎokàn le.
talk voice both . . . and . . . high PEF complexion good PEF
{The voice has become louder, and the complexion has turned better.}

"*yě . . . yě . . . yě . . .*" can be used if there are three clauses about similar or related matters, as in the following example:

(56) 回家去，酒<u>也</u>好，菜<u>也</u>香，喝得<u>也</u>清净，多好。
Huí jiā qù, jiǔ <u>yě</u> . . <u>yě</u> . . <u>yě</u> . . . hǎo, cài <u>yě</u> xiāng, hē de <u>yě</u>
return home go booze . . . and . . . and . . . good food delicious drink SP

qīngjìng,   duō   hǎo.
undisturbed   how   good
{(Let's) go home (and have a drink). The booze is good, the food is delicious, and besides nobody will disturb us while (we are) drinking (at home). Won't that be nice?}

In "yě...yě...yě..." sentences, if all the clauses are affirmative, they have different subjects, as shown in (56). However, if the clauses are all negative, they can have the same or different subjects. The following are two examples:

(57)　听说你病啦，饭也吃不下，觉也睡不好。
Tīngshuō nǐ   bìng la, fàn yě...yě... chī-bù-xià, jiào yě
hear   you be sick MP food both...and... be unable to eat sleep
shuì-bù-hǎo.
cannot sleep well
{(I) heard that you are sick, and that you can't eat or sleep well.}

(58)　也宝也不哭，也不笑，也不说话，只是紧紧地抱着奶奶。
Yěbǎo yě...yě...yě... bù kū, yě bù xiào, yě bù shuōhuà, zhǐshì
Yebao ...and...and... NEG cry NEG smile NEG speak just
jǐn-jǐn de bào-zhe   nǎinai.
tight   SP hold-PRG   grandmother
{Yebao didn't cry, smile, or speak but just held Granny tightly.}

The clauses with yě in both (57) and (58) are in the negative form. In (57), the two clauses have different subjects, whereas the three ones in (58) share the same subject.

If the "yě...yě..." construction can form a complex sentence independently; that is, there is no other clause preceding or following the construction, the word *le* needs to occur at the end of both clauses if they are affirmative in form. However, if they are in the negative form, *le* does not need to be present. The following are two examples:

(59)　鸡也飞了，蛋也打了。
Jī   yě...yě...   fēi-le,   dàn   yě   dǎ-le.
hen both...and...   fly-PEF   egg   break-PEF
{The hen has flown away, and the eggs have been broken.}

(60)　你也别发火，我也不要生气。
Nǐ   yě...yě...   bié   fāhuǒ,   wǒ   yě   bù   yào   shēngqì.
you both...and... do not lose temper I   NEG   will take offence
{Please don't lose your temper, and I will not take offense, either.}

In (59), the two clauses, both of which are positive in form, make up a complex sentence, and *le* occurs at the end of either clause. In (60), the two clauses, both of which are negative in form, also form a complex sentence.

"jǐ p, yòu q" and relevant forms 17

In sentences in the form of *"yě p, yě q"*, there exists a coordinate relationship between the clauses, and *"yě . . . yě . . ."* is employed to highlight this relationship.

1.4.2 Differences between "yě p, yě q" and "yòu p, yòu q"

First, the two clauses joined by *"yòu . . . yòu . . ."* usually share the same subject, whereas the two clauses linked by *"yě . . . yě . . ."* tend to have different subjects. Compare the following two examples:

(61) 你我相处半月，酒也呷了，烟也抽了，这两分船钱本来不应该收你的。
Nǐ wǒ xiāngchǔ bàn yuè, jiǔ <u>yě</u> . . . <u>yě</u> . . . xiā le, yān <u>yě</u>
you I be together half month booze both . . . and . . . drink PEF cigarette both
chōu-le, zhè liǎng fēn chuán qián běnlái bù yīnggāi shōu nǐ de.
smoke-PEF this two cent ferry charge certainly NEG should charge you MP
{You have hung around with me for half a month, drinking and smoking, so I certainly ought not to charge you the two-cent fare for the ferry.}

(62) 你我相处半月，又呷酒，又抽烟，这两分船钱本来不应该收你的。
Nǐ wǒ xiāngchǔ bàn yuè, <u>yòu</u> . . . <u>yòu</u> . . . xiā jiǔ <u>yòu</u> chōuyān,
you I be together half month both . . . and . . . drink booze smoke
zhè liǎng fēn chuán qián běnlái bù yīnggāi shōu nǐ de.
this two CL ferry charge certainly NEG should charge you MP
{You have hung around with me for half a month, drinking and smoking, so I certainly ought not to charge you the two-cent fare for the ferry.}

In (61), *"yě . . . yě . . ."* joins two clauses, whose subjects are *jiǔ* and *yān*, and in (62), *"yòu . . . yòu . . ."* links two clauses that share the same subject—*"nǐ wǒ."*

Second, the two clauses linked by *"yě . . . yě . . ."* can have the same predicate, while the two clauses joined by *"yòu . . . yòu . . ."* have different predicates. For example:

(63) 山也绿，水也绿，真是一片绿色的世界！
Shān <u>yě</u> . . . <u>yě</u> . . . lǜ, shuǐ yě lǜ, zhēn shì yī piàn lǜsè
mountain both . . . and . . . green water green really COP one CL green
de shìjiè!
SP world
{The mountains are green, and the waters are also green. It's such a green color world!}

The first and the second clauses in (63) have the same predicate; i.e., *lǜ,* so *"yòu . . . yòu . . ."* cannot take the place of *"yě . . . yě . . ."* in this sentence.

Third, sometimes either *"yě p, yě q"* or *"yòu p, yòu q"* can occur, but they each have their own emphases: *"yě p, yě q"* indicates that the two matters are closely related and puts the emphasis on the correlation between them, while *"yòu p, yòu q"* highlights the coexistence of two different matters. Compare the two following two examples:

(64) 他家是冒尖户，钱<u>也</u>多，粮<u>也</u>足，日子过得红火极了！
Tā jiā shì màojiān hù, qián <u>yě</u>...<u>yě</u>... duō, liáng <u>yě</u> zú, rìzi guò de hónghuo jí le!
his family COP stand out household money both...and... a lot food abundant life lead SP prosperous extremely MP
{His family is a rich one, with a lot of income and food grain, so they live an extremely prosperous life!}

(65) 他家是冒尖户，钱<u>又</u>多，粮<u>又</u>足，日子过得红火极了！
Tā jiā shì màojiān, hù, qián <u>yòu</u>...<u>yòu</u>... duō, liáng <u>yòu</u> zú, rìzi guò de hónghuo jí le!
his family COP stand out household money both...and... a lot food abundant life lead SP prosperous extremely MP
{His family is a rich one, not only having a high income but also producing abundant food grain, so they live an extremely prosperous life!}

In (64), "*yě...yě...*" emphasizes the correlation between the two matters: a lot of money and abundant food. The two clauses can be rephrased as "*qián yě duō, liáng yě duō*" ('a lot of money and a lot of food grain') or "*qián yě zú, liáng yě zú*" ('plenty of money and plenty of food grain'). In (65), "*yòu...yòu...*" highlights the coexistence of having lots of money and having lots of food grain, so the two clauses can be rewritten as "*yòu yǒu qián, yòu yǒu liáng*" ('not only has lots of money but also lots of food grain').

Last, "*yě...yě...*" can only link clauses that are logically coordinate, but "*yòu...yòu...*" can join clauses that are logically coordinate, adversative, or successive.

1.5 "*yībiān p, yībiān q*"

The form of "*yībiān p, yībiān q*" indicates that two actions are in progress at the same time; therefore, it is also a form of coordinate complex sentences.

1.5.1 Linguistic form

In sentences in the form of "*yībiān p, yībiān q*," the predicate of either clause is acted by a verb, which can be followed by *zhe*, as in the following example:

(66) 迟大冰<u>一边</u>漫无目的地走着，<u>一边</u>遥望着广漠的绿野。
Chí Dàbīng <u>yībiān</u>...<u>yībiān</u>... mànwú-mùdì de zǒu-zhe, yībiān yáowàng-zhe *guǎngmò de lǜ yě.*
CHI Dabing meanwhile aimless SP walk-PRG look into the distance-PRG vast SP green field
{CHI Dabing looked at the vast green fields in the distance as he was walking aimlessly.}

More often than not, one of the two verbs is followed by *zhe*, and the other is not, but there are instances in which neither verb is followed by *zhe*, as in the following three examples:

(67) 鲁玉枝一边笑着，一边闪到一颗老枫树后……
Lǔ Yùzhī   yībiān   yībiān   xiào-zhe,   yībiān   shǎn   dào   yī
LU Yuzhi   meanwhile   giggle-PRG   meanwhile dodge   arrive one
kē   lǎo   fēngshù   hòu…
CL   old   maple   behind
{LU Yuzhi dodged behind an old maple tree as she was giggling.}

(68) 苏老师一边说，一边对他微微地笑着。
Sū lǎoshī   yībiān…   yībiān…   shuō,   yībiān   duì   tā   wēi-wēi   de
teacher SU   meanwhile   talk   meanwhile at   him   slightly-REDP SP
xiào-zhe.
smile-PRG
{Teacher SU smiled at him while talking.}

(69) 顾新雨一边洗脸，一边听宋伯伯向那女同志介绍。
Gù Xīnyǔ   yībiān…   yībiān…   xǐ   liǎn,   yībiān   tīng   Sòng bóbo   xiàng
GU Xinyu   meanwhile   wash   face   meanwhile listen SONG uncle   to
nà   nǚ   tóngzhì   jièshào.
that   female comrade   brief
{While washing his face, GU Xinyu listened to Uncle SONG, who was briefing the lady.}

For each additional concurrent action, there can be one occurrence of *yībiān* or *tóngshí* ('meanwhile'). The following are three examples:

(70) 她一边说，一边笑，一边就跑。
Tā   yībiān…   yībiān…   yībiān…   shuō,   yībiān   xiào,   yībiān   jiù   pǎo.
she   meanwhile   meanwhile   talk   meanwhile laugh   meanwhile just   run
{Talking and laughing, she just started to run.}

(71) 他一边吃饭，一边用眼睛往远处看，一边头脑里想着许多事，许今天和今后该办的事；……
Tā   yībiān…   yībiān…   yībiān…   chī   fàn,   yībiān   yòng   yǎnjīng   wǎng
he   meanwhile   meanwhile   eat   food   meanwhile use   eye   towards
yuǎnchù   kàn,   yībiān   tóunǎo-li   xiǎng-zhe   xǔduō   shì,   xǔduō   jīntiān
faraway place look meanwhile in mind   think-PRG   many   matter   many   today
hé   jīnhòu   gāi   bàn   de   shì;…
and   future   should   do   SP   matter
{While he is eating, he looks far away, thinking about many things that need to be done today and later…}

(72) 他一边把黑胖子扶下条案，一边问，同时拿眼睛盯住那欲逃不逃继续犯横的小男孩儿。
Tā   yībiān…   yībiān…   tóngshí…   bǎ   hēipàngzi   fú-xià
he   meanwhile   meanwhile   BA   black fattie help someone get down
tiáo'àn,   yībiān   wèn,   tóngshí   ná   yǎnjīng   dīngzhù   nà   yù   táo
long narrow table   ask   meanwhile with eye   stare   that   want   run away

bù   táo   jìxù   fānhèng   de   xiăo   nánháir.
NEG   run away   continue be unreasonable   SP   little   boy
{He asked the dark-skinned fat man questions as he was helping him get down from the table, and meanwhile staring at the young boy who was still being unreasonable and hesitating to run away.}

In some cases, *yībiān* does not occur in pairs. More detailed discussions on these cases can be found in Chapter 2, Volume II.

Besides, "*yībiān p, yībiān q*" can be rewritten as "*biān p, biān q*" in some cases. The following are two examples:

(73) 青年们边望我微笑，边互相窃窃私语。

Qīngnián-men   biān ... biān ...   wàng   wŏ   wēixiào,   biān   hùxiāng
young person-PL   meanwhile   at   me   smile   mutually
qièqiè-sīyŭ.
whisper to each other
{While whispering to each other, the young people smiled at me.}

(74) 伊品超边遐想着，边细针密线地缝着。

Yī Pĭnchāo   biān ... biān ...   xiáxiăng-zhe,   biān
YI Pinchao   meanwhile   daydream-PRG
xìzhēn-mìxiàn   de   féng-zhe.
fine needle and small stitches   SP   sew-PRG
{YI Pinchao daydreamed while sewing something with small stitches.}

1.5.2 *Logical basis*

The logical basis for sentences in the form of "*yībiān p, yībiān q*" is the coordinate relationship in the sense that two actions are in progress concurrently. The occurrence of this form helps to highlight the coordinate relationship. However, there are, in fact, two different situations of simultaneity.

First, the two separate actions are in progress without interfering with each other. For this reason, the relationship between the two clauses is typically coordinate, as shown in the following two examples:

(75) 是那天，我拉着孩子在外面一边晒太阳，一边看着水泥篮球场上的飞行员们做预习准备。

Shì   nà   tiān,   wŏ   lā-zhe   háizi   zài   wàimiàn   yībiān ... yībiān
COP that   day   I   lead-PRG child   on   outside   meanwhile
shàitàiyáng,   yībiān   kàn-zhe   shuĭní   lánqiú   chăng-shàng   de
sunbathe   look-PRG   concrete   basketball   on court   SP
fēixíngyuán-men   zuò   yùxí   zhŭnbèi.
pilot-PL   do   practice   preparation
{It was on the day when I took the kids outside to sunbathe while watching the pilots doing their ground training on the concrete basketball court.}

(76) 唯独三女儿有点害羞，一边含着手指，一边跟在她父亲的后边。
Wéidú   sān nǚ'ér   yǒudiǎn hàixiū,   yībiān . . . yībiān . . .   hán-zhe
only   the third daughter a little shy   meanwhile   suck-PRG
shǒuzhǐ, yībiān   gēn   zài tā   fùqīn   de   hòubiān.
finger   follow   at   her father SP   behind
{Only the third daughter was a bit shy. She followed her father, sucking her finger.}

In (75), "sunbathing" and "watching . . . the training on the concrete basketball court" are two actions taking place at the same time without interfering with each other, and this is also the case for the two actions of "sucking her finger" and "following her father" in (76).

The second situation is that two actions are in progress consecutively at a given time; therefore, the relationship is coordinate in the sense of alternation, as in the following example:

(77) 我和两个客人，一边饮酒，一边吸烟，一边畅谈。
Wǒ   hé   liǎng   gè   kèrén,   yībiān . . . yībiān . . . yībiān . . .   yǐnjiǔ,
I   and two   CL   guest   meanwhile . . . meanwhile   drink
yībiān   xīyān,   yībiān   chàngtán.
         smoke   talk freely
{The two guests and I talked as we were drinking and smoking.}

During the given time, the three actions, drinking, smoking, and talking, are in progress alternately rather than simultaneously, in the strict sense.

1.5.3 Non-connective "yībiān . . . yībiān . . ."

In some sentences, "*yībiān . . . yībiān . . .*" is not a paired conjunction that joins the clauses in a complex sentence but a pair of correlated locative nouns. In those sentences, each *yībiān* either precedes the word *shì* and acts as the subject or precedes a subject–predicate phrase as an adverbial. As a pair of correlated locative nouns, "*yībiān . . . yībiān . . .*" can be replaced by such expressions as "*zuǒbiān . . . yòubiān . . .*" ('the left side . . . the right side . . .') or "*zhè biān . . . nà biān . . .*" ('this side . . . that side . . .'), as in the following two examples:

(78) 这里连接着一条后楼房的水泥走廊，一边是水泥栏杆，一边是佣人和孩子住的后房。
Zhèlǐ liánjiē-zhe   yī   tiáo hòu   lóufáng de   shuǐní   zǒuláng, yī   biān   shì
here   connect-PRG one CL   back building SP   cement   corridor one side   COP
shuǐní   lángān,   yī   biān   shì   yōngrén hé   háizi zhù de   hòu   fáng.
cement   handrail one side   COP   servant and child live SP   back room
{There is a concrete corridor connected to the rear of the building, with a concrete handrail on one side and rear rooms for the servants and children on the other.}

(79) 一边，战士们和警卫员顶牛；一边，战士们和张辉孟对着吸烟，说着掏心肝的亲切话。

Yī biān zhànshì-men hé jǐngwèiyuán dǐngniú; *yī biān* zhànshì-men hé
one side solider-PL and guard poker game one side solider-PL and
Zhāng Huīmèng duì-zhe xīyān, shuō-zhe tāo xīn'gān de qīnqiè huà.
ZHANG Huimeng face-PRG smoke say-PRG heartfelt SP kind word
{On one side, some soldiers were playing poker with the guards; on the other side, other soldiers and ZHANG Huimeng were smoking and talking cordially with each other.}

In the above two examples, *yībiān* occurs twice and acts as the subject in (78) and an adverbial in (79).

1.6 "*yīmiàn p, yīmiàn q*"

Another coordinate form is "*yīmiàn p, yīmiàn q*," which indicates that two acts are in progress concurrently or that two recurrent activities are taken at the same time.

1.6.1 Comparisons between "*yīmiàn p, yīmiàn q*" and "*yībiān p, yībiān q*"

In some sentences, "*yīmiàn p, yīmiàn q*" is used to link two acts performed at the same time, as in the following two examples:

(80) 杜丽一面拭汗，一面瞅着徐竹卿和那些大汽车小汽车。

Dù Lì *yīmiàn* . . . *yīmiàn* . . . shì hàn, *yīmiàn* chǒu-zhe Xú Zhúqīng
DU Li meanwhile wipe sweat look at-PRG XU Zhuqing
hé nàxiē dà qìchē xiǎo qìchē.
and those big vehicle small vehicle
{DU Li looked at XU Zhuqing and those big and small vehicles as she was wiping her sweat.}

(81) 老熊一面走，一面用前掌拨开一路的树叶。

Lǎo xióng *yīmiàn* . . . *yīmiàn* . . . zǒu, *yīmiàn* yòng qiánzhǎng bō-kāi
old bear meanwhile walk use forepaw push aside
yīlù de shùyè.
all the way SP tree leaf
{The old bear kept pushing the tree leaves aside with its forepaws as it was walking.}

In other sentences, "*yīmiàn p, yīmiàn q*" is used to join two recurrent activities. The following are two examples:

(82) 一面绝不滥用浪费，一面努力发展生产。

Yīmiàn . . . *yīmiàn* . . . jué bù lànyòng làngfèi, *yīmiàn* nǔlì
meanwhile absolutely NEG abuse waste strive

fāzhǎn   shēngchǎn.
develop   production
{(We) must not abuse or waste (resources), and meanwhile, we must strive to raise production.}

(83) 因为家里穷，他<u>一面</u>帮家里做农活，<u>一面</u>跟父亲念点儿书。
Yīnwèi   jiā-li   qióng, tā   <u>yīmiàn</u> . . . <u>yīmiàn</u> . . . bāng   jiā-li   zuò
because   in family poor   he   meanwhile   help   in family do
nónghuó, <u>yīmiàn</u>   gēn   fùqīn   niàn diǎnr shū.
farmwork   with   father   do some reading
{Because his family was poor, he studied with his father a bit while helping his family with the farmwork.}

If "*yīmiàn . . . yīmiàn . . .*" links two acts, it can be replaced by "*yībiān . . . yībiān . . .*" For instance, "*yīmiàn . . . yīmiàn . . .*" in (80) can be replaced by "*yībiān . . . yībiān . . .*"

If there are three acts performed concurrently, "*yīmiàn . . . yīmiàn . . . yīmiàn . . .*" can be used to link them all, for example:

(84) 照旧例，近年是每逢节根或年关的前一天，他一定须在夜里十二点钟才回家，<u>一面</u>走，<u>一面</u>掏着怀中，<u>一面</u>大声地叫道："喂，领来了！"
Zhào   jiù   lì,   jìn   nián   shì   měi   féng
according to old   practice recent year   COP   every time meet
jiégēn   huò niánguān   de qián yī   tiān, tā yīdìng xū
day before a festival or New Year's Eve SP before one day he surely need
zài yè-lǐ shí'èr diǎn zhōng cái huí jiā, <u>yīmiàn</u> . . . <u>yīmiàn</u> . . . <u>yīmiàn</u> . . .
at   night 12 o'clock   late go home meanwhile . . . meanwhile
zǒu, <u>yīmiàn</u> tāo-zhe   huái-zhōng, <u>yīmiàn</u> dàshēng de jiàodào: "Wèi,
walk   pull-PRG   in chest   loud voice SP shout   hello
lǐng-lái le!"
receive MP
{As a routine, he didn't come home until midnight the day before a holiday or New Year's Eve, without exception. He would reach into his inside pocket as he walked, shouting loudly, "Hey, I've got it (my salary)!"}

If "*yīmiàn . . . yīmiàn . . .*" is employed to join two recurrent activities, it cannot be or can be hardly substituted by "*yībiān . . . yībiān . . .*" For example, "*yīmiàn . . . yīmiàn . . .*" in (82) cannot be replaced by "*yībiān . . . yībiān . . .*" The following is another example:

(85) 她<u>一面</u>读书，<u>一面</u>做着零零星星的活计，用自己的力量养活自己。
Tā <u>yīmiàn</u> . . . <u>yīmiàn</u> . . . dúshū,   <u>yīmiàn</u> zuò-zhe línglíng-xīngxīng de
she meanwhile   go to school   do-PRG   sporadic   SP
huójì, yòng zìjǐ   de lìliàng   yǎnghuó zìjǐ.
job   with oneself SP strength   support oneself
{While she was going to school, she did odd jobs to support herself.}

In the above example, "going to school" and "doing odd jobs to support herself" are both recurrent activities, therefore "*yīmiàn . . . yīmiàn . . .*" is more suitable than "*yībiān . . . yībiān . . .*". However, if the sentence was "She was knitting a jumper while reading.", then "*yībiān . . . yībiān . . .*" can be used, because "reading" and "knitting a jumper" are both temporary acts.

1.6.2 Logical basis

The logical basis for "*yīmiàn p, yīmiàn q*" that links two concurrent acts is the same as that for "*yībiān p, yībiān q*," both of which denote a coordinate relationship between the clauses.

However, if "*yīmiàn p, yīmiàn q*" links two recurrent activities, it has two possible types of logical basis.

The first type is a coordinate relationship. For instance, between "*juébù lànyòng làngfèi*" ('must not abuse or waste') and "*nǔlì fāzhǎn shēngchǎn*" ('striving to raise production') in (82), and between "*bāng jiālǐ zuò nónghuó*" ('helping the family with the farmwork') and "*gēn fùqīn niàn diǎnr shū*" ('studying with his father') in (83). In this case, "*yīmiàn p, yīmiàn q*" stresses the coordinate relationship. The following is an example:

(86) 他在原地手搭凉棚观察了我片刻后，便<u>一面</u>对我叫着"阿美利加、阿美利加"，<u>一面</u>朝我这个方向跑将过来。

Tā zài yuán dì shǒu dā liángpéng
he in originally spot place a hand flat on the forehead to block out the sun
guānchá-le wǒ piànkè hòu, biàn <u>yīmiàn</u> . . . <u>yīmiàn</u> . . . duì wǒ
observe-PEF me short moment after then meanwhile to me
jiào-zhe "Āměilìjiā, Āměilìjiā", <u>yīmiàn</u> cháo wǒ zhè gè fāngxiàng
shout-PRG America America toward me this CL direction
pǎo-jiāng guòlái.
run-DC come over
{He stood in place, put his hand on his forehead to observe me, and after a while, he called out to me "America, America" as he was running towards me.}

The second type is an adversative relationship. In this case, "*yīmiàn p, yīmiàn q*" is employed to transform the adversative relationship into the coordinate relationship, and thus, a coordinate complex sentence is formed to emphasize the coexistence of the two actions. The following are three examples:

(87) <u>一面</u>在口头上宣称实行"民主"，"还政于民"，<u>一面</u>又在实际上残酷地压迫人民的民主运动，不愿意实行<u>丝毫</u>的民主改革。

<u>Yīmiàn</u> . . . <u>yīmiàn</u> . . . zài kǒutóu-shàng xuānchēng shíxíng "mínzhǔ",
meanwhile at verbally claim practice democracy
"huánzhèngyúmín", <u>yīmiàn</u> yòu zài shíjì-shàng cánkù
return the political power to the public and in factual cruelly
de yāpò rénmín de mínzhǔ yùndòng, bù
SP oppress people SP democratic movement NEG

yuànyì   shíxíng   sīháo   de   mínzhǔ   gǎigé.
be willing implement slightest SP democratic reform
{On one hand, (they) claim to practice "democracy" and to "return the political power to the public," but on the other hand, (they) cruelly suppress people's democratic movements and are unwilling to implement any democratic reforms in the slightest.}

(88) (当时，武汉的环境是困难的，在敌人封锁、内部动摇的情况下，把最后的希望押在冯玉祥身上，……) 冯玉祥<u>一面</u>与武汉来的这些人应付，<u>一面</u>宣布他要去徐州会蒋介石。
(Dāngshí, Wǔhàn de huánjìng shì   kùnnán de, zài dírén   fēngsuǒ,
back then Wuhan SP environment COP difficult SP at enemy blockade
nèibù   dòngyáo de qíngkuàng-xià, bǎ zuìhòu de xīwàng yā zài Féng Yùxiáng
inside waver SP in situation BA last   SP hope   bet at FENG Yuxiang
shēn-shàng,...) Féng Yùxiáng   <u>yīmiàn</u> ... <u>yīmiàn</u> ... yǔ   Wǔhàn lái de
on body   FENG Yuxiang meanwhile   with Wuhan come SP
zhèxiē rén   yìngfu,   <u>yīmiàn</u> xuānbù   tā yào qù   Xúzhōu huì
these   person deal with   announce he will go to Xuzhou meet
Jiǎng Jièshí.
CHIANG Kai Shek.
{[At that time, the situation in Wuhan was difficult. Due to the enemy's blockade and internal wavering, (the Communist International) saw FENG Yuxiang as its last hope...] On one hand, FENG Yuxiang was dealing with those people from Wuhan, but on the other hand, he announced that he would go to Xuzhou to meet CHIANG Kai Shek.}

(89) 这时的心情便有些复杂，<u>一面</u>不由地加快了步伐，<u>一面</u>又希望脚下的路程更长一些，以便有足够的心理准备，好面对仰慕已久的龙湫之水。
Zhè shí   de xīnqíng   biàn yǒuxiē fùzá,   <u>yīmiàn</u> ... <u>yīmiàn</u> ...
this time SP mood   then a little complicated meanwhile
bùyóu   de jiākuài-le   bùfá, <u>yīmiàn</u> yòu xīwàng jiǎo-xià de
can't help SP speed up-PEF pace   and hope   underfoot SP
lùchéng gèng cháng yīxiē, yǐbiàn yǒu zúgòu de xīnlǐ zhǔnbèi,   hǎo
journey more long a little so that have enough SP mind preparation be easy to
miànduì yǎngmù yǐ   jiǔ   de lóngqiū zhī shuǐ.
face   admire already long time SP Longqiu SP water
{At this time, (my) feelings are mixed. On one hand, I couldn't help but speed up my pace, but on the other hand, I wished that the journey were a little longer so that I could be mentally prepared to face Longqiu Waterfall, which I had long admired.}

If the logical basis for "*yīmiàn p, yīmiàn q*" is an adversative relationship, *dàn* or other adversative connectives can be used before the second *yīmiàn* so that the inherent adversative relationship between the clauses becomes even more conspicuous. More discussions can be found in Chapter 3, Volume III.

1.7 "*yī fāngmiàn p, lìng yī fāngmiàn q*"

Another coordinate form is "*yī fāngmiàn p, lìng yī fāngmiàn q*," which juxtaposes two aspects of the same action.

1.7.1 Linguistic form

The connective "*yī fāngmiàn . . . lìng yī fāngmiàn . . .*" is a marker for coordinate sentences. Such words as *yòu* or *yě* often collocate with "*lìng yī fāngmiàn*", as in the following two examples:

(90) 一方面他觉得苏青很爱他，另一方面又觉得苏青说不爱他就可能不爱他了。

Yī fāngmiàn . . . lìng yī fāngmiàn . . .   tā   juéde   Sū Qīng   hěn   ài
both . . . and . . .   he   feel   SU Qing   very much   love
tā,   lìng yī fāngmiàn   yòu   juéde   Sū Qīng   shuō   bù   ài   tā   jiù   kěnéng
him   but feel   SU Qing   say   NEG   love   him   just   may
bù   ài   tā   le.
NEG   love   him   MP

{On one hand, he thinks that SU Qing loves him so much, but on the other hand, he is afraid that if SU Qing says that she doesn't love him, because after all she means what she says.}

(91) 上面所说的那些，一方面是由于幼稚而来，另一方面也是由于责任心不足而来的。

Shàngmiàn   suǒ   shuō   de   nàxiē,   yī fāngmiàn . . . lìng yī fāngmiàn . . .   shì
above   PAP   say   SP   those   both . . . and . . .   COP
yóuyú   yòuzhì   ér   lái,   lìng yī fāngmiàn   yě   shì   yóuyú
due to   naive   then   come   also   COP   due to
zérènxīn   bù   zú   ér   lái de.
sense of responsibility   NEG   enough   then   come SP

{The above mentioned is due to naivety as well as lack of a sense of responsibility.}

If the two clauses share the same logical subject, the subject usually occurs in the anterior clause only and precedes "*yī fāngmiàn . . . ,*" but it is absent in the posterior clause, as in the following example:

(92) 我们一方面实行开放政策，另一方面仍坚持建国以来毛主席一贯倡导的自力更生为主的方针。

Wǒ-men   yī fāngmiàn . . . lìng yī fāngmiàn . . .   shíxíng   kāifàng
we   both . . . and . . .   implement   open up
zhèngcè,   lìng yī fāngmiàn   réng   jiānchí   jiànguó   yǐlái
policy   still   insist   form a country   since then
Máo zhǔxí   yīguàn   chàngdǎo   de   zìlì-gēngshēng   wéi   zhǔ
MAO chairman   consistent   advocate   SP   rely on oneself   be   primary
de   fāngzhēn.
SP   policy

{We implement the policy of opening up meanwhile adhering to the principle of self-reliance, which Chairman MAO had always advocated since the founding of our country.}

If the two clauses each have their own subjects, "*yī fāngmiàn*" and "*lìng yī fāngmiàn*" respectively precede the subjects, as in the following two examples:

(93) 在解放区，<u>一方面</u>，军队应实行拥政爱民的工作，<u>另一方面</u>，民主政府应领导人民实行拥军优抗的工作，更大地改善军民关系。

Zài jiěfàng qū, <u>yī fāngmiàn</u> ... <u>lìng yī fāngmiàn</u> ... **jūnduì** yīng shíxíng
in   liberated area both ... and ...   army   should do
yōngzhèng-àimín   de gōngzuò, <u>lìng yī fāngmiàn</u>,
support the government and love the people SP work
mínzhǔ   **zhèngfǔ**   yīng   lǐngdǎo   rénmín   shíxíng
democratic   government   should   lead   people   do
yōngjūn-yōukàng
support the army and give preferential treatment to the families with members fighting the Japanese invaders
de gōngzuò, gèng dà   de   gǎishàn jūnmín   guānxì.
SP   work   more good SP improve   military and civilian relationship
{In the liberated areas, the army should support the government and love the common people, and meanwhile, the democratic governments should lead the common people to support the army and give preferential treatment to the families with members fighting the Japanese invaders, so as to better improve the relationship between the army and the people.}

(94) 在这种非常复杂的形势下，<u>一方面</u>我们没有在大敌当前犯进攻"自家人"的错误，<u>另一方面</u>我们也没有在反共顽固派武装进攻面前，犯毫不抵抗、一味退让的右倾机会主义的错误。

Zàizhè zhǒngfēichángfùzá dexíngshì-xià,<u>yī fāngmiàn</u> ... <u>lìng yī fāngmiàn</u> ...
in this type very   complex SP in situation both ... and ...
wǒ-men méiyǒu   zài   dàdí-dāngqián   fàn
we   NEG   when   be confronted with a formidable enemy make
jìngōng   "zìjiārén"   de cuòwù, <u>lìng yī fāngmiàn</u> **wǒ-men**
attack   people on one's own side SP mistake   we
yě   méiyǒu zài ... miànqián fǎn   gòng   wángùpài   wǔzhuāng
also   NEG   in front of   anti   Communist Party   diehard   arm
jìngōng miànqián, fàn   háo bù   dǐkàng, yīwèi   tuìràng de   yòuqīng
attack   make a bit NEG resist   simply retreat   SP   right deviation
jīhuìzhǔyì   de cuòwù.
opportunism   SP mistake
{In this very complex situation, we have not made the mistake of attacking "our own people" when confronted with a formidable enemy, nor have we made the mistake of being right opportunists—we have not given in or retreated in the face of the armed attacks by the anti-Communist diehards.}

The word *yī* can be omitted in "*lìng yī fāngmiàn*," as in the following example:

(95) 党<u>一方面</u>必须对于错误思想进行严肃的斗争，<u>另方面</u>又必须充分地给犯错误的同志留有自己觉悟的机会。

Dǎng <u>yī fāngmiàn</u> ... <u>lìng fāngmiàn</u> ... bìxū   duìyú cuòwù   sīxiǎng jìnxíng
party both ... and ...   must   again wrong   thoughts conduct
yánsù   de dòuzhēng, <u>lìngfāngmiàn</u> yòu   bìxū   chōngfèn de   gěi   fàn
serious SP fight   and   must   full   SP   to   make
cuòwù   de tóngzhì liú   yǒu   zìjǐ   juéwù   de   jīhuì.
mistake SP comrade keep   have   oneself realize SP   opportunity

28 *"jì p, yòu q" and relevant forms*

{(Our) Party must wage a campaign against wrong thoughts but, meanwhile, we must give those comrades who have made mistakes enough chances to realize their own mistakes.}

The word *lìng* in *"lìng yī fāngmiàn"* can be replaced by *yòu*, as in the following example:

(96) 中央认为应使干部对于党内历史问题在思想上完全弄清楚，同时对于历史上犯过错误的同志在作结论时应取宽大的方针，以便<u>一方面</u>，彻底了解我党历史经验，避免重犯错误；<u>又一方面</u>，能够团结一切同志,共同工作。

Zhōngyāng rènwéi yīng shǐ gànbù duìyú dǎng-nèi lìshǐ
central committee believe should make cadre about within party history
wèntí zài sīxiǎng-shàng wánquán nòng qīngchǔ, tóngshí duìyú lìshǐ-shang
issue at in ideology fully make clear same time for in history
fàn-guò cuòwù de tóngzhì zài ... shí ... zuò jiélùn shí yīng
make-EXP mistake SP comrade when draw conclusion should
qū kuāndà de fāngzhēn, yībiàn <u>yī fāngmiàn</u> ... <u>yòu yī fāngmiàn</u>
adopt lenient SP principle so that both ... and ...
chèdǐ liǎojiě wǒ dǎng lìshǐ jīngyàn, bìmiǎn
thoroughly understand our party history experience avoid
chóng fàn cuòwù; <u>yòu yī fāngmiàn</u>, nénggòu tuánjié yīqiē tóngzhì,
repeatedly make mistake can unite all comrade
gòngtóng gōngzuò.
together work

{The Central Committee believes that the cadre of the Party should fully understand the historical issues about the Party, and that the principle of leniency should be adopted when the conclusion about their mistake is drawn. By so doing, those comrades can have a good understanding of the historical experience of the Party and avoid making the same mistakes repeatedly, and all comrades can be united and work together.}

Sometimes, *"lìng yī fāngmiàn"* is present in the second clause, but *"yī fāngmiàn"* is absent in the first clause, as in the following example:

(97) 那个"对象目标"就算真像兄弟夸的那么流油光，也得让她当妈的看着顺眼、符合心意，还得让女儿高兴；<u>另一方面</u>，人家男方那头也得同意才行呀！

Nà gè "duìxiàng mùbiāo" jiùsuàn ... yě ... zhēn
that CL person that someone is dating target even if really
xiàng xiōngdi kuā de nàme liú yóuguāng, yě děi ràng tā dāng mā
like brother praise SP so gloss flows need make she be mother
de kàn-zhe shùnyǎn, fúhé xīnyì, hái děi ràng
SP look-PRG pleasing to the eye agree with mind still need make
nǚ'ér gāoxìng; <u>lìng yī fāngmiàn</u>, rénjiā nánfāng nà tóu yě
daughter happy and the other person the man that side also
děi tóngyì cái xíng ya!
need agree just okay MP

{Even if the target boyfriend being matched (with my daughter) is really as perfect as my brother has claimed, he still needs to look pleasing to my eyes and make satisfy my daughter, and my daughter needs to like him as well. And meanwhile, the boy's family needs to agree!}

In some cases, the word *lìng* in "*lìng yī fāngmiàn*" can be left out, that is, "*yī fāngmiàn . . . yī fāngmiàn . . .*," as in the following two examples:

(98) 那时候<u>一方面</u>和平了，<u>一方面</u>又埋伏了文章。
Nà   shíhou <u>yī fāngmiàn</u> . . . <u>yī fāngmiàn</u> . . . hépíng   le,   <u>yī fāngmiàn</u>   yòu
that   time   both . . . and . . .   peace   PEF   and
máifú-le   wénzhāng.
hide-PEF   complex situation
{At that time, on one hand, peace came, and on the other hand, there was a great deal behind it.}

(99) 但是我们<u>一方面</u>取之于民，<u>一方面</u>就要使人民经济有所增长，有所补充。
Dànshì   wǒ-men   <u>yī fāngmiàn</u> . . . <u>yī fāngmiàn</u> . . .   qǔ   zhī   yú   mín,
but   we   both . . . and . . .   get   it   from   people
<u>yī fāngmiàn</u> jiù   yào   shǐ   rénmín jīngjì   yǒu suǒ zēngzhǎng, yǒu
                   then need make people economy have PAP increase   have
suǒ   bǔchōng.
PAP   supplement
{However, while taking from the people, we must also make sure that their economy grows and expands.}

1.7.2 Logical basis

In some cases, the two clauses in "*yī fāngmiàn . . . lìng yī fāngmiàn . . .*" sentences are coordinate in the usual sense, as in the following two examples:

(100) 这块读书人的"宝地"之所以书肆昌盛，<u>一方面</u>是它比邻文庙、学宫、贡院、书院，借着各路的文气和书卷气；<u>另一方面</u>是它受着状元府第浓郁的仕途官气的庇荫，……
Zhè kuài dúshū rén de   "bǎodì"   zhī suǒyǐ   shūsì   chāngshèng,
this CL   scholar   SP   treasure trove the reason why bookstore prosperous
<u>yī fāngmiàn</u> . . . <u>lìng yī fāngmiàn</u> . . . shì   tā   bǐlín   wénmiào,
both . . . and . . .   COP   it   be adjacent temple of Confucius
xuégōng,   gòngyuàn,   shūyuàn,
institution of higher learning examination complex academy of classical learning
jiè-zhe   gè   lù   de   wénqì   hé
rely on-PRG each direction   SP   atmosphere of literary study   and
shūjuàn qì;   <u>lìng yī fāngmiàn</u>   shì   tā   shòu-zhe
academic atmosphere   COP   it   get-PRG
zhuàngyuán
Number One Scholar (title conferred on the one who came first in the highest imperial examination)
fǔdì   nóngyù de   shìtú   guānqì
mansion   strong   SP   career as a government official successful official career
de   bìyìn, . . .
SP   bless
{The reason this scholars' "treasure trove" is lined with bookstores is that it is adjacent to the Confucian Temple, the Examination Institute, and academies, surrounded by the atmosphere of literary study, and it is blessed by the successful official career of the champion in the imperial examination . . . }

30 *"jì p, yòu q" and relevant forms*

(101) 一方面，用武力掩护了群众的生产；另一方面，又用劳力进行了普遍的帮助。

Yī fāngmiàn ... lìng yī fāngmiàn ..., yòng wǔlì yǎnhù-le qúnzhòng
both ... and ...   use   force protect-PEF the masses
de shēngchǎn; lìng yī fāngmiàn, yòu yòng láolì jìnxíng-le pǔbiàn
SP productive activity   and use   labor offer-PEF   general
de bāngzhù.
SP help
{(We) have used armed forces to protect the productive activities of the masses and meanwhile helped them with labor.}

In other cases, the logical basis for sentences in the form of "*yī fāngmiàn p, lìng yī fāngmiàn q*" is adversative, indicating that *p* and *q* are contrary to each other, as in the following two examples:

(102) 一方面是投降派们连妓女都不如的民族气节的丧失，另一方面是江南士子们无力的呻吟和反抗。

Yī fāngmiàn ... lìng yī fāngmiàn ... shì tóuxiángpài-men lián ... dōu
both ... and ...   COP capitulationist-PL even
jìnǚ   dōu bùrú   de mínzú   qìjié   de sàngshī,
prostitute not be as good as SP national integrity SP lose
lìng yī fāngmiàn shì jiāngnán   shìzǐ-men
                   COP regions south of the Yangtze River scholar-PL
wúlì   de shēnyín hé   fǎnkàng.
be feeble SP groan   and resist
{On one hand, the capitulationists, who are even worse than prostitutes, have lost their national integrity, and on the other, the southern scholars are groaning and resisting (the Japanese invaders) feebly.}

(103) 及至五十年后，方苞以戴名世《南山集》案罹祸，不死却以布衣值南书房，一方面其心中对亡明不无遗老之念，另一方面又感皇恩浩荡。

Jízhì wǔshí nián hòu, Fāng Bāo yǐ   Dài Míngshì 'nánshānjí'
until   fifty   year after FANG Bao because of DAI Mingshi Nanshan Collection
àn   líhuò,   bù   sǐ   què yǐ bùyī   zhí   nánshūfáng,
case suffer a mishap NEG die but as non-official work at the emperor's study
yī fāngmiàn ... lìng yī fāngmiàn ... qí   xīn-zhōng   duì wáng míng
both ... and ...   his heart-LOC   for past   Ming dynasty
bùwú   yílǎo
have more or less old person who remains loyal to the previous dynasty
zhī niàn,   lìng yī fāngmiàn   yòu gǎn
SP   miss   and feel grateful
huáng'ēn-hàodàng.
the emperor's graciousness is infinite
{Fifty years after, FANG Bao suffered a mishap for his involvement in the case of DAI Mingshi's *Nanshan Collection*. However, he was not sentenced to death, instead, he was employed in the emperor's study without official titles. On one hand, he was nostalgic for the past Ming dynasty, but on the other, he was grateful for the current emperor's infinite graciousness.}

If the clauses in a sentence in the form of "*yī fāngmiàn p, lìng yī fāngmiàn q*" are inherently adversative, an adversative connective, for instance, *dàn*, can occur before "*lìng yī fāngmiàn*." The adversative connective transforms the coordinate relationship into the adversative one. More discussions can be found in Chapter 3, Volume III.

1.7.3 Differences between "*yī fāngmiàn . . . lìng yī fāngmiàn . . .*" and "*yīmiàn . . . yīmiàn . . .*"

When linking two continual actions, a sentence in the form of "*yīmiàn p, yīmiàn q*" can be rewritten as "*yī fāngmiàn p, (lìng) yī fāngmiàn q*." For instance, "*yīmiàn . . . yīmiàn . . .*" in (88) can be replaced by "*yī fāngmiàn . . . lìng yī fāngmiàn . . .*" However, these two forms are quite different in other aspects.

First, in sentences in the form of "*yī fāngmiàn p, (lìng) yī fāngmiàn q*," "*yī fāngmiàn*" can precede the subject, whereas *yīmiàn* in "*yīmiàn p, yīmiàn q*" usually follows the subject.

Second, "*yī fāngmiàn . . . (lìng) yī fāngmiàn . . .*" can only link two clauses, while "*yīmiàn . . . yīmiàn . . .*" can join more than two clauses if extended to "*yīmiàn . . . yīmiàn . . . yīmiàn . . .*"

Third, "*yīmiàn . . . yīmiàn . . .*" can link two acts, but "*yī fāngmiàn . . . (lìng) yī fāngmiàn . . .*" cannot. For instance, (104a) cannot be rewritten as (104b).

(104) a 施芬兰<u>一面</u>说，<u>一面</u>往外走。
Shī Fēnlán <u>yīmiàn</u> <u>yīmiàn</u> *shuō,* <u>yīmiàn</u> *wǎng wài zǒu.*
SHI Fenlan meanwhile   talk   toward out walk
{SHI Fenlan walked out as she was talking.}

b* 施芬兰一方面说，另一方面往外走。
Shī Fēnlán *yī fāngmiàn* *lìng yī fāngmiàn* *shuō,* *lìng yī fāngmiàn*
SHI Fenlan both . . . and . . .   talk
wǎng wài zǒu.
toward outside walk

Fourth, when linking two recurrent actions, "*yī fāngmiàn . . . (lìng) yī fāngmiàn . . .*" emphasizes that the two actions are the two aspects of the same matter, whereas "*yīmiàn . . . yīmiàn . . .*" stresses that the two actions are in progress at the same time. Compare:

(105) 她<u>一方面</u>苦苦练琴，<u>一方面</u>也选修中国古典诗词。
Tā <u>*yī fāngmiàn*</u> <u>*yī fāngmiàn*</u> *kǔ-kǔ liàn qín,*
she both . . . and . . .   hard-REDP practice musical instrument
<u>*yī fāngmiàn*</u> *yě xuǎnxiū* *Zhōngguó gǔdiǎn shīcí.*
        also take . . . as an elective course Chinese classical poetry
{She practiced musical instruments very hard and took Chinese classical poetry as an elective course.}

(106) 她一面苦苦练琴，一面选修中国古典诗词。
   Tā yīmiàn . . . yīmiàn . . . kǔ-kǔ liàn qín, yīmiàn
   she meanwhile hard-REDP practice musical instrument
   xuǎnxiū Zhōngguó gǔdiǎn shīcí.
   take as an elective course Chinese classical poetry
   {While taking Chinese classical poetry as an elective course, she practiced musical instruments very hard.}

In (105), two different aspects of "her study" are reflected, while in (106) more emphasis is placed on "her two learning activities", which are in progress concurrently.

1.8 Other coordinate sentence forms

The seven coordinate forms that have been discussed and their varieties all juxtapose *p* and *q*, therefore all of them can be regarded as juxtapositional sentence forms. Besides, there are two other subtypes of coordinate sentences, that is, contrastive sentences and annotative sentences.

1.8.1 Contrastive sentence forms

Contrastive sentences are those in which the clauses contrast semantically with each other. These sentences can be further divided into two subtypes.

 First, complementary or contextual antonyms are used in the anterior and posterior clauses, as in the following two examples:

(107) 北方太冷，南方太热。
   Běifāng tài lěng, nánfāng tài rè.
   north too cold south too hot
   {The north is too cold, while the south is too hot.}

(108) 敌人一天天烂下去，我们一天天好起来。
   Dírén yītiāntiān làn xiàqù, wǒ-men yītiāntiān hǎo qǐlái.
   enemy day by day bad continue we day by day good continue
   {The enemy is getting weaker day by day, while we are getting stronger day after day.}

 Second, the anterior and the posterior clauses are respectively marked by *shì* and *bùshì* or *bùshì* and *érshì*, i.e., "*shì* . . . *bùshì* . . ." or "*bùshì* . . . *érshì* . . .". The following are two examples:

(109) 这里是大学校园，不是你们可以胡闹的场所！
   Zhèlǐ shì dàxué xiàoyuán, bù shì nǐ-men kěyǐ húnào
   this place COP university campus NEG COP you-PL Can run wild
   de chǎngsuǒ!
   SP place
   {This is a college campus, not a place where you can run wild!}

(110) 你<u>不是</u>一个小孩，<u>而是</u>一个国家干部！
Nǐ   bù   shì yī gè xiǎohái, ér   shì yī gè guójiā gànbù!
you NEG COP one CL child   but COP one CL state   official
{You are not a child but a government official!}

1.8.2 Annotative sentence forms

Annotative sentences are another subtype of coordinate sentences, in which one clause annotates the other or the two of them annotate each other. There are mainly three types of annotations.

First, the second clause annotates the first one with such expressions as "*zhè jiùshì shuō*" or "*huàn jù huà shuō*," as in the following two examples:

(111) 文如其人，<u>这就是说</u>，什么样的人就写什么样的文章。
Wén rú   qí rén, zhè jiùshì shuō, shénme yàng de rén   jiù xiě
writing resemble its author this is to say what kind SP person just write
shénme yàng de wénzhāng.
what   kind SP article
{The writing mirrors the author, that is to say, the style of someone's writing reflects their personality.}

(112) 受事句不一定都用"被"字，<u>换句话说</u>，受事句不一定都是"被"字句。
Shòushìjù   bù yīdìng   dōu yòng "bèi" zì,
patient subject sentence NEG necessarily all use   by   character
huàn jù huà shuō,   shòushìjù   bù   yīdìng   dōu
in other words   patient subject sentence NEG necessarily all
shì   "bèi"zìjù.
COP   "by" character sentence
{The character *bèi* does not have to occur in all patient-subject sentences. Or, to put it another way, not all patient-subject sentences have to be *bèi*-sentences.}

Second, the posterior clause annotates a key word in the anterior clause.
In some cases, the annotation is a direct explanation, and "*zhè*" ('this') or "*nà*" ('that') often occurs in the posterior clause, as in the following example:

(113) 大婶抚养过<u>三个孤儿</u>，这三个孤儿现在都参加工作了。
Dàshěn fǔyǎng-guò sān gè gū'ér, zhè sān gè gū'ér xiànzài dōu cānjiā
aunt   raise-EXP three CL orphan this three CL orphan now   all join
gōngzuò le.
workforce PEF
{Aunt has brought up three orphans, all of whom are now working.}

In some cases, the annotation is general-specific or specific-general, as shown in the following two examples:

(114) 大姊有两个儿子，一个参加了工作，一个在北京上大学。

Dàshěn yǒu liǎng gè érzi, yī gè cānjiā-le gōngzuò, yī gè zài Běijīng shàng dàxué.
aunt have two CL son one CL join-PEF workforce one CL in Beijing attend university
{Aunt has two sons, one of whom is working, and the other is going to college in Beijing.}

(115) 天保二十五，玉璐二十三，他们都是硕士研究生。

Tiānbǎo èrshíwǔ, Yùlù èrshísān, tā-men dōu shì shuòshì yánjiūshēng.
Tianbao twenty-five Yulu twenty-three they both COP master postgraduate
{Tianbao is 25, and Yulu is 23, both of whom are graduate students studying for a master's degree.}

The annotation is a specification in (114) and a generalization in (115). As a matter of fact, this kind of complex sentences are dual-layer ones. If the annotation is a specification, there exists a second layer of coordinate relationship between the clauses within the annotation; if the annotation is a generalization, the second layer of coordinate relationship exists between the clauses within what is annotated.

Third, the anterior clause annotates the posterior clause with a metaphor, as in the following two examples:

(116) 一根麻线难搓绳，一人难办大事情。

Yī gēn máxiàn nán cuō shéng, yī rén nán bàn dà shìqíng.
one CL hemp fiber difficult rub rope one person difficult do great thing
{It's hard to make a great achievement by one individual, as it is hard to make a rope with one hemp fiber.}

(117) 生铁百炼成好钢，军队百战无敌挡。

Shēngtiě bǎi liàn chéng hǎo gāng, jūnduì bǎi zhàn wú dí dǎng.
pig iron hundred temper become good steel army hundred battle there not be enemy withstand
{It takes hundreds of battles for an army to become invincible, just as it takes hundreds of times of tempering for pig iron to become good steel.}

Summary

First, this chapter discusses seven coordinate sentence forms: "*jì p, yòu q*"; "*jì p, yě q*"; "*yòu p, yòu q*"; "*yě p, yě q*"; "*yībiān p, yībiān q*"; "*yīmiàn p, yīmiàn q*," and "*yī fāngmiàn p, lìng yī fāngmiàn q*." In addition, the contrastive and annotative sentence forms, which also mark the coordinate relationship between the clauses, are discussed as well.

Second, the seven forms can be divided into two groups. One group includes "*jì p, yòu q*"; "*jì p, yě q*"; "*yòu p, yòu q*"; and "*yě p, yě q*"; the other group has "*yībiān p, yībiān q*"; "*yīmiàn p, yīmiàn q*"; and "*yī fāngmiàn p, lìng yī fāngmiàn q*." The forms within the same group share more semantic similarities with each other than with any forms in the other group. Therefore, there is a certain arbitrariness in choosing "*jì p, yòu q*" as the representative for all the coordinate forms.

Third, within the two groups, each form has its unique meaning and use. Knowledge about the subtle differences between "*jì p, yòu q*" and "*jì p, yě q*," between "*yòu p, yòu q*" and "*yě p, yě q*," and between "*yībiān p, yībiān q*" and "*yīmiàn p, yīmiàn q*", among others, greatly enhances the understanding of coordinate complex sentences in Chinese.

NB Some examples in this chapter are cited from literary works, political essays, articles, and so on. The sources are listed as follows:

1   *Baihuazhou* (《百花洲》) 1998(3), including Examples (71), (89), (100), and (102);
2   *Chang Literature* (《长江》) 1982(3), including (79);
3   *Changcheng* (《长城》) 1982(1), including (1), (6), (18), (35), (42), and (105); 1982(3), including (52);
4   *Chinese* for Junior High School Students, Book 3, including (46); Book 6, including (2), (10), (11), (15), and (29);
5   *Chinese* for Primary School Students, including (83);
6   *Chinese* for Senior High School Students, Book 1, including (3), (9), and (17); Book 4, including (91);
7   *Chunfeng* (《春风》) 1982(1), including (21), (39), and (97);
8   *Dangdai* (《当代》) 1982(3), including (20), (28), (37), (41), (47), (72), and (81); 1983(1), including (59); 1983(4), including (70);
9   *Dragon Boat Festival* (《端午节》) by LU Xun (鲁迅), including (84);
10 *Fiction Monthly* (《小说月报》) 1981(12), including (56); 1982(1), including (25); 1982(2), including (45); 1982(3), including (80); 1982(6), including (61); 1982(7), including (75); 1996(12), including (8), (14), (19), (23), (24), (76), and (86);
11 *Flower City* (《花城》) 1983(3), including (68) and (77);
12 *Harvest* (《收获》) 1982(2), including (26) and (27); 1982(4), including (58) and (78); 1983(3), including (44); 1983(4), including (66) and (67);
13 *Lotus* (《芙蓉》) 1983(4), including (4), (22), and (74);
14 *October* (《十月》) 1982(2), including (40); 1982(3), including (32) and (85);
15 *People's Literature* (《人民文学》) 1982(3), including (5), (30), (36), (38), (43), and (69);
16 *Qingming* (《清明》) 1983(3), including (7); 1999(5), including (103);
17 *Selected Stories* (《小说选刊》) 1997(1) (supplement), including (31); 1998(11), including (12);
18 *Selected Works of DENG Xiaoping* (1975–1982) (《邓小平文选(1975–1982年)》), including (92);

19 *Selected Works of Excellent Chinese Short Stories in 1980* (《1980年全国优秀短篇小说评选获奖作品集》), including (54), (55), (57), and (73);
20 *Selected Works of LIU Shaoqi* (《刘少奇选集》), including (94), (5), (9), (31), (44), (55), (59), (61), and (63);
21 *Selected Works of MAO Tse-tung* (《毛泽东选集》), including (82), (87), (93), (95), (96), (99), and (101);
22 *Selected Works of ZHOU Enlai* (《周恩来选集》), including (88) and (98);
23 *Short Stories Since the Foundation of People's Republic of China* (《建国以来短篇小说》), including (60);
24 *Zhongpian Xiaoshuo Xuankan* (《中篇小说选刊》) 1997(3), including (16) and (90); 1997(4), including (13);
25 *Zuopin yu Zhengming* (《作品与争鸣》) 1982(7), including (53).

2 Paired and single occurrences of the connective *yībiān*

In discussions of coordinate complex sentences in grammar books, *yībiān* always occurs in pairs, i.e., "*yībiān* . . . *yībiān* . . . ," which seems to imply that *yībiān* always occurs in pairs as a marker for the coordinate relationship between the clauses. However, this is not always the fact. The connective *yībiān* can actually occur in the following three sentence forms:

Form A: "*yībiān p, yībiān q*"
Form B: "Ø *p, yībiān q*"
Form C: "*yībiān p,* Ø *q*"

As can be seen, *yībiān* occurs in pairs in Form A, singly in the posterior clause in Form B, and singly in the anterior clause in Form C. The following are three examples:

(1) a 他们<u>一边</u>挥着鲜花，<u>一边</u>飞也似的冲了过去。
Tā-men <u>yībiān</u> . . . <u>yībiān</u> . . . huī-zhe xiānhuā, <u>yībiān</u> fēi yě shìde
they   meanwhile   wave-PRG flower   fly just like
chōng-guòqu le. guòqu.
rush over   PEF
{They waved flowers while rushing over.}

b 他们挥着鲜花，<u>一边</u>飞也似的冲了过去。
Tā-men huī-zhe   xiānhuā, <u>yībiān</u>   fēi yě shìde chōng-guòqu le guòqu.
they   wave-PRG flower   meanwhile fly just like rush over   PEF
{They waved flowers while rushing over.}

c <u>一边</u>挥着鲜花，他们飞也似的冲了过去。
<u>Yībiān</u>   huī-zhe   xiānhuā, tā-men fēi yě shìde chōng-guòqu le guòqu.
meanwhile wave-PRG flower   they   fly just like rush over   PEF
{They waved flowers while rushing over.}

Only one or two example sentences in Form B can be found in *Modern Chinese Dictionary*,[1] *Eight Hundred Words in Modern Chinese*,[2] *Interpretation of Grammatical Words in Modern Chinese*,[3] and *The Dictionary of Grammatical Words in Modern Chinese*.[4] However, no sentences in Form C can be found in

DOI: 10.4324/9781003362166-2

those academic works/dictionaries. On the other hand, in the author's *Complex Sentences and Connectives*,[5] all sentences in the three forms can be found, none of which, however, is thoroughly analyzed.

This chapter mainly deals with Forms B and C. The locative *yībiān* ('one side'), as in "*gē zài nà yībiān*" ('put something on the other side'), falls outside the scope of the discussion in this chapter.

2.1 Paired occurrence and single occurrence

The statistics that follow and the reflections on them will help understand the single and paired occurrences of the connective *yībiān*.

2.1.1 Statistics of Group A

Table 2.1 Statistics of Group A

Literary work	Author	Form A	Form B	Form C	Total
Venture into the Southeast	BU Guang	1	0	0	1
Nowhere to Bid Farewell	CHEN Ran	1	0	0	1
You Are a River	CHI Li	2	0	0	2
Endless Chores	LIU Zhenyun	3	0	0	3
Night talk by a Bandit	YOU Fengwei	3	0	0	3
King of Chess	Ah Chen	5	0	0	5

In this table, it can be seen that only Form A occurs in those literary works.

There are three additional notes on these statistics.

First, Form A occurs 27 times in the six primary school textbooks *Chinese* and 24 times in the six junior high school textbooks *Chinese*, but neither Form B nor Form C occurs in any of those textbooks. This indicates that Form A is the most common among the three forms.

Second, even Form A cannot be found in some literary works, such as *Hard Porridge* by WANG Meng, *Crying Colors* by BAI He, *Hideous Moonlight* by LIAN Sheng, and *The Dream of West Lake* by YU Qiuyu. This suggests that the connective *yībiān* is not omnipresent despite its high frequency of use.

Third, *yībiān* sometimes is written as *yībiānr*. In some cases, *yībiān* occurs more than twice, for example, "*yībiān* . . . *yībiān* . . . *yībiān* . . . ," as in the following two examples:

(2) 打手势或者画画儿要用手，手就不能同时做别的事，说话用嘴，可以<u>一边</u>儿说话，<u>一边</u>儿劳动。

Dǎ   shǒushì huòzhě huà   huàr   yào yòng shǒu, shǒu jiù   bù   néng
make gesture or   draw picture need use   hand hand then NEG can
tóngshí   zuò biéde shì,   shuōhuà yòng zuǐ,   kěyǐ <u>yībiānr</u> . . . <u>yībiānr</u> . . .
same time do   other thing talk   use   mouth can   meanwhile
shuōhuà, <u>yībiānr</u> láodòng.
talk   do physical work

Paired and single occurrences of the connective yībiān 39

{When someone is making gestures or drawing pictures with their hands, they can't do anything else at the same time; whereas while they are talking, they can do physical work.}

(3) 我一边说，一边写，一边注意她用的信封。
Wǒ yībiān ... yībiān ... yībiān ... shuō, yībiān xiě, yībiān zhùyì tā yòng
I meanwhile ... meanwhile talk write notice she use

de xìnfēng.
SP envelope
{I took notice of the envelope that she used as I was talking and writing.}

2.1.2 Statistics of Group B

Table 2.2 Statistics of Group B

Literary work	Author	Form A	Form B	Form C	Total
Home of Teachers	JIANG Chunguang	10	8	0	18
Playful People	WANG Shuo	8	1	0	9
Lonely Wives	BAI Fan	6	1	0	7
Old Stories about Provisional Capital	MO Huaiwei	5	2	0	7

Both Form A and Form B occur in the works in Group B.

The following two aspects should be taken into account.

First, Form B does not occur as frequently as Form A in general. For example, in WANG Shuo's *Playful People*, there is only one occurrence of Form B, but there are eight occurrences of Form A. Nevertheless, this is not always the case, for instance, in his other book, *The Troubleshooters*, Form A occurs once, but Form B occurs twice. Another example is YAN Guaiyu's *Burying a Buffalo*, in which Form A occurs only once but Form B occurs five times.

Second, there are literary works in which only Form B can be found, although such cases are rare. For instance, in HE Yuru's *Gate of Fear*, there is one occurrence of Form B but no occurrence of Form A or Form C, and in JIANG Yun's *Run away from the Scene*, there are three occurrences of Form B but no occurrence of the other two forms.

2.1.3 Statistics of Group C

Table 2.3 Statistics of Group C

Literary Work	Author	Form A	Form B	Form C	Total
Love Is Not Enough for a Marriage	ZHANG Xin	2	1	1	4
Danger	MO Shen	5	1	6	12
Emperor Yongzheng: Nine Princes Fight for the Throne	ERYUE He	44	13	52	109

In these works, there are occurrences of all three forms.

There are three points worth noticing.

First, in general, Form A is used most frequently, and Form C is rarely used. However, the data in Table 2.3 indicate that in a few works the frequency of Form C is close to or even higher than Form A.

Second, the conclusion of the present author's long-term observation indicates that there are more works in which Form B can be found than those in which Form C can be found. However, Form C is more frequently used in certain works than Form B. Moreover, Form B does not occur in some works in which Form A and Form C can be found. For instance, in both CHEN Chong's *Fast Tracking without Feedback* and WANG Liyun's *Girl Named Chuner*, there are three occurrences of Form A and one occurrence of Form C but no occurrence of Form B.

Third, the connective *yībiān* rarely occurs in the senior high school textbooks *Chinese* published by People's Education Press in the 1980s. However, in Book Two, there is one occurrence of Form C, but no occurrences of Form A or Form B. The following is the aforementioned sentence in Form C:

(4) 蓬头，赤脚，一边扣着钮扣，几个还没睡醒的"懒虫"从楼上冲下来了。

Péngtóu, chìjiǎo, <u>yībiān</u> kòu-zhe niǔkòu, jǐ gè hái
tangled hair bare foot meanwhile button-PRG button several CL still
méi shuìxǐng "lǎnchóng" cóng lóu-shàng chōng-xiàlái le.
NEG wake up lazybones from upstairs rush down PEF
{Tangled-haired and barefooted, several "lazybones" who were only half awake sprinted down the stairs as they were buttoning up.}

The above example can be rewritten in Form A, as follows:

(5) 蓬头，赤脚，几个还没睡醒的"懒虫"一边扣着钮扣，一边从楼上冲下来了。

Péngtóu, chìjiǎo, jǐ gè hái méi shuìxǐng de "lǎnchóng"
tangled hair bare foot several CL still NEG wake up SP lazybones
<u>yībiān</u> . . . <u>yībiān</u> . . . kòu-zhe niǔkòu, <u>yībiān</u> cóng lóu-shàng chōng-xiàlái
meanwhile   button-PRG button   from upstairs rush down
le.
PEF
{Tangled-haired and barefooted, several "lazybones" who were only half awake sprinted down the stairs as they were buttoning up.}

The coexistence of all the three forms can be found in some famous vernacular Chinese literary works. For example, in the first 80 chapters in *Dream of the Red Chamber* by CAO Xueqing, the connective *yībiān* occurs in six sentences, which are listed as follows, in the order of their occurrences.

(6) 一边说，一边催他穿了衣服，同鸳鸯往前面来见贾母。

<u>Yībiān</u> . . . <u>yībiān</u> . . . shuō, <u>yībiān</u> cuī tā chuān-le yīfu, tóng Yuānyang
meanwhile   talk   urge him put on-PEF clothes with Yuanyang

Paired and single occurrences of the connective yībiān 41

```
wǎng    qiánmiàn    lái    jiàn    Jiǎ mǔ.
go to   front       come   meet    Lady Dowager
```
{As (Xiren) was talking, she urged him to put on his clothes so that he could go to the front with Yuanyang to meet Lady Dowager.}

(7) 不言卜家夫妇，且说贾芸赌气离了母舅家门，一径回归旧路，心下正自烦恼，<u>一边</u>想，<u>一边</u>低头只管走，不想一头就碰在一个醉汉身上，把贾芸唬了一跳。

```
Bù    yán        Bǔ jiā     fūfù,     qiěshuō  Jiǎ Yún  dǔqì           lí-le
NEG   talk about BU family  couple    mention  JIA Yun  act in a fit of pique  leave-PEF
mǔjiù          jiāmén,   yījìng     huíguī  jiù lù,   xīn-xià  zhèng        zì   fánnǎo,
maternal uncle house     directly   go back old road  in heart in progress  self annoyed
yībiān       yībiān    xiǎng,  yībiān  dītóu                    zhǐguǎn        zǒu,  bù   xiǎng
meanwhile              think   yībiān  lower the head focusing on walk   NEG  expect
yǔtóu      jiù    pèng    zài yī  gè zuìhàn       shēn-shàng,  bǎ Jiǎ Yún hǔ-le
suddenly   then   bump into one   CL drunken man  on body      BA JIA Yun scare-PEF
yī    tiào.
one   jump
```
{Let's not talk about the BU couple, but JIA Yun only. He left his uncle's house in a fit of pique, going straight back along the road, very upset. He thought as he walked without looking up, but suddenly he bumped into a drunken man and scared himself.}

(8) <u>一边</u>说，<u>一边</u>将一个锦匣举起来。

```
Yībiān        yībiān    shuō,  yībiān  jiāng  yī   gè   jǐnxiá        jǔ-qǐlái.
meanwhile               talk           BA     one  CL   brocade box   lift up
```
{(JIA Yun) talked as he lifted up a brocade box.}

(9) 史湘云<u>一边</u>摇着扇子，笑道："自然你能会宾接客，老爷才叫你出去呢。"

```
Shǐ Xiāngyún   yībiān     yáo-zhe      shànzi,  xiào  dào:  "Zìrán     nǐ
SHI Xiangyun   meanwhile  shake-PRG    fan      smile say         certainly  you
néng            huìbīn-jiēkè,            lǎoye  cái   jiào  nǐ   chūqu  ne."
be capable of   meet guests and receive visitors  master  then  ask   you  go out MP
```
{As SHI Xiangyun was fanning herself, she said with a smile, "The master asked you to come out certainly because you are good at welcoming and receiving guests."}

(10) 李纨收过，<u>一边</u>吩咐内库上人说："等太太回来看了再收。"

```
Lǐ Wán  shōu-guò,  yībiān      fēnfu     nèikù-shàng rén       shuō:  "Děng tàitai
LI Wan  take       meanwhile   instruct  in storehouse person  say    wait  madam
huílái  kàn-le      zài    shōu."
return  check-PEF   then   put in storage
```
{As LI Wan took (the gifts), she told the storehouse staff, "They (the gifts) won't be put in storage until Madame comes back and checks."}

(11) 一边想，一边便走过来蹲下笑道："你在这里作什么呢？"
   Yībiān... yībiān... xiǎng, yībiān biàn zǒu-guòlái dūn-xià xiào dào: "Nǐ zài
   meanwhile   think   meanwhile then walk over squat down smile say you at
   zhèli zuò shénme ne?"
   here do what MP
   {(Xueyan) thought, as she came over and squatted down. "What are you up to here?" she asked with a smile.}

Among the above six examples, four are in Form A, i.e., (6), (7), (8), and (11); one in Form B, i.e., (10); and one in Form C, that is, (9). The A:B:C ratio is 4:1:1, which presents a general picture of the frequency of the use of the three forms in modern Chinese.

2.2 Form B: "Ø p, yībiān q"

In Form B, *yībiān* occurs singly in the posterior clause. In the anterior clause, Ø is the slot for the connective. According to the meaning and structure combined, there are three types of "Ø p."

2.2.1 Type 1: Ongoing action in the anterior clause

If the anterior clause indicates that an action is ongoing, the "S-V *zhe* (O)" form is often used, and the posterior clause is very likely to include *yībiān*. Compare:

(12) a* 大娘笑，一边连连点头。(?)
   Dàniáng xiào, yībiān lián-lián diǎntóu.
   aunt   smile meanwhile repeatedly-REDP nod

   b 大娘笑着，一边连连点头。(+)
   Dàniáng xiào-zhe, yībiān lián-lián diǎntóu.
   aunt   smile-PRG meanwhile continuously-REDP nod
   {Aunt smiled while nodding.}

There are two findings after similar example sentences have been analyzed.

First, the use of "V *zhe* (O)" in the anterior clause clearly shows that an action is ongoing and provides a semantic condition for the occurrence of *yībiān* in the posterior clause, which indicates that the action stated in the posterior clause takes place at the same time as the one stated in the anterior clause. The following are two examples:

(13) （小禄……手里拿着个洗干净的萝卜，）利落地切着，一边笑说："你们福气！我打量借不来米呢……"
   (Xiǎo Lù... shǒu-li ná-zhe gè xǐ-gānjìng de luóbo,) liluò de qiē-zhe,
   Xiaolu   in hand hold-PRG CL wash...clean SP radish nimble SP cut-PRG
   yībiān   xiào shuō: "Nǐ-men fúqì! Wǒ dǎliang jiè bù lái mǐ ne..."
   meanwhile smile say you-PL luck I think   can't borrow rice MP
   {[Xiaolu... holding a washed radish in his hand,] said with a smile, "You guys are lucky! I had thought no one would lend you rice," as he was cutting the radish neatly...}

(14) 我在心里诅咒着他的肥胖，一边轻盈地躲闪着街上的行人和车辆。
Wǒ zài xīn-li zǔzhòu-**zhe** tā de féipàng, **yībiān** qīngyíng de
I in in heart curse-PRG he SP obese as light SP
duǒshǎn-zhe jiē-shàng de xíngrén hé chēliàng.
dodge-PRG on street SP pedestrian and vehicle
{I lightly dodged the pedestrians and vehicles on the street as I was cursing him in my heart for his obesity.}

In either of the two examples above, the occurrence of *zhe* in the anterior clause indicates that the action in the posterior clause took place concurrently with the one in the anterior clause, and both sentences can be rewritten in the form of "*yībiān p, yībiān q*."

Besides, if two or more verbs occur consecutively in the anterior clause, then *p* can take the form of "V *zhe* (O) + V *zhe* (O)" or "V *zhe* (O) + V (O)", as in the following example:

(15) 老板（见他前言不搭后语，满口柴胡，极怕生事，只好着意周旋，）捧着香茶，拧着热毛巾侍候着，一边逗他说话出酒气："爷不知道？今儿法场出事了，刀下留人！"
Lǎobǎn (jiàn tā qiányánbùdāhòuyǔ, mǎnkǒucháihú, jí pà shēngshì,
owner see him talk incoherently talk nonsense extremely fear make trouble
zhǐhǎo zhuóyì zhōuxuán,) pěng-**zhe** xiāng chá, nǐng-**zhe** rè máojīn
necessarily carefully deal with hold-PRG fragrant tea twist-PRG hot towel
shìhòu-**zhe**, **yībiān** dòu tā shuōhuà chūjiǔqì: "Yé bù zhīdào? Jīnr
wait on-PRG meanwhile tease him talk sober up sir NEG know today
fǎchǎng chūshì le, dāo-xià liú rén!"
execution ground something be up MP under knife save person
{[Seeing that he was talking nonsense, and therefore might cause trouble, the (restaurant) owner had to deal with him carefully.] Holding fragrant tea, twisting a hot towel, and waiting on him, he tried to sober him up by tricking him into talking, "Sir, you haven't heard? Something was up on the execution ground today. The death-row convict didn't get executed at the last minute!"}

The word *zhe* occurs three times in a row in the above example, i.e., "V *zhe* O + V *zhe* O + V *zhe*". The following are another two examples:

(16) "市委领导同志"满面红光地微笑着向群众致意，一边把麦克风递给杨重："活该，谁让你们把麦克风给我让我讲话的。"
"Shìwěi lǐngdǎo tóngzhì" mǎnmiàn-hóngguāng de wēixiào-**zhe**
municipal party committee leader comrade ruddy-faced SP smile-PRG
xiàng qúnzhòng zhìyì, **yībiān** bǎ màikèfēng dì gěi Yáng Zhòng:
to the masses salute meanwhile BA microphone pass to YANG Zhong
"Huógāi, shuí ràng nǐ-men bǎ màikèfēng gěi wǒ ràng wǒ jiǎnghuà de."
deserve who ask you-PL BA microphone give me task me speak MP
{Smiling and ruddy-faced, the "leading comrade of the Municipal Party Committee" saluted the audience. While handing the microphone to YANG Zhong, he said, "It serves you right for giving me the microphone and asking me to speak."}

(17) 他只是咧着大嘴呵呵笑，一边招手：“上来，你上来。”
 Tā zhǐshì liě-*zhe* dà zuǐ hē-hē
 he just extend the corners of the mouth to the sides-PRG big mouth ha-REDP
 xiào, *yībiān* zhāoshǒu: "Shànglái, nǐ shànglái."
 laugh meanwhile wave hand come up you come up
 {Grinning from ear to ear, he beckoned, "Come up, you, come up."}

In the two examples above, *zhe* occurs only once respectively: "V *zhe* + V" in (16) and "V *zhe* O + V" in (17).

Second, if *zhe* is absent in the anterior clause, namely *p* is in the form of "V (O)," it can be inserted to form "V *zhe* (O)." Even without the presence of *zhe*, *p* still suggests an ongoing action and provides a semantic condition for the occurrence of *yībiān* in the posterior clause. The following are three examples:

(18) 有没来得及拖下去的伤兵，在冒着烟的焦炭中爬动，一边咬牙切齿地骂着："狗娘养的，丢老子在这里呀？！"
 Yǒu méi láidejí tuō xiàqu de shāngbīng, zài
 there be NEG have time for doing something drag go down SP wounded soldier in
 mào-zhe yān de jiāotàn-zhōng pá-dòng, *yībiān* yǎoyá-qièchǐ
 give off-PRG smoke SP through coke crawl meanwhile gnash the teeth in anger
 de mà-zhe: "Gǒuniángyǎngde, diū lǎozi zài zhèli ya?!"
 SP swear-PRG son of a bitch dump me at here MP
 {The wounded soldiers who had not yet been carried off (the battlefield) crawled through the smoking coke as they swore, teeth clenched, "Son of a bitch! Get me out of here!"}

(19) 她蹲在窗台上擦玻璃，一边还哼着小曲儿。
 Tā dūn zài chuāngtái-shàng cā bōli, *yībiān* hái hēng-zhe xiǎoqǔr.
 she squat on on windowsill clean glass meanwhile also hum-PRG little tune
 {As she squatted on the windowsill cleaning the glass, she hummed a little tune to herself.}

(20) 小白人掩嘴笑个不停，一边热烈地和冯小刚握手，"舒坦了舒坦了，从未有过的舒坦。"
 Xiǎobáirén yǎn zuǐ xiào gè bù tíng, *yībiān* rèliè
 small white person cover mouth giggle CL NEG stop meanwhile warm
 de hé Féng Xiǎogāng wòshǒu, "Shūtan le shūtan le, cóngwèi
 SP with FENG Xiaogang shake hands at ease PEF at ease PEF never
 yǒu-guò de shūtan."
 occur-EXP SP at ease
 {As the small white man (someone who looked like an albino) kept giggling, with one hand covering his mouth, he warmly shook hands with FENG Xiaogang, "Now I'm at ease, and I have never felt as comfortable as now."}

The word *zhe* could occur in the anterior clause in each of the three examples above. In (18), *zhe* could occur after *pá-dòng*, thus *p* would be in the form of "V *zhe*"; in (19), *zhe* could occur after the verb *cā*, thus *p* would be in the form of "V *zhe* O"; and in (20), *zhe* could occur after *yǎn*, thus *p* would be in the form of "V *zhe* V."

In some cases, a temporal adverb *zhèng* or *zhèngzài*, which has the same function as the word *zhe*, can occur in the anterior clause, as in the following example:

(21) 中午，司马婉卓正在煤气灶上炒菜，一边收听着收音机里的长篇小说连播节目。

Zhōngwǔ,	Sīmǎ Wǎnzhuó	**zhèng**	zài	... shàng	méiqìzào	shàng
noon	SIMA Wanzhuo	in progress	on		gas stove	

chǎocài,	yībiān	shōutīng-zhe	shōuyīnjī-li	de	chángpiān-xiǎoshuō
cook	meanwhile	listen-PRG	on radio	SP	novel

liánbō	jiémù.
be broadcast in succession	program

{At noon, SIMA Wanzhuo cooked on the gas stove while listening to a novel series on the radio.}

2.2.2 Type 2: Course of an action in the anterior clause

If the anterior clause takes the form of "V + directional verb", *p* denotes the course of an action, and "*yībiān* + *q* (V)" is likely to occur in the posterior clause. Compare the following two examples:

(22) *a 大娘吃完饺子，一边乐呵呵地笑。(?)

Dàniáng	chīwán	jiǎozi,	yībiān	lèhēhē	de	xiào.
aunt	eat up	dumpling	meanwhile	happily	SP	laugh

b 大娘端出饺子，一边乐呵呵地笑。(+)

Dàniáng	duān-chū	jiǎozi,	yībiān	lèhēhē	de	xiào.
aunt	bring out	dumpling	as	happily	SP	laugh

{Auntie laughed merrily as she brought out the dumplings.}

The study of similar sentences has revealed the following three rules:

First, the "V + directional verb" structure in the anterior clause indicates that an action is in progress, and it provides the semantic condition for the occurrence of the action marked by *yībiān* in the posterior clause. In other words, this type of complex sentence suggests that while the action in the anterior clause is in progress, the action in the posterior clause occurs at a certain point. The following are two examples:

(23) 叫老易的兵（就松弛下来，）慢慢走回方才自己睡的地方，坐下，一边故作大方地说："也就是大肉炖萝卜了，什么好东西，……"

Jiào	Lǎo Yì de bīng	(jiù sōngchí-xiàlái,)	màn-màn	zǒu-**huí**	fāngcái
named old YI SP soldier	then become relaxed	slowly-REDP	walk back	just now	

zìjǐ	shuì de dìfang,	zuò-xia,	yībiān	gù zuò dàfāng	de shuō:
oneself	sleep SP place	sit down	meanwhile	pretend be generous	SP say

"Yě jiù shì dàròu dùn luóbo le, shénme hǎo dōngxi, ..."
just pork stew radish MP nothing good thing

{The soldier named Old YI [, who had just become relaxed] pretended to be generous, "Just pork stew with radishes, nothing rare . . ." while he was walking slowly back to where he had just slept and then sitting down.}

(24) 事已至此，刘国璋也只得收起自己的种种奇思异想，**一边**观察别人怎么当的班主任。

*Shìyǐzhìcǐ,   Liú Guózhāng   yě zhǐděi   shōu-**qǐ**   zìjǐ   de   zhǒng-zhǒng*
at this point LIU Guozhang   have to   put away   oneself   SP   kind-REDP
*qísīyìxiǎng,   **yībiān**   guānchá biérén zěnme dāng de bānzhǔrèn.*
strange idea meanwhile observe others how   be   SP teacher in charge of a class
{As LIU Guozhang was observing how others worked as the teacher in charge of a class, he had to brush away all his various strange ideas at this point.}

In the anterior clause of (23), *zǒu-huí* ('walk back to') indicates a course of spatial displacement, and the action stated in the posterior clause started toward the end of the course, while in the anterior clause of (24) *shōu-qǐ* suggests a course of time shift, and the action in the posterior clause might have continued throughout the course.

Second, the cooccurrence of a directional verb and a directional preposition can make the spatial displacement more evident. The following are two examples:

(25) 秀秀娘忙不迭地**到**灶间**去**烧菜，**一边**叫道："秀子！秀子！"

*Xiùxiu niáng   mángbùdié de   **dào**   zàojiān   **qù**   shāocài, **yībiān**   jiàodào:*
Xiuxiu mother hurried   SP towards kitchen go   cook   meanwhile shout
"*Xiùzi!   Xiùzi!*"
 Xiuzi   Xiuzi
{As Xiuxiu's mother hurried to the kitchen to cook, she shouted, "Xiuzi! Xiuzi!"}

(26) "我给你看看去。" 老太太站起来，**往**厨房走，**一边**对于观说，"你好长时间没来了。"

"*Wǒ   gěi   nǐ   kàn-kàn-qu.*"   *Lǎotàitai zhàn-**qǐlái**, **wǎng**   chúfáng   zǒu,*
 I   for you   go to have a look old lady   stand up   toward   kitchen   walk
yībiān *duì   Yú Guān   shuō,   "Nǐ   hǎo   cháng   shíjiān   méi   lái   le.*"
  as   to   YU Guan   say   you   very   long   time   NEG   come   MP
{"I'll go and have a look for you," the old lady said to YU Guan, as she stood up and walked toward the kitchen, "you haven't been here for ages."}

In the anterior clause of (25), "*dào zàojiān qù*" ('go to the kitchen') is in the form of "preposition + V" (directional verb), and in (26) *zhàn-qǐlái*, a "V + directional verb" structure, occurs first, and then "*wǎng chúfáng zǒu*" ('walk toward the kitchen'), a "prepositional phrase + verb," occurs.

Directional prepositions include *wǎng, cháo, xiàng, dào,* and *gěi*, among others. In some cases, only a "preposition + V" structure occurs in the anterior clause, but a directional verb can be present, for example, "*wǎng chúfáng zǒu*" can be rewritten as "*wǎng chúfáng zǒu qù*." The following are two more examples:

(27) 他摇摇晃晃朝工棚里面走，**一边**回头瞪着小满。

*Tā   yáoyáo-huànghuàng cháo   gōngpéng   lǐmiàn   zǒu,   **yībiān**   huítóu*
he   stagger   toward   shed   inside walk   meanwhile look back
dèng-zhe   Xiǎomǎn.
stare-PRG   Xiaoman
{He looked back and then stared at Xiaoman as he was staggering to the inside of the shed.}

Paired and single occurrences of the connective yībiān 47

(28) 文峰（用手拂一下已经很整齐的分头，）往旁边挪挪屁股，给姑娘让座，<u>二边</u>又凑近了，轻言细语和她说话。

Wénfēng (yòng shǒu fú yīxià yǐjīng hěn zhěngqí de fēntóu,) **wǎng**
Wenfeng with hand brush once already very neat SP parted hair to
pángbiān **nuó-nuó** pìgu, gěi gūniang ràngzuò, <u>yībiān</u>
aside move-REDP buttocks for girl make room for a seat meanwhile
yòu còujìn le, qīngyán-xìyǔ hé tā shuōhuà.
also get closer PEF speak softly with her talk
{Wenfeng [brushed his already neatly parted hair with his hand and] moved his bum to the side to make a seat for the girl, and almost at the same time (as she sat down) he moved closer to her and talked to her softly.}

The directional verb *qù* can be added and placed after *zǒu* in (27), and the directional verb *kāi* can replace the second *nuó* in (28).

However, if a preposition occurs after "V," then there is no space for a directional verb. The following are two examples:

(29) 大家奔向大海，<u>一边</u>高声欢呼。
Dàjiā bēn-**xiàng** dàhǎi, <u>yībiān</u> gāoshēng huānhū.
everybody rush to sea meanwhile loudly cheer
{Everyone cheered loudly as they ran to the sea.}

(30) 他把钱还给我，一边不停地说谢谢。
Tā bǎ qián huán-**gěi** wǒ, <u>yībiān</u> bù tíng de shuō xièxiè.
he BA money return to me meanwhile NEG stop SP say thanks
{He kept saying thanks as he returned the money to me.}

Third, in some cases, *le* can occur in the anterior clause, either following the verb, i.e., "V *le* + directional verb," or following the directional verb, i.e., "V + directional verb+ *le*," as in the following two examples:

(31) 大娘端出了面条，一边乐呵呵地笑。
Dàniáng duān-chū **le** miàntiáo, yībiān lèhēhē de xiào.
old aunt bring out PEF noodles meanwhile happy SP smile
{Aunt smiled happily as she brought out the noodles.}

(32) 小魁站了起来，一边向我眨眼睛。
xiǎokuí zhàn-qǐlái **le** qǐlái, yībiān xiàng wǒ zhǎ yǎnjīng.
Xiaokui stand up PEF meanwhile at I blink eye
{Xiaokui winked at me as he stood up.}

The cooccurrence of *le* and directional verb is meant to stress both the presence and the continuation of the action. The following are two examples:

(33) "我们全家都是用的这种篾块。" 说完，那学生就把头低了下去，<u>一边</u>用脚尖在地上划拉。
"*Wǒ-men quán jiā dōu shì yòng de zhè zhǒng mièkuài.*" Shuō wán,
we whole family all COP use SP this type bamboo cane speak finish

*nà xuéshēng jiù bǎ tóu **dī**-xiàqu, **le xiàqu**, <u>yībiān</u> yòng jiǎojiān*
that student then BA head lower down PEF meanwhile with tiptoe
zài dì-shàng huála.
on ground scratch
{The student said, "All my family use this kind of bamboo cane." After that, he "swept" the ground with the tip of his toes as he lowered his head down.}

(34) 当下三人在门口解装，一个麻脸伙计早提着灯迎了出来，<u>一边</u>帮着卸骡子，……

Dāngxià sān rén zài ménkǒu jiězhuāng, yī gè má liǎn huǒji
then three person in doorway unload one CL pockmarked face clerk
*zǎo tí-zhe dēng **yíng**-chūlái **le chūlai**, <u>yībiān</u> bāng-zhe*
early hold-PRG lantern come out to welcome PEF as help-PRG
xiè luózi, ...
unload mule
{At the moment, the three men were unloading baggage (from mules) in the doorway. Carrying a lantern, a pockmarked clerk came out to welcome them and helped to unload the mules ...}

The above two examples indicate that the actions of *dī* ('lower') and *yíng* ('welcome') have occurred and that the states of *dī-xiàqù* and *yíng-chūlái* are continuing, which justifies the occurrence of *yībiān* in the posterior clause.

2.2.3 Type 3: Quoting in the anterior clause

In this type, the anterior clause is a quotation, and the verb is usually *shuō* ('say') or one of its synonyms. In such sentences, "*yībiān* + *q* (V)" is likely to occur in the posterior clause, as in the following two examples:

(35) 她说："别走！" <u>一边</u>拉住他的手。

Tā shuō: "Bié zǒu!" <u>Yībiān</u> lā-zhù tā de shǒu.
she say do not go meanwhile hold he SP hand
{Holding his hand, she said, "Don't go!"}

(36) "来人呀！" 她大声叫喊，<u>一边</u>顺手捡起一块砖头。

"Lái rén ya!" Tā dàshēng jiàohǎn, <u>yībiān</u> shùnshǒu jiǎn-qǐ yī
come person MP she loudly shout meanwhile conveniently pick up one
kuài zhuāntou.
CL brick
{"Help!" She shouted, as she conveniently picked up a brick.}

Three conclusions can be drawn from the analysis of sentences in similar and related structures.

First, the anterior clause provides information about who says what in a particular form, which contains two basic elements, that is, "S + *shuō* verb" and a direct quotation. The use of "*yībiān*..." in the posterior clause is meant to emphasize the concurrence of the speaking and the mental activity or body action of the speaker, that is, while the speaking is in progress, the mental activity or physical movement occurs at a certain point. The following are two examples:

(37) 我说："还要莫斗人，不吃人家的麦子和小菜，懂了没有？" 一边还轻轻地在他头上拍了一巴掌。
Wǒ shuō: "*Hái yào mò dǒu rén, bù chī rénjiā de màizi hé*
I say also need do not gore person NEG eat others SP wheat and
xiǎocài, dǒng-le méiyǒu?" Yībiān hái qīng-qīng de zài
young vegetables understand-PEF NEG meanwhile also gentle-REDP SP at
tā tóu-shàng pāi-le yī bāzhang.
his on head pat-PEF one palm
{"Don't gore people (with your horns), and don't eat people's wheat (growing in the fields) or vegetables (growing in the gardens). Do you understand me?" I said, gently patting him on the head.}

(38) 黄丽的哥哥很忠于职守地说："好的，我等你考虑。" 一边摸出烟，点燃火，很有架势地吸起来。
Huáng Lì de gēge *hěn zhōngyú-zhíshǒu de shuō:* "***Hǎode,***
HUANG Li SP elder brother very be devoted to one's duty SP say okay
wǒ děng nǐ kǎolǜ." Yībiān mō-chū yān,
I await you think meanwhile fumble for something and take it out cigarette
diǎnrán huǒ, hěn yǒu jiàshì de xī-qǐlái.
light fire very have posture SP start to smoke
{HUANG Li's brother fumbled for a cigarette, lit it, and smoked ostentatiously, as he said in a very-devoted-to-his-duty tone, "All right, I'll wait for you to think about it."}

In (37), the concurrence of the speaking and the body action is suggested, and in (38) the occurrence is also suggested, although it is hard to determine when exactly the body action occurs.

Second, *mà* ('swear'), *hǎn* ('shout'), *wèn* ('ask'), *huídá* ('answer'), *fēnfù* ('instruct'), and so on, can be regarded as the synonyms of *shuō*. They take neither *zhe* nor any directional verbs but can take objects, such as *yījù* ('a sentence'), *yīshēng* ('one sound'), and so forth, as in the following example:

(39) 他没听清楚她说什么，他问，"什么？" 一边向前探着身子。
Tā méi tīng-qīngchǔ tā shuō shénme, ***tā wèn,*** "*Shénme?" Yībiān xiàng*
he NEG hear clearly she say what he ask what meanwhile toward
qián tàn-zhe shēnzi.
front lean-PRG body
{He didn't quite catch what she had said, so he leaned forward as he asked her, "What did you say?"}

In the anterior clause of (39), an object *yījù* can be added and placed after *wèn*. The following is another example:

(40) 胡石大乐，他笑得喷饭，他大骂一声，操！<u>一边</u>把呼机举到林则眼前。
*Hú Shí dà   lè,   tā xiào de pēnfàn, **tā dà   mà   yī shēng**, cāo!*
HU Shi loudly laugh he laugh SP spew food he loudly swear one sound fuck
<u>*Yībiān*</u>   bǎ   hūjī   jǔ-dào Lín Zé   yǎn-qián.
meanwhile BA pager raise to LIN Ze before eye
{HU Shi burst into laughter, and he laughed so hard that food was spewed out from his mouth. "Fuck!" he swore loudly, as he raised the pager to LIN Ze's eyes.}

In (40) *mà* takes *yīshēng* as its object.

Third, in some cases, a direct quotation occurs before, instead of after, "S *shuō*"; thus, *p* is immediately followed by *q*, as in the following example:

(41) "我来给我儿子，寄 …… 寄一点钱。"他回答，<u>一边</u>把手从衣襟里抽出来，掌心里有一个小纸包，包得严严实实。
*"Wǒ lái   gěi wǒ érzi, jì . . . jì   yīdiǎn qián." **Tā huídá**, <u>yībiān</u>   bǎ*
I   come to   my son send   send a little money   he reply   meanwhile BA
shǒu cóng yījīn-li   chōu-chūlái, zhǎngxīn-li yǒu   yī gè xiǎo zhǐ
hand from inside lapel pull out   in palm   there be one CL small paper
bāo, bāo   de yányán-shíshí.
bag wrap SP tightly
{"I've come to send . . . send some money to my son," he replied, as he pulled his hand out of his jacket. In his palm was a tightly wrapped paper bag.}

A direct quotation occurs before "S *shuō*" in (41). Quotation marks generally need to be placed around the direct quotation, but they can be left out if the context is clear enough. For example, *cāo* in (40) does not have quotation marks around it. The following is another example:

(42) 现在你先等一会儿。我会付双倍的等候费。老安慷慨地说，<u>一边</u>盘算着。
Xiànzài nǐ   xiān děng yīhuìr. Wǒ huì fù shuāng bèi de děnghòu fèi.
now   you first wait a moment I will pay double time SP wait time fee
Lǎo Ān kāngkǎi   de   shuō, <u>*yībiān*</u>   *pánsuàn-zhe.*
old AN generous SP   say   meanwhile calculate-PRG
{"Now please wait a moment. I will pay double the wait time fee," said old AN generously, as he calculated in his mind.}

As can be seen in (42), there are no quotation marks around the direct quotation.

2.3   Form C: "*yībiān p, Ø q*"

In Form C, *yībiān* occurs in the anterior clause only, and Ø in the posterior clause indicates the slot for the connective *yībiān*. There are similarities as well as differences between "Ø *p*" in Form B and "Ø *q*" in Form C.

2.3.1   *Similarities*

There are similarities between "Ø *p*" and "Ø *q*," and "Ø *q*" also denotes an ongoing action, course of an action and quoting, as in the following three examples:

(43) 一边跑，他脑子里不停地转着念头。
 Yībiān   pǎo,   tā   nǎozi-li   bù   tíng   de   zhuǎn-zhe   niàntou.
 meanwhile run   he   in mind   NEG   stop   SP   think-PRG   idea
 {He kept thinking as he ran.}

(44) 一边看，他不由自主地流下了眼泪。
 Yībiān   kàn,   tā   bùyóu-zìzhǔ   de   liúxià-le   yǎnlèi.
 meanwhile watch he   cannot help but   SP   shed-PEF   tear
 {As he was watching, he could not help but shed tears.}

(45) 他一边朝前走，口中答道："我不在乎！"
 Tā _yībiān_   cháo   qián   zǒu, kǒu-zhōng dá-dào: "Wǒ bù   zàihu!"
 he meanwhile toward front walk in mouth   reply   I   NEG   care
 {"I don't care!" he replied as he walked along.}

There are three different indications of "Ø q."
First, it can denote an ongoing action, usually with the presence of *zhe* in the sentence. The progressiveness of the action stated in the anterior clause makes it possible for "Ø q" to act as the posterior clause, although with limitations. The following are two examples:

(46) （胤禛）一边说，苦笑着摇了摇头，……
 (Yìnzhēn)   _yībiān_   shuō,   kǔxiào-_zhe_   yáoleyáo tóu,...
 Yinzhen   meanwhile   talk   have a wry smile-PRG shake one's head
 {As [Yinzhen] was talking, he shook his head with a wry smile ...}

(47) 金玉泽一边命人给邬思道打水取换洗衣服,自坐着吃茶，（出了半天神方叹道：……）
 Jīn Yùzé   _yībiān_   mìng   rén   gěi   Wū Sīdào   dǎ   shuǐ   qǔ
 JIN Yuze meanwhile   order   other person for   WU Sidao   get   water fetch
 huànxǐ yīfu,   zì   zuò-_zhe_   chī   chá, (chūshén-le
 clothes to be changed for washing   self   sit-PRG   drink tea   be lost in thought-PEF
 bàntiān   shén   fāng   tàn   dào:...)
 quite a while late   as   sigh say
 {As JIN Yuze asked someone to get water and clean clothes for WU Sidao, he sat down and drank tea, [and sighed after he awoke from his trance:...].}

In both (46) and (47), *zhe* occurs. However, in both examples *zhe* needs to be followed by another action, that is, "*yáoleyáo tóu*" in (46) and "*chī chá*" in (47). Otherwise, words such as *réngrán* ('still') or *háizài* ('still') needs to be present. The following are two examples:

(48) （胤禛）一边说，仍然苦笑着。
 (Yìnzhēn)   _yībiān_   shuō,   **réngrán**   kǔxiào-_zhe_.
 Yinzhen   meanwhile   talk   still   have a wry smile-PRG
 {As [Yinzhen] was talking, still smiling wryly.}

52 *Paired and single occurrences of the connective yībiān*

(49) 金玉泽一边命人给邬思道打水取换洗衣服，仍然坐着。
Jīn Yùzé yībiān   mìng rén   gěi   Wū Sīdào dǎ shuǐ qǔ
JIN Yuze meanwhile order other person for WU Sidao get water fetch
huànxǐ yīfu,   réngrán zuò-zhe
clothes to be changed for washing still   sit-PRG
{As JIN Yuze asked someone to get water and clean clothes for WU Sidao, he was still sitting.}

The following is another example:

(50) （他们走进餐厅。）一边走，方亮的心里仍在不停地翻腾。
(Tā-men zǒu-jìn   cāntīng.) Yībiān   zǒu, Fāng Liàng de xīn-li réng
they   walk into restaurant meanwhile walk FANG Liang SP in heart still
zài   bù   tíng de fānténg.
in progress NEG   stop SP change drastically
{[They were walking into the restaurant.] FANG Liang's state of mind kept swinging as he was walking.}

In (50) *zhe* does not occur, but "*réng zài*" does, which suggests that the action is in progress. Moreover, even with the presence of "*réng zài*", *zhe* can still occur, i.e., "*Yībiān zǒu, FANG Liàng de xīn-lǐ réng zài bùtíng de fānténg-zhe*."

Second, "Ø *q*" sometimes suggests the course of an action, which is often indicated by a directional verb. The significance of "Ø *q*" justifies its occurrence after "*yībiān p*," as shown in the following example:

(51) 一边挥着鲜花，他们飞也似的冲了过去。
Yībiān   huī-zhe   xiānhuā, tā-men fēi yě shìde chōng-guòqu le   guòqu.
meanwhile wave-PRG   flower   they   fly just like   rush over   PEF
{As they waved flowers, they rushed over there.}

In the example above, *guòqu* in the posterior clause signifies the process of spatial displacement. The following are another two examples:

(52) "…… 你不是说，你特别喜欢花吗？" 一边说，双手恭恭敬敬地把花献上。
"*… Nǐ bù   shì shuō, nǐ   tèbié   xǐhuān huā   ma?"   Yībiān   shuō,*
 you NEG COP say   you really   like   flower MP   meanwhile say
shuāng shǒu gōnggōng-jìngjìng de bǎ   huā   xiàn-shàng.
both   hand respectful   SP BA flower raise and present
{"… didn't you say that you really liked flowers?" (Someone) said while presenting the flowers respectfully with both hands.}

(53) （晓燕叫智雄切萝卜，自己在一旁择豆角。）一边择，冷不丁笑了出来，（智雄道，"什么事这么好笑？"）
(Xiǎoyàn jiào Zhìxióng qiē luóbo, zìjǐ zài yīpáng zhái dòujiǎo.) Yībiān
Xiaoyan ask Zhixiong cut radish self at aside select been   meanwhile
zhái,   lěngbùdīng xiào-chūlái, le   chūlai, (Zhìxióng dào, "shénme shì   zhème
select suddenly   laugh out loud PEF   Zhixiong say   what   matter so

hǎoxiào?")
funny
{[Xiaoyan asked Zhixiong to cut the radishes and she, herself, was selecting the beans aside.] She burst into laughter as she was selecting (the beans), [Zhixiong asked, "What's so funny?"]}

The occurrence of the directional verb *shàng* in (52) suggests the course of spatial displacement, and in (53) the use of the directional verb *chūlai* indicates the course of time shift.

Third, "Ø q" sometimes suggests quoting, in the form of "*shuō* + direct quotation." An example can be found in *Dream of the Red Chamber* (Example (9)). The following are two more examples:

(54) 刘燮一边笑着给刘文运斟酒，说道，"脸都叫踢白了！……"
*Liú Xiè yībiān xiào-zhe gěi Liú Wényùn zhēn jiǔ, **shuō-dào**, "Liǎn dōu*
LIU Xie meanwhile smile-PRG for LIU Wenyun pour wine say face even
jiào tī bái-le!..."
PASSIVE kick pale-PEF
{As LIU Xie smiled and poured wine for LIU Wenyun, he said, "(His rejection of your offer) has made you so embarrassed! . . ."}

(55) 戴铎一边想，笑道："就是四爷这话！……"
*Dài Duó yībiān xiǎng, **xiào dào**: "Jiù shì Sìyé zhè huà!..."*
DAI Duo meanwhile think smile say just COP Fourth Prince this word
{As DAI Duo thought, he said with a smile, "You are right in saying that, Fourth Prince! . . ."}

In (54) and (55) the two synonyms of *shuō*, i.e., *shuō-dào* and *xiào-dào*, are both disyllabic, and they are each followed by a direct speech. For *shuō* or its monosyllabic synonym, other elements need to be supplemented before or after it, as shown in the following example:

(56) （于是司马婉卓看见了他胳膊上的受伤处，那里正汩汩地冒着血。）她（急忙上前扶住胳膊，）一边采取措施止血，顺口问了句："怎么伤成这样？"
(Yúshì Sīmǎ Wǎnzhuó kànjiàn-le tā gēbo-shàng de shòushāng chù, nàli
then SIMA Wanzhuo see-PEF his in arm SP be injured place there
zhèng gǔ-gǔ de mào-zhe xuè.) Tā (jímáng shàng-qián fú-zhù
in progress gurgle-REDP SP spurt-PRG blood she hurriedly go forward hold
*gēbo,) yībiān cǎiqǔ cuòshī zhǐ xuè, shùnkǒu **wèn**-le jù: "Zěnme*
arm meanwhile take measures stop blood naturally ask-PEF sentence how
shāng chéng zhèyàng?"
be injured become so
{[Then SIMA Wanzhuo saw that the wound in his arm was gurgling with blood.] "How did your arm get injured like this?" she asked, as she [got close to hold his arm and] took steps to stop the bleeding.}

In (56), the verb *wèn* is preceded by *shùnkǒu* and followed by "*le jù*"; if not, *wèn* would need to be replaced by a disyllabic word, for instance, *wèn-dào*, and that part could be rewritten as in the following example:

(57) 她<u>一边</u>采取措施止血，问道："怎么伤成这样？"
Tā <u>yībiān</u>   cǎiqǔ cuòshī zhǐ xuè, **wèn-dào** "Zěnme shāng
she meanwhile take   measure stop blood ask   how   be injured
chéng zhèyàng?"
become so
{While taking steps to stop the bleeding, she asked, "How did your arm get injured like this?"}

2.3.2 Differences in meaning and structure

Differences also exist between "Ø *p*" and "Ø *q*". The following are three sentences:

(58) <u>一边</u>吆喝，他已采取了守势。
<u>Yībiān</u>   yāohe, tā **yǐ**   cǎiqǔ-le   shǒushì.
meanwhile shout   he already adopt-PEF defensive posture
{He had already adopted the defensive posture as he shouted.}

(59) <u>一边</u>表演，他突然变了花样。
<u>Yībiān</u>   biǎoyǎn, tā **tūrán**   biàn-le   huāyàng.
meanwhile perform   he suddenly change-PEF trick
{As he performed, he suddenly changed his tricks.}

(60) <u>一边</u>朝里走，我内心越来越不安。
<u>Yībiān</u>   cháo   lǐ   zǒu,   wǒ **nèixīn**   yuèláiyuè   bù'ān.
meanwhile toward inside walk   my inner world more and more uneasy
{As I walked inside, I became more and more uneasy.}

The study of sentences in the same structure and similar structures has resulted in the following conclusions.

First, the word *yǐ* ('already') or its synonym can occur in "Ø *q*," which stresses that the action stated in the posterior clause has already occurred and is in progress before the action stated in the anterior clause ends, whereas it is impossible for *yǐ* or its synonym to occur in "Ø *p*" in Form B. For this reason, (58) makes sense, but (61) does not.

(61) *他已采取了守势，一边*q*。
Tā **yǐ**   cǎiqǔ-le   shǒushì,   <u>yībiān</u>   *q*.
He already adopt-PEF defensive posture meanwhile

The following are four examples:

(62) 胤禔……<u>一边</u>寻思，口中已转了风："这事情不单要从字迹上想，……"
Yintí ... *yībiān* xúnsi, kǒu-zhōng **yǐ** zhuǎn-le fēng: "Zhè shìqíng
Yinti meanwhile think in mouth already change-PEF tone this matter
bùdān yào cóng zìjǐ-shàng xiǎng, ..."
not only need from in handwriting consider
{As Yinti ... was thinking, the tone of his voice had already changed, "This is not a matter only about the handwriting ..."}

(63) （康熙又转脸对张廷玉道："你拟旨，……"张廷玉素以行文敏捷办事迅速著称。）康熙<u>一边</u>说，他已在打腹稿。
(Kāngxī yòu zhuǎn liǎn duì Zhāng Tíngyù dào: "Nǐ nǐ zhǐ ..."
Kangxi then turn face to ZHANG Tingyu say you draft imperial edict
Zhāng Tíngyù sù yǐ xíngwén mǐnjié bànshì xùnsù zhùchēng.) Kāngxī
ZHANG Tingyu always for write sharp action quick be well known Kangxi
yībiān shuō, tā **yǐ** zài dǎ fùgǎo.
meanwhile say he already in progress make mental notes
{[(Emperor) Kangxi then turned to ZHANG Tingyu, who had a reputation for writing quickly and getting things done efficiently, and said, "You draft the edict ..."] ZHANG was already making mental notes as Kangxi spoke.}

(64) 戴铎<u>一边</u>说，胤禛已经移步往前走，……
Dài Duó *yībiān* shuō, Yìnzhēn **yǐjīng** yí bù wǎng qián zǒu, ...
DAI Duo meanwhile talk Yinzhen already move step toward forward walk
{As DAI Duo was talking, Yinzhen had already begun to walk ahead ...}

(65) （邬思道）<u>一边</u>说，已经进了店，……
(Wū Sīdào) *yībiān* shuō, **yǐjīng** jìn-le diàn, ...
WU Sidao meanwhile talk already enter-PEF hotel
{[WU Sidao] already walked into the hotel as (he) was talking ...}

The word *yǐ* occurs in the first two examples and *yǐjīng* in the latter two. Sometimes, the absence of *yǐ* or its synonyms affects the legitimacy of the posterior clause. The following is an example:

(66) <u>一边</u>说着，司马婉卓迅速准备好各种器具，和李惠芬一起出门了。
Yībiān shuō-zhe, Sīmǎ Wǎnzhuó xùnsù zhǔnbèi hǎo gèzhǒng qìjù,
meanwhile say-PRG SIMA Wanzhuo rapidly prepare finished all kinds device
hé Lǐ Huìfēn yīqǐ chūmén-le.
with LI Huifen together leave-PEF
{While SIMA Wanzhuo was speaking, she had quickly prepared all kinds of (medical) devices and gone out with LI Huifen.}

Example (67a), a shortened version of (66), is acceptable because of the presence of *chū*, which indicates the course of an action. On the other hand, (67b), another shortened version of (66), is unacceptable, but if *yǐ* occurred, it would be grammatically correct, as (67c).

(67) a 一边说着，司马婉卓和李惠芬一起出门了。
Yībiān   shuō-zhe, Sīmǎ Wǎnzhuó   hé   Lǐ Huìfēn   yīqǐ   chūmén-le.
meanwhile   say-PRG   SIMA Wanzhuo   with   LI Huifen   together   leave-PEF
{While SIMA Wanzhuo was speaking, she had gone out with LI Huifen.}

*b 一边说着，司马婉卓迅速准备好各种器具。
Yībiān   shuō-zhe, Sīmǎ Wǎnzhuó   xùnsù   zhǔnbèi-hǎo   gèzhǒng   qìjù.
meanwhile   say-PRG   SIMA Wanzhuo   rapidly finish preparing   all kinds device

c 一边说着，司马婉卓已迅速准备好各种器具。
Yībiān   shuō-zhe, Sīmǎ Wǎnzhuó   **yǐ**   xùnsù   zhǔnbèi-hǎo   gèzhǒng
meanwhile   say-PRG   SIMA Wanzhuo   already   rapidly   finish preparing all kinds
qìjù.
device
{While SIMA Wanzhuo was speaking, she had already quickly got all kinds of (medical) devices ready.}

Second, "Ø q" may stress suddenness with *tūrán* ('suddenly') or another word of similar meaning, which indicates that the action stated in the posterior clause suddenly occurs while the action stated in the anterior clause is in progress. By contrast, *tūrán* cannot occur in "Ø p" in Form B, and this is why (68a) is acceptable but (68b) is not.

(68) a 一边表演，他突然变了花样。
Yībiān   biǎoyǎn,   tā   **tūrán**   biàn-le   huāyàng.
meanwhile   perform   he   suddenly   change-PEF   trick
{As he performed, he suddenly changed his tricks.}

*b 他突然变了花样，一边表演。
Tā   tūrán   biàn-le   huāyàng,   yībiān   biǎoyǎn.
he   suddenly   change-PEF   trick   meanwhile   perform

The following are three more examples:

(69) 一边斟酒，她突然给我丢了一个眼色。
Yībiān   zhēn jiǔ,   tā   **tūrán**   gěi wǒ diū yǎnsè le   yī   gè   yǎnsè.
meanwhile   pour wine   she suddenly   at me   wink   PEF one CL
{While she was pouring the wine, she suddenly winked at me.}

(70) 一边往前带球，他突然抽筋倒在地上。
Yībiān   wǎng   qián   dàiqiú,   tā   **tūrán**   chōujīn   dǎo
meanwhile   toward front   run with the ball he   suddenly   have a cramp fall
zài dì-shàng.
on ground
{As he was running with the ball forward, he fell to the ground with a cramp.}

(71) 一边和谈，他们突然发动了进攻。
*Yībiān   hétán,   tā-men **tūrán**   fādòng-le   jìngōng.*
meanwhile hold peace talks they suddenly launch-PEF attack
{They suddenly launched an attack while peace talks were in progress.}

In some cases, the absence of *tūrán* may affect the legitimacy of the posterior clause, for example:

(72) 只听两个道人低声谈论，对明日比武之约似乎胜算在握，<u>一面</u>解衣上炕，突然皮清玄叫了起来："啊，被窝中湿漉漉的是甚麽？啊，好臭，姬师兄，你这麽懒，在被窝中拉尿？"
Zhǐ   tīng liǎng gè   dàorén   dī   shēng tánlùn,   duì   míngrì
only hear two CL Taoist priest low voice discuss about tomorrow
bǐwǔ   zhī yuē   sìhū   shèngsuàn-zàiwò,
martial arts competition SP appointment seemingly have the games in hands
<u>*yīmiàn*</u> *jiě   yī   shàng   kàng,   **tūrán**   Pí Qīngxuán jiào-qǐlái le*
meanwhile unbutton clothes get onto bed suddenly PI Qingxuan cry out PEF
qǐlái: Ā, bèiwō-zhōng shīlùlù   de   shì shènme? Ā, hǎo chou, Jī shīxiōng,
         ah in quilt   soaking wet SP COP what   ah so stinky JI big brother
nǐ   zhème lǎn,   zài   bèiwō-zhōng   lāniào?
you so lazy at in quilt pee
{The two Taoist priests were discussing the next day's martial arts competition in a low voice, and they seemed to have the game in their hands. As they undressed and went to the bed, PI Qingxuan suddenly called out, "Ah, what's soaking wet and stinky in the quilt? Brother JI, how lazy you are! Did you pee in the quilt?"}

In the anterior clause of the above example, the word *yīmiàn*, an equivalent of *yībiān*, occurs. In the posterior clause, the occurrence of *tūrán* not only emphasizes the suddenness of the action but also guarantees the correctness of the clause. Without *tūrán*, the clause would be defective. Therefore, in some cases, *tūrán* needs to be present even though there is a directional verb in the posterior clause.

Third, some instances of "Ø q" include *nèixīn* ('inner world/mind') or other similar words, such as *xīnlǐ* and *xīnxià*. Complex sentences in this structure underline the speaker's thoughts or perception in the course of the ongoing action stated in the anterior clause. Among all the example sentences collected by the author, neither *nèixīn* nor its synonym can be found in Form B. This is why (73a) is acceptable while (73b) is not.

(73) a 一边朝里走，我内心越来越不安。
*Yībiān   cháo   lǐ   zǒu,   wǒ   **nèixīn**   yuèláiyuè   bù'ān.*
meanwhile toward inside walk my inner world more and more uneasy
{As I was walking inside, I became more and more uneasy.}

*b 我内心越来越不安，一边朝里走.
*Wǒ **nèixīn**   yuèláiyuè   bù'ān,   <u>yībiān</u>   cháo   lǐ   zǒu.*
my inner world more and more uneasy meanwhile toward inside walk

The following is another example:

(74) 令狐冲一面运功，心下暗自奇怪："怎地雪花落在脸上，竟然不消融？"
Línghú Chōng   yīmiàn   yùngōng,
LINGHU Chong   meanwhile   use one's own energy by practicing qi gong
                               (a form of Chinese martial arts)
xīn-xià ànzì   qíguài: "Zěnde xuěhuā luò zài liǎn-shàng, jìngrán
in mind to oneself strange how come snowflake fall at on face unexpectedly
bù   xiāoróng?"
NEG   melt
{As LINGHU Chong was using his energy (to dispel the cold from inside his friends' bodies), he wondered why the snowflakes on his face were not melting.}

Sometimes, *nèixīn* or its synonym is absent, but it is implied, as in the following two examples:

(75) （司马婉卓缓缓地转过身，走出去。）一边走，她感到自己的脚步很沉重，几乎有一种抬不起来的感觉。
(Sīmǎ Wǎnzhuó huǎn-huǎn de zhuǎn-guò shēn, zǒu-chūqu.) Yībiān   zǒu,
SIMA Wanzhuo   slow-REDP SP turn around body walk out   meanwhile   walk
tā gǎndào zìjǐ de jiǎobù   hěn chénzhòng, jīhū yǒu yī zhǒng tái bù qǐlái
she feel   self SP footstep very heavy   nearly have one type can't lift
de gǎnjué.
SP feeling
{[SIMA Wanzhuo slowly turned around and walked out.] As she was walking, her feet felt so heavy that they could hardly be lifted.}

(76) 我一边说着，思前想后，也忍不住冒泪花儿了。
Wǒ yībiān   shuō-zhe, sīqián-xiǎnghòu, yě rěn bù zhù   mào lèihuār le.
I   meanwhile speak-PRG think through   also can't hold back shed tear   PEF
{As I spoke, I thought it through and burst into tears, too.}

In the two examples above, *nèixīn-lǐ* can be inserted and placed before *gǎndào* in (75) and *sīqián-xiǎnghòu* in (76).

2.3.3 Difference in subject location

In Form B ("Ø *p, yībiān q*"), the subject is absent in the posterior clause, while it sometimes is present in the posterior clause in Form C (*yībiān p, Ø q*), hence the form of "*yībiān p, S Ø q*." Quite a number of examples in this form can be found in the previous discussions. The following is another example:

(77) "……知识分子当我的大哥，我服！"一边说，他端起杯子，豪气十足地："……来，干杯！"
"...Zhīshifènzǐ dāng wǒ de dàgē, wǒ fú!" Yībiān   shuō, tā duān-qǐ bēizi,
intellectual be I SP boss I accept   meanwhile say he raise   glass

Paired and single occurrences of the connective yībiān 59

háoqì-shízú   de: "... Lái,   gānbēi!"
full of boldness SP come on bottom up
{"... An intellectual being my boss, I accept!" Raising his glass, he said boldly,
"... Come on, bottoms up!}

As can be seen, the subject *tā* is present in the posterior clause.

The presence of the subject in the posterior clause indicates that the action in the anterior clause and the one in the posterior clause are relatively independent of each other. The following are another two examples:

(78) "王主任，你看见他来了吗？在哪儿看见的？" <u>一边</u>说，她侧过脸，拼命向王维力使眼色。

"Wáng zhǔrèn, nǐ   kànjiàn tā   lái-le   ma? Zài nǎr   kànjiàn de?" Yībiān
director WANG you see him come-PEF MP at where see MP meanwhile
shuō, tā   cè-guò   liǎn, pīnmìng   xiàng Wáng Wéilì   shǐ yǎnsè.
say she turn face trying hard at WANG Weili wink
{"Director WANG, did you see him coming? Where did you see that?" As she was speaking, she turned her face to WANG Weili and tried hard to wink at him.}

(79) 胤禛也点点头道："先生说的是，这字神韵不足。" <u>一边</u>说，二人随着戴铎进来。

Yìnzhēn yě   diǎn-diǎn tóu   dào: "Xiānsheng shuō de shì,   zhè zì
Yinzhen also nod-REDP head say sir say SP correct this character
shényùn   bùzú."   Yībiān   shuō,   èr   rén   suí-zhe
romantic charm insufficient meanwhile speak two person follow-PRG
Dài Duó   jìnlái.
DAI Duo come in
{Yinzhen also nodded and said, "Sir, you are right in saying that these characters are lacking in romantic charm." While he was speaking, the two men followed DAI Duo in.}

Undoubtedly, the subject could occur in the anterior clause in the two examples above, nevertheless, compared with "S *yībiān* V, V," "*yībiān* V, SV" can highlight the action in the posterior clause.

Summary

First, among complex sentences that include the connective *yībiān*, Form A ("*yībiān p, yībiān q*") is the regular one, and Forms B ("Ø*p, yībiān q*") and C ("*yībiān p,* Ø*q*") are abbreviated forms. In Form A, *p* or *q* is not limited by terms or conditions as they are in Forms B and C, and besides, "*yībiān p . . . yībiān q* . . ." can often be condensed into "*yībiān p yībiān q*" or "*biān p biān q*." Moreover, it can even be extended to "*biān p biān q biān r . . .* ," in which commas can be absent. The following are two examples, (80a) and (81), whose phraseology is impossible in Form B and Form C.

(80) a 一边作一边学。

    <u>Yībiān</u> . . . <u>yībiān</u> . . . zuò   <u>yībiān</u> xué.
    meanwhile   do   learn
    {As (he) works, he learns.}

→b 边作边学。

    <u>Biān</u> . . . <u>biān</u> . . . zuò   <u>biān</u> xué.
    meanwhile   do   learn
    {As (he) works, he learns.}

(81) 春儿边听边问边叹气。

    Chūn'ér   <u>biān</u> . . . <u>biān</u> . . . <u>biān</u> . . . tīng   <u>biān</u>   wèn   <u>biān</u>   tànqì.
    Little Chun meanwhile   listen   ask   sigh
    {As Little Chun listened, she asked questions and sighed.}

Second, there are semantic and structural requirements for the use of Form B ("Ø *p, yībiān q*"); that is, the anterior clause denotes an ongoing action, or the course of an action, or quoting. In other words, if any of these requirements is met, *yībiān* can be absent in the anterior clause. The following are two examples:

(82) 他<u>一边</u>用浴巾擦着身子，<u>一边</u>心不在焉地回答佩如的故意搭讪。

    Tā <u>yībiān</u> . . . <u>yībiān</u> . . . yòng yùjīn   cā-zhe   shēnzi, <u>yībiān</u> xīnbù-zàiyān
    he meanwhile   with bath towel wipe-PRG body   absent-minded
    de   huídá   Pèirú   de   gùyì   dāshàn.
    SP   respond Peiru   SP   intentional chat
    {As he was wiping himself with a bath towel, he absentmindedly dealt with Peiru's chat.}

(83) 队长就<u>一边</u>往兵的面前走，<u>一边</u>脸上堆起讨好的笑来。

    Duìzhǎng jiù <u>yībiān</u> . . . <u>yībiān</u> . . . wǎng bīng   de miànqián zǒu, <u>yībiān</u>
    captain   just meanwhile   toward soldier SP front   walk
    liǎn-shàng duī-qǐlai tǎohǎo de   xiào   lái.
    on face   pile up   ingratiate SP smile
    {As the captain was walking to the front of the soldiers, he smiled ingratiatingly.}

The anterior clause in (82) denotes an ongoing action and in (83) the process of an action. Therefore, they can be written as respectively (84) and (85).

(84) 他用浴巾擦着身子，<u>一边</u>心不在焉地回答佩如的故意搭讪。

    Tā yòng yùjīn   cā-*zhe*   shēnzi, <u>yībiān</u> xīnbù-zàiyān de huídá
    he with bath towel wipe-PRG body   meanwhile absent-minded SP respond
    Pèirú   de   gùyì   dāshàn.
    Peiru   SP   intentional chat
    {As he was wiping himself with a bath towel, he absentmindedly dealt with Peiru's chat.}

(85) 队长就往兵的面前走(去)，一边脸上堆起讨好的笑来。
Duìzhǎng jiù wǎng bīng de miànqián zǒu-qù, <u>*yībiān*</u> *liǎn-shàng*
captain just toward soldier SP front walk over there meanwhile on face
duī-qǐlai tǎohǎo de xiào lái.
pile up ingratiate SP smile
{As the captain was walking to the front of the soldiers, he smiled ingratiatingly.}

In some cases, the omission of *yībiān* might cause a change in layer demarcation, therefore what form to be used depends on the actual need, for example:

(86) 那两条牧羊犬总是Ø在牦牛四周来回跑动，<u>一边</u>警惕地观察着四野，<u>一边</u>帮主人监视着牦牛以及有可能掉下来的货物。
Nà liǎng tiáo mùyángquǎn zǒngshì Ø zài máoniú-sìzhōu láihuí pǎo-dòng,
that two CL shepherd dog always at around yak back and forth run
<u>*yībiān*</u> <u>*yībiān*</u> *jǐngtì de guānchá-zhe sìyě,* <u>*yībiān*</u> *bāng*
meanwhile vigilant SP observe-PRG surrounding ground help
zhǔrén jiānshì-zhe máoniú yǐjí yǒu kěnéng diào-xiàlái de huòwù.
owner keep watch-PRG yak and there be possibility drop SP goods
{The two shepherd dogs always ran around the yaks, vigilantly keeping watch on the vast expanse of open ground while helping the owner to keep a close eye on the yaks and goods that might drop.}

Made up of three clauses, the above complex sentence is in Form A ("*yībiān p, yībiān q*"), which indicates that the action in the second clause and the action in the third clause are concurrent. However, if the first *yībiān* is absent, the sentence will be in Form B and the layer segmentation will be different: the first two clauses and the third clause (as opposed to the first clause and the last two clauses) are coordinated.

Third, there are semantic and structural limitations on the use of Form C ("*yībiān p, Ø q*"), i.e., the action in the anterior clause should be an ongoing action, referring to the course of an action, or be a quotation. Besides, such words as *yǐ, tūrán,* or *nèixīn*, and so on may occur in the posterior clause. If one of these requirements is satisfied, *yībiān* can be absent in the posterior clause, as in the following example:

(87) 此刻，他<u>一边</u>小口小口地抿酒，<u>一边</u>睁大眼睛往远处看。
Cǐkè, tā <u>*yībiān*</u> <u>*yībiān*</u> *xiǎokǒu-xiǎokǒu de mǐn jiǔ,* <u>*yībiān*</u>
this moment he meanwhile sip by sip SP sip wine
zhēng-dà yǎnjīng wǎng yuǎnchù kàn.
open wide eye toward distance look
{At this moment, he drank sip by sip while looking out into the distance with his eyes wide open.}

The posterior clause in (87) denotes an ongoing action, which allows the occurrence of *zhe*. If *yībiān* in the posterior clause is omitted, the sentence can be rewritten as (88):

(88) 此刻，他<u>一边</u>小口小口地抿酒，睁大(着)眼睛往远处看（着）。
Cǐkè,　tā　yībiān　xiǎokǒu-xiǎokǒu de mǐn jiǔ, yībiān zhēng-dà (zhe)
this moment he meanwhile sip by sip　　SP sip wine　　open wide PRG
yǎnjīng wǎng yuánchù kàn (zhe).
eye　　toward distance look PRG
{At this moment, he drank sip by sip while looking out into the distance with his eyes wide open.}

The absence of *yībiān* in some cases can change the segmentation between the clauses, thus the choice of the form should be made according to actual need. The following is an example:

(89) "可是！"秀秀娘也慢搭搭拐过来，<u>一边</u>将锥尖儿在头皮上磨磨，使劲儿在鞋底上扎一锥子，然后挑出麻线的头儿来，缠在手指上，吱地一声拉出好长，<u>一边</u>说，"比那淑贞，她可是差了天地！"
"Kěshì!" Xiùxiù niáng　yě　màndādā guǎi-guòlái, yībiān　　yībiān... jiāng
but　　Xiuxiu's mother also slow　turn around meanwhile　　　　BA
zhuī jiānr zài tóupí-shàng mó-mó,　shǐjìnr zài xiédǐ-shàng zhā yī zhuīzi, ránhòu
awl tip　on scalp　　rub-REDP　hard　on sole　　　stab one awl　then
tiāo-chū　máxiàn　de tóur lái, chán zài shǒuzhǐ-shàng, zhī　de yī shēng
pick out　linen thread SP head　wrap on finger　　　　squeak SP one sound
lā-chū　hǎo cháng, yībiān shuō, "Bǐ nà Shūzhēn, tā kěshì chà le tiāndì!"
pull out very long　　say　　than that Shuzhen she indeed bad MP a lot
{"But!" Xiuxiu's mother also turned around slowly. As she rubbed the tip of the owl on her scalp, forced it into the shoe sole (that she was making), picked out the head of the thread, wrapped it around her finger, and then pulled out a good length of the thread with a squeak, she said, "She is really much worse than Shuzhen!"}

Composed of three clauses, the above example is in Form A (*yībiān* . . . *yībiān* . . .), which indicates that the two actions in the second and the third clauses are concurrent. However, if the second *yībiān* is absent, the sentence will be in Form C.

Fourth, there is pragmatic consideration for the choice of Form B or Form C.

Form B is intended to ensure the smooth flow of speech and to explicate the relationship between the actions in the clauses, which can be illustrated by the following example:

(90) ……林则从抽屉里取出现金，交给了她，<u>一边</u>庄重地说："夫人，愿我们不断发展我们两国之间的贸易关系。"
. . . Lín Zé cóng chōuti-li qǔ-chū xiànjīn, jiāo-gěi le tā, yībiān
LIN Ze from drawer　take out cash　hand to PEF her meanwhile
zhuāngzhòng de shuō: "Fūren, yuàn wǒ-men búduàn　fāzhǎn wǒ-men
solemn　　　SP say　　madam hope we　continuously develop our
liǎng　guó　　zhījiān　de　màoyì　guānxi."
two　country　between　SP　trade　relationship
{. . . Taking the cash out of the drawer and handed it to her, LIN Ze said solemnly, "Madam, may we continue to develop the trade relationships between our two countries."}

Paired and single occurrences of the connective yībiān 63

The absence of *yībiān* in the anterior clause guarantees a smooth speech flow from the preceding text. The presence of *yībiān* in the posterior clause is meant to highlight the concurrence between the two actions and play down the successiveness. In addition, if "S + *shuō* + direct quotation" occurs in the anterior clause, *yībiān* is often omitted; otherwise, the two occurrences of *yībiān* would be too far apart.

The use of Form C is intended to manifest the relationship between the actions in the two clauses and out of consideration for syntax, as illustrated by the following example:

(91) 周用诚几步到门口，扶着哭得泪人似的七十四进来，<u>一边</u>让他坐了，说道："你先别伤心，……"

Zhōu Yòngchéng   jǐ   bù   dào   ménkǒu, fú-zhe   kū   de
ZHOU Yongcheng a few step arrive doorway hold-PRG cry   SP
lèirén   shìde   Qīshísì jìnlái, <u>yībiān</u>
person whose face is covered with tears like Qishisi come in meanwhile
ràng tā   zuò-le, shuōdào: "Nǐ   xiān bié   shāngxīn,..."
ask   him sit-MP   say   you   first do not be grieved
{ZHOU Yongcheng hurried to the door, held the tearful Qishisi and let him in. As he asked him to be seated, he said, "Please calm down . . ."}

In the above example, the occurrence of *yībiān* in the anterior clause foreshadows a concurrent action rather than a consecutive one later in the sentence. The absence of *yībiān* in the posterior clause is for syntactic diversity, namely, to avoid monotonousness and rigidity.

Last, paired occurrences of connectives are common in modern Chinese. Nevertheless, for many words, such as *yībiān*, single occurrences and paired occurrences coexist. Therefore, in order to study complex sentences in Modern Chinese in depth, it is necessary to have a good understanding of the single occurrence of various paired connectives. This research is very complicated but essential.

NB Some examples in this chapter are cited from literary works, political essays, articles, and so on. The sources are listed as follows:

1 *All Beans and Wheat* (《遍地菽麦》) by DENG Yiguang (邓一光), including Example (18), (23), and (83);
2 *Bonded Labour* (《包身工》) by XIA Yan (夏衍), including (4);
3 *Burying a Buffalo* (《瘞牛记》) by YAN Guaiyu (严怪愚), including (37);
4 *Chinese* for Junior High School Students, Book 6, including (2);
5 *Dangdai* (《当代》) 1982(3), including (76);
6 *Dangerous Situation* (《危情》) by MO Shen (莫伸), including (21), (52), (56), (66), (75), (77), and (78);
7 *Divine Eagle, Galant Knight* (《神雕侠侣》) by JIN Yong (金庸), including (72);
8 *Dream of the Red Chamber* (《红楼梦》) by CAO Xueqi (曹雪芹), including (6), (7), (8), (9), (10), and (11);

9. *Emperor Yongzheng* (《雍正皇帝》) by Eryuehe (二月河), including (13), (15), (34), (46), (47), (54), (55), (62), (63), (64), (65), (79), and (91);
10. *Fiction Monthly* (《小说月报》) 1996(12), including (27) and (86); 1997(6), including (39), (40), (82), (87), and (90);
11. *Harvest* (《收获》) 1987(6), including (16) and (26); 1992(2), including (20);
12. *Home of Teachers* (《教工之家》) by JIANG Chunguang (蒋春光), including (24), (28), (33), and (38);
13. *Love is Not Enough for Marriage* (《仅有爱情是不能结婚的》) by ZHANG Kangkang (张抗抗), including (53);
14. *Not Serious at All* (《一点正经没有》) by WANG Shuo (王朔), including (17);
15. *October* (《十月》) 1982(4), including (50); 1998(1), including (14);
16. *Old Stories about Provisional Capital* (《陪都旧事》) by MO Huaiwei (莫怀威), including (19);
17. *People's Literature* (《人民文学》) 1987(5), including (25) and (89);
18. *State of Divinity* (《笑傲江湖》) by JIN Yong (金庸), including (74);
19. *White Poppies* (《白罂粟》) by ZHANG Kangkang (张抗抗), including (41);
20. *Xiao Shuo Jia* (《小说家》) 1997(3), including (3);
21. *Zhongpian Xiaoshuo Xuankan* (《中篇小说选刊》) 1995(2), including (42).

Bibliography

[1] Institute of Language, Chinese Academy of Social Sciences. *Modern Chinese Dictionary* (《现代汉语词典》). The Commercial Press, 1978.
[2] LV Shuxian (吕叔湘). *Eight Hundred Words in Modern Chinese* (《现代汉语八百词》). The Commercial Press, 1980.
[3] Department of Chinese Language and Literature, Peking University. *Interpretations of Grammatical Words in Modern Chinese* (《现代汉语虚词例释》). The Commercial Press, 1982.
[4] *The Dictionary of Grammatical Words in Modern Chinese* (《现代汉语虚词词典》).
[5] XING Fuyi (邢福义). *Complex Sentences and Connectives* (《复句与关系词语》). Heilongjiang People's Press, 1985.

3 "p, jiēzhe q" and relevant forms

In this chapter, various forms of successive complex sentences are discussed, with *jiēzhe* selected as a typical marker.

This chapter is divided into three parts, each of which is devoted to a discussion of one of the successive complex sentence forms: "*p, jiēzhe q*"; "*p, ránhòu q*"; and "*p, zhè cái q.*"

3.1 "*p, jiēzhe q*"

"*p, jiēzhe q*" is a form for successive sentences, which indicate a type of successiveness of actions. In a successive sentence, the actions follow each other chronologically with or without interruption.

3.1.1 Linguistic form

In sentences in the form of "*p, jiēzhe q,*" the word *jiēzhe* occurs at the beginning of the posterior clause, as in the following two examples:

(1) 隔壁传来倒茶的响声，接着是警卫员喊首长接电话。
　　Gébì　　　　chuán-lái dào chá de xiǎngshēng, jiēzhe shì jǐngwèiyuán
　　next door room come　pour tea SP sound　　　then　COP guard
　　hǎn shǒuzhǎng jiē　　diànhuà.
　　call chief　　answer phone call
　　{From next door came the sound of tea pouring, followed by a guard calling the chief to answer the phone.}

(2) 灰白色的沉重的晚云中间时时发出闪光，接着一声钝响，是送灶的爆竹；……
　　Huībáisè　de　chénzhòng de　wǎn　　yúnzhōngjiān shí-shí
　　gray white SP heavy　　　SP evening clouds middle from time to time-REDU
　　fāchū　　shǎnguāng, jiēzhe yī　shēng dùn xiǎng,　shì
　　give off flash　　　then　one CL　dull sound　COP

DOI: 10.4324/9781003362166-3

```
              sòngzào              de   bàozhú; . . .
              bid farewell Kitchen God  SP   firecracker
```
{From time to time, among the gray and heavy evening clouds, flashes of light shine, followed by a dull thud—the sound of a firecracker bidding farewell to the Kitchen God.}

In written language, *jiēzhe* is sometimes followed by a comma, as in the following two examples:

(3) 邹丽梅眼睛湿润了，<u>接着</u>，两滴硕大的泪珠涌出眼帘。
```
    Zōu Lìméi   yǎnjing  shīrùn-le,  jiēzhe,  liǎng dī    shuòdà de lèizhū   yǒng-chū
    ZOU Limei   eye      moist-PEF   then     two   drop  huge   SP teardrop well up
    yǎnlián.
    eye
```
{ZOU Limei's eyes became teary, and then two large tears welled up.}

(4) 走了一会，就听到前面响起一阵粗野的吆喝声，<u>接着</u>，就出现了十多个便衣，押着一个人从山坡上下来了。
```
    Zǒu-le       yīhuì,   jiù   tīng-dào  qiánmiàn  xiǎng-qǐ      yī   zhèn  cūyě  de
    walk-PEF    a while   then  hear       front     start to sound one  CL    rude  SP
    yāohe shēng, jiēzhe, jiù   chūxiàn-le   shíduō       gè   biànyī,
    shout sound  then          appear-PEF  more than ten CL   person in plain clothes
    yā-zhe        yī   gè   rén    cóng  shānpō-shàng  xiàlái-le.
    escort-PRG   one  CL   person from  on slope       come down-PEF
```
{After walking for a while, (they) heard a rude shout from ahead, and then (they) saw a dozen plainclothes men escorting someone down the slope.}

Besides, *jiēzhe* can often collocate with an adverb, such as *yòu* ('again'), *jiù* ('just'), and *biàn* ('then'), among which *yòu* and *jiù* usually follow *jiēzhe*, hence "...*jiēzhe yòu*..." and "...*jiēzhe jiù (biàn)*...". However, sometimes *yòu* precedes *jiēzhe*, hence "...*yòu jiēzhe*...," as in the following six examples:

(5) （亚女）微微地蹙起了眉尖，摇了摇头，<u>接着</u>又打起了我无论如何也不明白的手势。
```
    (Yà'nǚ)  wēi-wēi        de  cù-qǐ           le  méijiān, yáoleyáo tóu,   jiēzhe yòu
    Yanv     slight-REDP    SP  start to frown  PEF eyebrow  shake one's head then
    dǎ-qǐ              le  wǒ  wúlùn-rúhé yě bù   míngbai de  shǒushì.
    start to make PEF      I   anyhow         NEG understand SP gesture
```
{[Yanv] slightly frowned, shook her head, and then started to make gestures that I wouldn't be able to understand anyhow.}

(6) 我给那些因为在近旁而极响的爆竹声惊醒，看见豆一般大的黄色的灯火光，<u>接着</u>又听得毕毕剥剥的鞭炮，是四叔家正在"祝福"了；……
```
    Wǒ   gěi       nàxiē  yīnwèi   zài  jìnpáng       ér   jí          xiǎng  de
    I    PASSIVE   those  because  in   nearby place  and  extremely   loud   SP
```

"p, jiēzhe q" and relevant forms 67

bàozhú   shēng   jīngxǐng, kànjiàn   dōu   yībān dà de huángsè de
firecracker sound wake up   see   soybean same big SP yellow   SP
dēnghuǒguāng, <u>jiēzhe</u> **yòu** tīng-de   bìbì-bōbō de biānpào,   shì
lamplight   then   hear   crackle   SP firecracker COP
sìshū   jiā   zhèngzài   "zhùfú"   le; . . .
the fourth uncle family   in progress pray   MP
{I was awakened by an extremely loud sound of firecrackers nearby and saw yellow lamplight as big as soybeans, and then a burst of crackling firecrackers followed—it was Fourth Uncle's family praying . . . }

(7) 她跳起来，搂住朋友的脖子，狂热地亲她，<u>接着</u>就带着这件宝物跑了。
Tā   tiào-qǐlái, lǒu-zhù   péngyǒu de bózi, kuángrè de qīn tā,
she jump up   hold . . . in one's arms friend SP neck excited SP kiss her
<u>jiēzhe</u> **jiù** dài-zhe   zhè jiàn bǎowù   pǎo-le.
then   take-PRG this CL   treasure   run-PEF
{She sprang up, threw her arms around her friend's neck, kissed her enthusiastically, and then ran away with the treasure.}

(8) 冷风穿透一层层衣服，收干了皮肤上的热汗，<u>接着</u>就侵入肌肤，刺向骨干。
Lěng fēng chuāntòu yī   céng-céng yīfu,   shōu-gān-le   pífū-shàng
cold wind penetrate one layer-REDP clothes absorb all-PEF on skin
de rè   hàn, <u>jiēzhe</u> **jiù** qīnrù   jīfū,   cì   xiàng gǔgàn.
SP hot sweat   then   enter   skin and muscle stab at   bone
{The cold wind penetrated all layers of clothes, sucked all the hot sweat on the skin, and then entered the skin and muscles, forcing its way into the bones.}

(9) 我到了自家的房外，我的母亲早已迎着出来了，<u>接着</u>便飞出了八岁的侄儿宏儿。
Wǒ dào-le   zìjiā   de fángwài,   wǒ de mǔqīn   zǎo
I   arrive-PEF oneself SP outside of the house I SP mother earlier
yǐ   yíng-zhe   chūlái-le,   <u>jiēzhe</u> **biàn** fēi-chū   le   bā   suì   de
already welcome-PRG come out-PEF   then   fly out   PEF eight CL   SP
zhí'ér   Hóng'ér.
nephew   little Hong
{When I got to my house, my mother had already come out to welcome me, and then my eight-year-old nephew Hongr rushed out.}

(10) 老人家说到这里，停了一会，又<u>接着</u>说下去：……
Lǎorénjia   shuō   dào   zhèli,   tíng-le   yīhuì,   **yòu** <u>jiēzhe</u> shuō-xiàqu: . . .
old person speak arrive here   stop-PEF a while   then   continue to say
{The old person paused for a moment, and then continued to speak . . . }

In some cases, the word *xiān* ('first') occurs in the anterior clause, forming the form of "*xiān* . . . *jiēzhe (yòu/jiù)* . . . ". The following are three examples:

(11) 我先是诧异，接着是很不安，似乎这话于我有关系。
Wǒ xiān shì chàyì, jiēzhe shì hěn bù'ān, sìhū zhè huà yú wǒ
I first COP surprised then COP very uneasy as if this words with me
yǒu guānxi.
have relation
{I was surprised first, and then felt very uneasy, as if what was said had something to do with me.}

(12) 我先是一怔，接着便明白过来了：……
Wǒ xiān shì yī zhèng, jiēzhe biàn míngbai-guòlái-le: ...
I first COP once startled then understand-PEF
{I was startled, and then I understood ...}

(13) 到了公元1190年，南宋有个名叫赵惇的人，他先在这里当王，接着又当上了皇帝，真是喜庆双重，……
Dào-le gōngyuán 1190 nián, nánsòng yǒu gè
arrive-PEF Anno Domini 1190 year Southern Song dynasty there be CL
míng jiào Zhào Dūn de rén, tā xiān zài zhèli dāng wáng,
name called ZHAO Dun SP person he first at here be seignior
jiēzhe yòu dāng-shàng le huángdì, zhēnshì xǐqìng shuāngchóng,...
then become- PEF Emperor really happy event double
{In the Southern Song dynasty, a man named ZHAO Dun who was first the seignior here and then became the emperor in 1190 A.D., which was indeed double happy events (for him) ...}

3.1.2 Function

The "*p, jiēzhe q*" form emphasizes that the actions follow one another chronologically without interruption, which is the main difference from "*p, ránhòu q*."

The word *jǐn* ('close') sometimes precedes *jiēzhe*, forming a phrasal word, i.e., "*jǐn jiēzhe*." For this reason, "*jǐn jiēzhe*" further emphasizes that the acts are in rapid succession. The following are three examples:

(14) 一个茶房送来了茶碗，紧接着就有人送上一块洒了香水的热毛巾。
Yī gè cháfáng sònglái-le cháwǎn, jǐn jiēzhe jiù yǒu rén
one CL waiter bring-PEF teacup close follow then there be person
sòng-shàng yī kuài sǎ-le xiāngshuǐ de rè máojīn.
hand one CL spray-PEF perfume SP hot towel
{A waiter brought the teacup, and then someone else handed a hot scented towel.}

(15) 她飞也似地来到了五光十色的五洲电料行，把情况说完，紧接着问："三十分钟能不能办好？"
Tā fēi yě shìde lái-dào le wǔguāng-shísè de wǔzhōu diànliàoháng, bǎ
she fly just like come PEF colorful SP Wuzhou Electricals BA
qíngkuàng shuō-wán, jǐn jiēzhe wèn: "Sānshí fēnzhōng néng bù néng
situation finish saying close then ask thirty minute can NEG can

bàn-hǎo?"
finish doing
{She rushed to the colorful Wuzhou Electricals, explained the situation, and then asked, "Can we get it done within 30 minutes?"}

(16) 随着钢鼓乐团艺术指导宋庆中老师的指挥，缓慢的钢鼓乐声伴随一串渗透着忧伤情感的"啊"声飘出来，<u>紧接着</u>钢鼓乐声速度加快，乐曲转入节奏明快的旋律。
Suízhe gānggǔ yuètuán yìshù zhǐdǎo Sòng Qìngzhōng lǎoshī de zhǐhuī,
with   steel band   artistic director SONG Qingzhong teacher SP conduct
huǎnmàn de gānggǔ yuèshēng bànsuí yī chuàn shèntòu-zhe yōushāng
slow   SP steel band music accompany one string permeate-PRG sad
qínggǎn de "ā" shēng piāo-chūlái, <u>jǐn jiēzhe</u> gānggǔ yuèshēng sùdù
emotion SP ah sound float out   close then steel band music speed
jiākuài,   yuèqǔ zhuǎn-rù jiézòu míngkuài de xuánlǜ.
become faster music change to rhythm bright   SP melody
{Under the direction of Mr. SONG Qingzhong, the artistic director of the steel band, the slow steel band music came out with a string of "ah" sounds permeated with sadness, and then music picked up speed and turned into a melody of bright rhythm.}

3.2 "p, ránhòu q"

Another form of successive complex sentences is "*p, ránhòu q*", which slightly differs from "*p, jiēzhe q*."

3.2.1 Linguistic form

In sentences in the form of "*p, ránhòu q,*" the connective *ránhòu* occurs at the beginning of the posterior clause. In written language, a comma sometimes follows *ránhòu*, as in the following three examples:

(17) 他在落实了我的身份之后对我说，你等着，<u>然后</u>把电话给了另一个人。
Tā zài luòshí-le wǒ de shēnfèn zhīhòu duì wǒ shuō, nǐ děng-zhe, <u>ránhòu</u>
he at confirm-PEF I SP identity after to me say you wait-PRG then
bǎ diànhuà gěi-le lìng yī gè rén.
BA phone pass-PEF another one CL person
{After confirming my identity, he asked me to wait, and then passed the phone to someone else.}

(18) 欧阳慧看着大家，<u>然后</u>她端起一碗，捧到刘乂面前，……
Ōuyáng Huì kàn-zhe   dàjiā,   <u>ránhòu</u> tā duān-qǐ yī wǎn,
OUYANG Hui look at-PRG everyone then she lift one bowl
pěng-dào   Liú Yì miànqián, ...
hold something to LIU Yi before face
{OUYANG Hui looked at everyone, and then she lifted a bowl (of something) and held it (with both hands) before LIU Yi ...}

(19) 卫伟愣了一小会儿，<u>然后</u>，悄悄地把资料夹回了乐谱里。
　　　Wèi Wěi　lèng-le　　　　yī　xiǎo　huìr,　<u>ránhòu</u>,　qiāo-qiāo　de　bǎ
　　　WEI Wei　be stunned-PEF　one little　while　then　　secret-REDP　SP　BA
　　　zīliào　　jiā-huí　le　yuèpǔ-lǐ.
　　　document　put back　PEF　in music folder
　　　{WEI Wei was stunned for a moment, and then secretly put the document back in the music folder.}

Often *ránhòu* collocates with such adverbs as *yòu, jiù* or *cái*, hense "... *ránhòu yòu (jiù/cái)* ...," as in the following example:

(20) 他从挎着的布包里取出一个装着蛋糕的纸袋递到黄成宾面前，让他过目，<u>然后</u>又放回布袋里。
　　　Tā cóng　kuà-zhe　de　bù　bāo-lǐ qǔ-chū　yī　gè zhuāng-zhe　dàn'gāo
　　　he　from　carry-PRG　SP　cloth in bag　take out　one　CL　contain-PRG　cake
　　　de zhǐ　dài　dì-dào　Huáng Chéngbīn　miànqián,　ràng tā　guòmù,
　　　SP paper　bag　hand to　HUANG Chengbin　before face　let　him　have a look
　　　<u>ránhòu</u> *yòu* fàng-huí bù　dài-lǐ.
　　　then　　　put back　cloth　in bag
　　　{From the cloth bag he was carrying (on his shoulder), he took out a paper bag that had cake in it, handed it to HUANG Chengbin to have a check, and then put it back in the cloth bag.}

In some cases, the word *xiān* ('first') occurs in the anterior clause, that is, "*xiān* ... *ránhòu (yòu/jiù)* ...," as in the following three examples:

(21) 林冲故事<u>先</u>提出全篇主眼，<u>然后</u>一步紧一步向顶点发展，……
　　　Lín Chōng　gùshi　<u>xiān</u>　tíchū　quánpiān　zhǔyǎn,　<u>ránhòu</u>　yībù jǐn yībù
　　　LIN Chong　story　first　present　whole article　main idea　then　step by step
　　　xiàng　dǐngdiǎn　fāzhǎn, ...
　　　to　climax　develop
　　　{The story of LIN Chong first presents the main point of the whole story and then develops to the climax step by step ...}

(22) 前天中午，前县委书记余正奇从地区打电话给他，<u>先</u>戏谑地说了声对不起，<u>然后</u>又倚老卖老地说老兄向你祝贺了。
　　　Qiántiān　　　zhōngwǔ,　qián　xiànwěi　　　shūjì
　　　day before yesterday　noon　former　County Party Committee　secretary
　　　Yú Zhèngqí　cóng　dìqū　dǎ diànhuà　gěi　tā,　<u>xiān</u>　xìxuè　de
　　　YU Zhengqi　from　prefecture　call　to　him　first　sarcastic　SP
　　　shuō-le　shēng　duìbùqǐ,　<u>ránhòu</u> *yòu* yǐlǎo-màilǎo　　　　　de
　　　say-PEF　CL　sorry　then　　　take advantage of one's seniority　SP
　　　shuō　lǎoxiōng　xiàng　nǐ　zhùhè　le.
　　　say　big brother　to　you　congratulate　MP
　　　{At noon the day before yesterday, YU Zhengqi, the former secretary of the County Party Committee, called him from the Prefecture (Party Committee). First, he said

sorry sarcastically, and then took advantage of his seniority and said, "Big brother congratulates you."}

(23) 我先送他上车，然后我们一块儿回去。
Wǒ   xiān   sòng tā   shàng chē, ránhòu wǒ-men yīkuàir   huíqu.
I   first send him   get on bus   then   we   together   go back
{I'll put him on the bus first, and then we'll go back together.}

3.2.2 Function

According to realis and irrealis moods, actions in "*p, ránhòu q*" can be divided into two types.

In the realis "*p, ránhòu q*," all the actions have been realized, and all the clauses are declarative ones, as in the following two examples:

(24) 我们隔着山谷一挥手，然后各奔前程。
Wǒ-men gé-zhe shāngǔ yī   huīshǒu, ránhòu gèbènqiánchéng.
we   across valley once wave   then   each pursues their onward journey
{We waved to each other across the valley, and then went our separate ways.}

(25) 我们在电话里又说了一会儿别的话，然后把电话挂了。
Wǒ-men zài diànhuà-lǐ yòu   shuō-le   yīhuìr biéde huà, ránhòu bǎ
we   at on phone   additionally talk-PEF   a while other words then   BA
diànhuà guà-le.
phone   hang up-PEF
{We talked about something else on the phone for a while, then hung up.}

In the irrealis "*p, ránhòu q*," the actions are to be realized, and the clauses are imperative or take an imperative tone, as in the following two examples:

(26) 《关于建国以来党的若干历史问题的决议》通过以后，要组织大家认真学习，然后要引导大家认真读点书。
"Guānyú jiànguó   yǐlái dǎng de ruògān lìshǐ   wèntí de juéyì"
about   establish a state since party SP certain history issue SP resolution
tōngguò yǐhòu, yào zǔzhī   dàjiā   rènzhēn xuéxí, ránhòu yào yǐndǎo
pass   after must organize everyone carefully study then   must guide
dàjiā   rènzhēn dú   diǎn shū.
everyone carefully read some book
{After the "Resolution on Certain Issues in the History of Our Party since the Founding of the People's Republic of China" is adopted, we must organize people to study it carefully and then guide them to further reading.}

(27) 下班前，你把老金送到我家门口，然后，就请你自便。
Xiàbān   qián, nǐ bǎ lǎo Jīn sòng-dào wǒ jiā   ménkǒu, ránhòu, jiù qǐng
finish work before you BA old JIN take to   my house doorway then   please

nǐ   zìbiàn.
you   do as one pleases
{Before you finish work, bring old JIN to my door, and then do as you wish.}

The connective *ránhòu* emphasizes that the actions follow the temporal order. For this reason, no matter whether the actions in the "...*ránhòu*..." construction are realis or irrealis, the construction denotes successiveness. Besides, the presence of *ránhòu* in different positions reflects the speaker's intention to emphasize that an act/action follows a particular one more closely than it follows another one. This can be illustrated by the following three examples, each of which consists of more than two clauses:

(28) 丁猛在屋里踱了个来回，<u>然后</u>走到桌前，把全部预算书摞到一块，往钱工面前一撂……
Dīng Měng zài wū-li duó-le gè láihuí, <u>ránhòu</u> zǒu-dào zhuō-qián,
DING Meng at in room pace-PEF CL round trip then walk to before desk
bǎ quánbù yùsuànshū luò-dào yīkuài, wǎng Qián Gōng
BA all budget document stack together to QIAN Engineer
miànqián yī liào...
before face once put down
{DING Meng paced back and forth in the room, then went to the desk, piled all the budget documents, and put them down before Engineer QIAN...}

(29) 心心胜利地挺直腰板，举起梅花扳手向她走远了的母亲示威地挥舞，<u>然后</u>赔不是地招呼乡亲们上车。
Xīnxīn shènglì de tǐng-zhí yāobǎn, jǔ-qǐ méihuābānshou xiàng tā
Xinxin victory SP straighten back hold up ring spanner at her
zǒuyuǎn-le de mǔqīn shìwēi de huīwǔ, <u>ránhòu</u> péi bùshì de
walk far away-PEF SP mother protest SP wave then apologize SP
zhāohu xiāngqin-men shàng chē.
call fellow villager-PL get on bus
{Bus Driver Xinxin straightened her back triumphantly, held up a ring spanner and waved at her mother, who had walked away, and then she apologized to the fellow villagers (passengers) and asked them to get on the bus.}

(30) 黄成宾摇摇头，取下眼镜揩拭水气，<u>然后</u>戴好，呆呆地看着洪老板出神。
Huáng Chéngbīn yáo-yáo tóu, qǔxià yǎnjìng kāishì shuǐqì, <u>ránhòu</u>
HUANG Chengbin shake-REDP head take off glasses wipe off moisture then
dài-hǎo, dāi-dāi de kàn-zhe Hóng lǎobǎn chūshén.
put on properly dull-REDP SP look at-PRG HONG boss be lost in thought
{HUANG Chengbin shook his head, took off his glasses and wiped the moisture on them, and then put them back on, and stared dully at Boss HONG, lost in thought.}

Among the three examples above, (28) is in the form of "*A, ránhòu B, C, D,*" in which *ránhòu* divides the acts into two groups by separating the first one from the other three; (29) is in the form of "*A, B, ránhòu C*," in which the position of *ránhòu* indicates that all the three acts follow the temporal order, but the second one follows the first one more closely than the third one follows the second one; (30) is in the form of "*A, B, ránhòu C, D*," in which *ránhòu* marks the successiveness of all the acts, and divides them into two processes—the first two in one process and the last two in the other.

The position of *ránhòu* is flexible and subject to the speaker's need. In other words, the position of *ránhòu* is determined by how the speaker intends to segment the course an the action. The following are four examples:

(31) 她下了草滩，一直走到婶婶湖边，铺了一张什么东西在跳板上，<u>然后</u>坐下来，弹响了吉他。
    Tā xià-le cǎotān, yìzhí zǒu-dào Shēnshen Hú biān, pū-le yī
    she go down-PEF grassland straight walk to side of Shenshen Lake spread one
    zhāng shénme dōngxi zài tiàobǎn-shàng, <u>ránhòu</u> zuò-xiàlái, tánxiǎng-le jíta.
    CL some stuff at on gangplank then sit down play-PEF guitar
    {She walked down the grass straight to Shenshen Lake, spread something on the gangplank, and then sat down, and started to play the guitar.}

(32) 她下了草滩，一直走到婶婶湖边，铺了一张什么东西在跳板上，坐下来，<u>然后</u>弹响了吉他。
    Tā xià-le cǎotān, yìzhí zǒu-dào Shēnshen Hú biān, pū-le yī
    she go down-PEF grassland straight walk to side of Shenshen Lake spread one
    zhāng shénme dōngxi zài tiàobǎn-shàng, zuò-xiàlái, <u>ránhòu</u> tánxiǎng-le jíta.
    CL some stuff at on gangplank sit down then play-PEF guitar
    {She walked down the grass straight to Shenshen Lake, spread something on the gangplank, sat down, and then started to play the guitar.}

(33) 她下了草滩，<u>然后</u>一直走到婶婶湖边，铺了一张什么东西在跳板上，坐下来，弹响了吉他。
    Tā xià-le cǎotān, <u>ránhòu</u> yìzhí zǒu-dào Shēnshen Hú biān, pū-le
    she go down-PEF grassland then straight walk to side of Shenshen Lake spread
    yī zhāng shénme dōngxi zài tiàobǎn-shàng, zuò-xiàlái, tánxiǎng-le jíta.
    one CL some stuff at on gangplank sit down play-PEF guitar
    {She came down the grass, and then walked straight to Shenshen Lake, spread something on the gangplank, sat down, and started to play the guitar.}

(34) 她下了草滩，一直走到婶婶湖边，<u>然后</u>铺了一张什么东西在跳板上，坐下来，弹响了吉他。
    Tā xià-le cǎotān, yìzhí zǒu-dào Shēnshen Hú biān, <u>ránhòu</u>
    she go down-PEF grassland straight walk to side of Shenshen Lake then
    pū-le yī zhāng shénme dōngxi zài tiàobǎn-shàng, zuò-xiàlái, tánxiǎng-le jíta.
    spread one CL some stuff at on gangplank sit down play-PEF guitar
    {She walked down the grass straight to Shenshen Lake, and then spread something on the gangplank, sat down, and started to play the guitar.}

74 *"p, jiēzhe q" and relevant forms*

Among these examples, (31) is in the form of "*A, B, C, ránhòu D, E*"; (32) is in "*A, B, C, D, ránhòu E*"; (33) is in "*A, ránhòu B, C, D, E*"; and (34) is in "*A, B, ránhòu C, D, E.*" It can be clearly seen that the position of *ránhòu* is flexible and that although it has exactly the same meaning in all the sentences, there exist subtle differences in how the course of the action is segmented.

If the word *xiān* occurs in the anterior clause, and thus the sentence is in the form of "*xiān . . . ránhòu . . .*," then the segmentation of the course of the action will be even clearer, as shown by the following example:

(35) 现在呢，<u>先</u>到办事处吃午饭，<u>然后</u>洗洗澡，睡个午觉。
Xiànzài ne, <u>xiān</u> dào bànshìchù chī wǔfàn, <u>ránhòu</u> xǐxǐzǎo, shuì
now   MP   first go to agency office eat lunch   then   take a shower sleep
gè   wǔjiào.
CL   afternoon nap
{Now, go to the agency office for lunch first, and then take a shower and a nap.}

Obviously, the acts in (35) are divided into two processes, that is, "*chī wǔfàn*" ('eat lunch'), and "*xǐzǎo + shuìwǔjiào*" ('take a shower + take a nap').

If *yòu* or *zài* occurs in the anterior or posterior clause, i.e., ". . . *yòu (zài)* . . . *ránhòu* . . ." or ". . . *ránhòu* . . . *yòu (zài)* . . . ," then it is clear that all the acts are divided into three parts regardless of how many clauses there are.

(36) 戴笠自己从衣钩上取下博士帽戴上，<u>又</u>客气了几句，<u>然</u>后握手而别。
Dài Lì   zìjǐ   cóng   yīgōu-shàng   qǔ-xià   bóshìmào   dài-shàng,   <u>yòu</u>
DAI Li   himself from   on coat hook   take off top hat   put on   and
kèqi-le   jǐ   jù,   <u>ránhòu</u>   wòshǒu   ér   bié.
say politely-PEF   several   sentence   then   shake hands   and   leave
{Dai Li took off the top hat from the hook and put it on, said a few polite words, and then shook hands and left.}

(37) 她利索地解下缠着的布带，把木盒放在矮凳上，<u>然后</u>把伤腿搁在木盒上，<u>再</u>用葛布罩着，闷住药气。
Tā   lìsuo de   jiě-xià chán-zhe   de   bù   dài, bǎ   mù   hé   fàng zài ǎi
she agilely SP untie   wrap-PRG   SP   cloth belt BA   wooden   box   put at   low
dèng-shàng, <u>ránhòu</u>   bǎ   shāng   tuǐ   gē   zài   mù   hé-shàng,   <u>zài</u>   yòng
on-stool   then   BA   injured   leg   put   at   wooden   on box   next   use
gébù   zhào-zhe,   mēn-zhù   yàoqì.
cloth made of Puerraia   cover-PRG   keep . . . from leaking air of medicine
{She quickly untied the bandage, placed the wooden box on a low stool, and then put her injured leg on the box and covered it with a piece of Pueraria cloth so as to keep the air of the medicine (coming out of the box) from leaking (to achieve the best treatment effect).}

3.2.3 Differences between "... jiēzhe ..." and "... ránhòu ..."

In general, *jiēzhe* and *ránhòu* are interchangeable with each other. However, the word *jǐn* ('close') can precede *jiēzhe*, i.e., "*jǐn jiēzhe*," but it cannot precede *ránhòu*. Moreover, *jiēzhe* can follow the subject, but *ránhòu* cannot. The following is an example:

(38) 吃完喝完，我们<u>接着</u>往前走。
Chī-wán   hē-wán,   wǒ-men   <u>jiēzhe</u>   wǎng   qián   zǒu.
finish eating finish drinking we   then   toward   front   walk
{After eating and drinking, we went on.}

Semantically, *jiēzhe* emphasizes successiveness, whereas *ránhòu* stresses the chronological order.

If the course of an action can be clearly segmented into two parts, *ránhòu* is more suitable than *jiēzhe*. For example, (39a) is clearly more natural than (39b).

(39) a 你先把她送走，<u>然后</u>请你自便。
Nǐ   xiān   bǎ   tā   sòngzǒu,   <u>ránhòu</u>   qǐng   nǐ   zìbiàn.
you   first BA   she   send away then   please   you   help oneself
{Send her away, and then do as you wish.}

b 你先把她送走，<u>接着</u>请你自便。
Nǐ   xiān   bǎ   tā   sòngzǒu,   <u>jiēzhe</u>   qǐng   nǐ   zìbiàn.
you   first BA   she   send away then   please   you   help oneself

The following is an example, in which *ránhòu* cannot be replaced by *jiēzhe*:

(40) 如果有人送点什么吃的给他，他总要工作人员先送给毛主席和我父亲一些，<u>然后</u>自己才肯吃。
Rúguǒ   yǒu   rén   sòng   diǎn   shénme   chī-de   gěi   tā,   tā   zǒng   yào
if   there be person give   some   any   food   to   him   he   always ask
gōngzuò   rényuán   xiān   sòng   gěi   Máo Zhǔxí   hé   wǒ   fùqin   yīxiē,
working   personnel first give   to   MAO Chairman and my   father some
<u>ránhòu</u>   zìjǐ   cái   kěn   chī.
then   self   then   be willing   eat
{If someone gave him something to eat, he would always ask the staff to share it with Chairman MAO and my father first, and then he would eat it.}

If successiveness is to be emphasized, *jiēzhe* is a better choice than *ránhòu*, as shown by the following example:

(41) 每天天还没亮，母亲就第一个起身，<u>接着</u>听见祖母起来的声音，<u>接着</u>大家都离开床铺，喂猪的喂猪，砍柴的砍柴，挑水的挑水。
Měitiān   tiān   hái   méi   liàng, mǔqīn jiù   dìyī gè   qǐshēn, <u>jiēzhe</u>
every day sky   still NEG   bright mother as early as   first CL   get up   then

	tīngjiàn	zǔmǔ	qǐlái	de	shēngyīn,	jiēzhe	dàjiā	dōu	líkāi	chuángpù,
	hear	grandma	get up	SP	sound	then	everyone	all	leave	bed

wèizhūde   wèi zhū, kǎncháide   kǎn chái,
person who feeds the pigs feed pig person who chops firewood chop firewood

tiāoshuǐde   tiāo shuǐ.
person who carries water carry water

{Every day before dawn, Mom was the first to get up, followed by Grandma, and then everyone left the bed to do their own job—some fed the pigs, some chopped firewood, and others fetched water.}

The two occurrences of *jiēzhe* in (41) emphasize that the acts are in quick succession and create a tense atmosphere, whereas *ránhòu* would be an awkward choice. Compare another two examples:

(42) （他刚下车，那一串）送煤进城，然后拉化肥回来（的大车队，正从他面前经过，……）

(Tā gāng xià chē, nà yī chuàn) sòng méi jìn chéng, ránhòu lā
he just get off bus that one CL deliver coal go to town then deliver
huàféi huílái (de dàchēduì, zhèng cóng tā miànqián
fertilizer come back SP horse and cart fleet in progress from his before face
jīngguò, ...)
pass

{[When he got off the bus, that fleet of] [horses and carts that] had delivered coal into town and then carried fertilizer on the way back [were just passing before him, ...]}

(43) （当我）目送亚女出了门，接着又分明望见小元的影子在自家的院子里晃动（时，我像吞了一个秤砣，立时愧疚得无地自容了，……）

(Dāng ... shí wǒ) mùsòng Yànǚ chū-le-mén, jiēzhe yòu
when I watch someone leave Yanv go out-PEF followed by
fēnmíng wàngjiàn Xiǎo Yuán de yǐngzi zài zìjiā de yuànzi-li
clearly see Xiao Yuan SP shadow at oneself SP in courtyard
huàngdòng (shí, wǒ xiàng yī tūn-le gè chèngtuó, lìshí
sway time I be like one swallow-PEF CL steelyard weight immediately
kuìjiù de wúdì-zìróng le, ...)
guilty SP nowhere to hide oneself MP

{[When I] watched Yanv going out the door, and then clearly saw Xiao Yuan's shadow sway in his courtyard [I felt so ashamed of myself as if I had swallowed a steelyard weight and that I wish I could find a place to hide myself . . .]}

In (42), there could be many other actions between "delivering the coal into the town" and "carrying fertilizer back," such as eating, resting, shopping, etc. The use of *ránhòu* emphasizes that delivering the coal into town happens prior to carrying the fertilizer back. In (43), "watching Yanv going out the door" is immediately followed by "seeing Xiao Yuan's shadow sway in his courtyard," and *jiēzhe* emphasizes that the two actions are in close succession. It would be inappropriate to replace *ránhòu* with *jiēzhe* in (42) or vice versa in (43).

It is true that *jiēzhe* can also segment the course of an action and emphasize that an act follows a particular one more closely than it follows another one in successive complex sentences. Nonetheless, between *jiēzhe* and *ránhòu*, the former focuses on successiveness while the latter focuses on chronology, as illustrated by the following example:

(44) 他吸了一口烟，又很快把烟筒里的烟灰吹掉，<u>接着</u>又吸，又吹。
Tā   xī-le   yī   kǒu   yān, yòu hěn kuài   bǎ yāntǒng-li de
he inhale-PEF one mouth smoke and very quickly BA in pipe   SP
yānhuī   chuī-diào, <u>jiēzhe</u> yòu   xī,   yòu   chuī.
tobacco ash blow off followed by inhale and   blow
{He took a puff at his pipe, quickly blew the ash out of the pipe, and then he smoked and blew again.}

In (44), *jiēzhe* segments the action into two steps—"inhaling and then blowing" and "inhaling and then blowing," but what it emphasizes is the short interval between the two steps and the shorter interval between "inhaling" and the "blowing" within each step. If *jiēzhe* was replaced by *ránhòu*, then the chronological order would be stressed.

It is common for *jiēzhe* and *ránhòu* to occur in collocation with each other, either in the form of "...*jiēzhe*...*ránhòu*..." or "...*ránhòu*...*jiēzhe*..." No matter how they are collocated, *jiēzhe* stresses successiveness and *ránhòu* highlights the chronological order. The following are three examples:

(45) 一篇文章或一篇演说，如果是重要的带指导性质的，总得要提出一个什么问题，<u>接着</u>加以分析，<u>然后</u>综合起来，指明问题的性质，给以解决的办法，......
Yī   piān wénzhāng huò yī   piān yǎnshuō, rúguǒ shì   zhòngyào de dài zhǐdǎo
one CL   article   or one CL speech   if   COP important SP have instruct
xìngzhì de, zǒng děi yào tíchū yī gè shénme wèntí, <u>jiēzhe</u> jiāyǐ
feature SP always need need raise one CL certain problem then   continue by
fēnxī, <u>ránhòu</u> zōnghé-qǐlái, zhǐmíng   wèntí de xìngzhì, gěi
analyze then   synthesize   clearly point out problem SP nature provide
yǐ   jiějué de bànfǎ,...
with solve SP approach
{If an article or a speech is important and instructive in nature, it is always necessary to raise a certain problem and analyze it, and then synthesize all the analyses, point out the nature of the problem and offer solutions...}

(46) 在座的长辈们都点头称是，<u>然后</u>由老四叔主持，换了庚帖，翁柯和茂漪饮了订婚酒，<u>接着</u>大家随便饮酒吃菜，夜深方散。
Zàizuò   de zhǎngbèi-men dōu diǎntóu chēng shì, <u>ránhòu</u> yóu lǎo sìshū
be present SP elder-PL   all nod   say   yes then   by old fourth uncle

78 *"p, jiēzhe q" and relevant forms*

```
zhǔchí,  huàn-le        gēngtiè,                        Wēng Kē  hé   Màoyī
host     exchange-PEF   eight-character horoscope card  WENG Ke  and  Maoyi
yǐn-le     dìnghūn       jiǔ,  jiēzhe  dàjiā      suíbiàn  yǐn    jiǔ   chī  cài,  yè
drink-PEF  engagement    wine  then    everyone   relaxed  drink  wine  eat  food  night
shēn  fāng        sàn.
late  as late as  leave
```
{After all the elders present nodded and said yes, Old Fourth Uncle presided over the exchange of the eight-character horoscope cards, and WENG Ke and Maoyi drank the engagement wine; then everyone started to eat and drink in a relaxed way and didn't leave until late at night.}

(47) 事情很麻烦，两个人都阴沉着脸，<u>然后</u>有了进展，<u>接着</u>一切就迎刃而解。
```
Shìqing  hěn   máfan,        liǎng gè rén     dōu   yīnchén-zhe  liǎn,  ránhòu
matter   very  troublesome   two   CL person  both  gloomy-PRG   face   then
yǒu-le        jìnzhǎn,   jiēzhe  yīqiē  jiù   yíngrèn-érjiě.
there be-PEF  progress   then    all    then  be easily solved
```
{Both of them had a gloomy face as the issue was quite troublesome, and then there was progress, followed by the resolution of the whole issue.}

In some cases, the permutation of *jiēzhe* and *ránhòu* seems to depend on rhetorical needs, and it is hard to tell the semantic differences between different permutations. The following is an example:

(48) 电话放下不久，我办公室的电话就响个不停，<u>最先</u>是王家物业有限公司董事长滕锦华打来的，<u>然后</u>是宝泰实业有限公司总经理徐方生打来的，<u>接着</u>是朋友出租汽车公司总经理占赋打来的，<u>最后</u>是大西部农庄的庄主程自祖打来的，他们的电话内容全部是一样的，……
```
Diànhuà  fàng-xia  bù    jiǔ,   wǒ  bàngōngshì  de  diànhuà  jiù   xiǎng  gè   bù
phone    hang up   NEG   long   my  office      SP  phone    then  ring   CL   NEG
tíng,  zuì   xiān   shì  Wángjiā Wùyè Yǒuxiàngōngsī              dǒngshìzhǎng
stop   most  early  COP  Wangjia Property Management Co., Ltd.  chairman
Téng Jǐnhuá    dǎ-lái de,  ránhòu  shì  Bǎotài Shíyè Yǒuxiàngōngsī
TENG Jinhua    call   MP   then    COP  Baotai Industrial Co., Ltd.
zǒngjīnglǐ        Xú Fāngshēng   dǎ-lái de,  jiēzhe  shì
general manager   XV Fangsheng   call   MP   then    COP
Péngyǒu Chūzūqìchē Gōngsī   zǒngjīnglǐ        Zhàn Fù   dǎ-lái de,  zuì   hòu
Friend Taxi Company          general manager  ZHAN Fu   call   MP   most  late
shì  Dàxībù Nóngzhuāng  de  zhuāngzhǔ  Chéng Zìzǔ    dǎ-lái de,  tā-men
COP  Great Western Farm  MP  owner      CHENG Zizu    call   MP   they
de  diànhuà     nèiróng   quánbù  shì  yīyàng de,...
SP  phone call  content   all     COP  same   MP
```
{Soon after (I) hung up, my office phone started and kept ringing, first from TENG Jinhua, Chairman of Wangjia Property Management Co., Ltd., then from XV Fangsheng, General Manager of Baotai Industrial Co., Ltd., followed by ZHAN Fu, General Manager of Friend Taxi Company, and last from CHENG Zizu, owner of Great Western Farm. All the calls were about the same thing.}

Example (48) is in the form of "*zuì xiān . . . ránhòu . . . jiēzhe . . . zuì hòu . . . ,*" and it would still make sense if this form was changed into "*zuì xiān . . . jiēzhe . . . ránhòu . . . zuì hòu . . .*" However, in terms of the rhetorical effect, the former seems better than the latter, because in this form *jiēzhe* separates *ránhòu* section from *zuìhòu* section and introduces *zuìhòu*, and *ránhòu* correlates with *zuìxiān*.

3.3 "*p, zhècái q*"

Another form of successive complex sentences is "*p, zhècái q*," which has a different semantic focus from "*p, jiēzhe q*" and "*p, ránhòu q*."

3.3.1 "*p, zhècái q*" and its function

In "*p, zhècái q*" sentences, *zhècái* is equivalent to *zhèshí cái* ('as late as that time'), meaning "not . . . until then." The following are two examples:

(49) 山虎如梦初醒，<u>这才</u>明白父女俩的心意。
Shānhǔ rúmèng-chūxǐng, <u>zhècái</u> míngbai
Shanhu as if awakening from a dream not . . . until then understand
fùnǚ liǎ de xīnyì.
father and daughter two SP intention
{Shanhu didn't understand the father and daughter's intention until then—it seemed that he had just awoken from dreams.}

(50) 亚女满意极了，双手接过捧在胸前，几乎是向我鞠躬似地点了一下头，<u>这才</u>迈着轻盈的脚步走了。
Yànǚ mǎnyì jí le, shuāng shǒu jiē-guò pěng zài xiōng-qián,
Yanv satisfied extremely MP double hand take over hold at in front of chest
jīhū shì xiàng wǒ jūgōng shìde diǎn-le yīxià tóu, <u>zhècái</u>
almost COP to me bow as if nod-PEF once head not . . . until then
mài-zhe qīngyíng de jiǎobù zǒu-le.
take-PRG light SP step walk away-PEF
{Yanv was extremely satisfied. She took it with both hands and held it in front of her chest. She nodded her head toward me almost as if bowing to me, and only then did she walk away with light steps.}

The clauses linked by *zhècái* can share the same subject or each have their own subjects. If the anterior and posterior clauses have different subjects, *zhècái* follows the subject in the posterior clause, as in the following example:

(51) 亚女红了脸，勇敢地跨出了矮墙，我<u>这才</u>鼓足了勇气，朝她家走去。
Yànǚ hóng-le liǎn, yǒnggǎn de kuà-chū le ǎi qiáng, **wǒ** <u>zhècái</u>
Yanv red-PEF face bravely SP step out PEF low wall I not . . . until then
gǔ-zú le yǒngqì, cháo tā jiā zǒu-qù.
pluck up PEF courage toward her house walk

{Yanv blushed, and bravely stepped across the low wall to the outside, and only then did I pluck up enough courage to walk to her house.}

Regardless of whether the anterior and posterior clauses share the same subject, the action introduced by *zhècái* is a reaction to the previous action. Therefore, in some cases, there is some kind of causality between the anterior and the posterior clauses. However, as a whole, "*p, zhècái q*" stresses the succession of the acts/actions. The following are two examples:

(52) 傍晌午，她瞧见在附近地里干活的社员都收工了，<u>这才</u>回到地边。
Bàngshǎngwǔ, tā   qiáojiàn zài fùjìn   dì-li   gànhuó de shèyuán
towards noon   she   see   at   nearby in field work   SP commune member
dōu shōugōng-le,   zhècái   huí-dào dì-biān.
all finish work-PEF not...until then return to edge of field
{She didn't return to the edge of the field until she saw that the commune members had all finished work in the nearby fields toward noon.}

(53) 这两年，我画了一百零八座影壁，有个八十八岁的老画师下乡走马看花，边看我十几幅影壁画，连叫十几声好，还要写一篇文章，替我刷个广告，文化馆<u>这才</u>打算给我举办影壁画展览会。
Zhè liǎng nián, wǒ huà-le   yībǎilíngbā zuò yǐngbì,   yǒu   gè bāshíbā
this two year I paint-PEF 108   CL screen wall there be CL 88
suì de lǎo huàshī xiàxiāng   zǒumǎ-kànhuā,   biān
CL SP old painter go to the countryside glance over things hurriedly while
kàn   wǒ shíjǐ   fú yǐngbìhuà,   lián   jiào
look at my more than ten CL screen wall painting continuously say loudly
shíjǐ   shēng hǎo, hái   yào   xiě   yī piān wénzhāng, tì
more than ten CL   good even   be going to write one CL   article   for
*wǒ shuā gè guǎnggào,   **wénhuàguǎn** zhècái   dǎsuàn*
me make CL advertisement cultural center not...until then plan
gěi wǒ jǔbàn yǐngbìhuà   zhǎnlǎnhuì.
for me hold screen wall painting exhibition
{In the past two years, I have painted 108 screen walls. An eighty-eight-year-old painter came to the countryside with the intention of having a quick look at the screen walls. When he saw the dozen of my screen wall paintings, he praised each one of them with a loud "good," and he was even going to write an article to promote my paintings, and only then did the cultural center plan to hold a screen-wall painting exhibition for me.}

Sometimes, *zhècái* collocates with *ránhòu*, with the former indicating a certain action that does not happen until a certain time, and the latter indicating the chronological order, as in the following example:

(54) 这就好比一人远远而来，<u>最初</u>我们只看到他穿的是长衣或短褂，<u>然后</u>又看清了他是肥是瘦，<u>然后</u>又看清了他是方脸或圆脸，<u>最后</u>，<u>这才</u>看清了他的眉目乃至音容笑貌：这时候，我们算把他全部看清了。

Zhè jiù hǎobǐ   yī rén   yuǎn-yuǎn ér lái, zuìchū wǒ-men zhǐ
this just be the same as one person walk from a distance first we   only

kàn-dào tā chuān de shì   chángyī huò duǎnguà, ránhòu yòu kàn-qīng-le
see   he wear SP COP   gown   or jacket   then   and see clearly-PEF

tā shì féi shì shòu, ránhòu yòu kàn-qīng-le   tā shì fāng liǎn huò
he COP fat COP thin, then and see clearly-PEF he COP square face or

yuán liǎn, zuìhòu, zhècái   kàn-qīng-le   tā de méimù
round face finally not...until then see clearly-PEF he SP eyebrow and eye

nǎizhì yīnróng-xiàomào: zhè shíhou, wǒ-men suàn bǎ tā
even   looks   this time   we   count BA him

quánbù   kàn-qīng le.
completely see clearly MP

{This is like a person coming from a distance. At first, we can only see whether he is wearing a gown or a jacket, then whether he is fat or thin, and then whether he has a square face or a round face. In the end, we can see the outline of his facial features and even details—only then can we say that we have seen the whole of him clearly.}

As a synonym of *zhècái*, "*zhèshí cái*" is also a marker for a successive complex sentence, but *zhèshí* and *cái* can be separated by the subject, whereas *zhè* and *cái* cannot. This indicates that *zhè* and *cái* have been merged into a unit similar to a phrasal word, and *zhèshí* and *cái* are much looser in structure, as can be shown in the following example:

(55) 阿鸽原路摇船回村，这时她才发现，身边少了什么。
Ā Gē yuán lù yáo chuán huí cūn, zhèshí ... cái ... tā cái fāxiàn,
A Ge original route row boat return village not...until then she   find

shēnbiān shǎo-le   shénme.
side   miss-PEF something

{A Ge rowed back to the village along the original route, and only then did she find that something around her was missing.}

In the above example, "*zhèshí tā cái...*" cannot be written as "*zhè tā cái...*"

3.3.2 Non-successive "... zhècái..." sentences

In some cases, *zhècái* does not indicate a succession of acts/actions, and it is quite different from "... *zhècái* ..." that indicates succession. The following are two examples:

(56) 应当把这一二年上边提倡说谎话所造成的影响，也写进去，这才完整。
Yīngdāng bǎ zhè yī'èr-nián shàngbiān tíchàng shuō huǎnghuà suǒ
should   BA this one or two-LC higher authority advocate tell lie   PAP

	zàochéng	de	yǐngxiǎng,	yě	xiě-jìnqu,	<u>zhè</u> <u>cái</u>	wánzhěng.
	cause	SP	impact	also	include in the writing	only this	complete

{The impact of the higher authority's advocate of telling lies during the past one or two years should also be included (in the report), and only by so doing is (the report) complete.}

(57) 路见不平，拔刀相助，<u>这才</u>是美人儿理想的情人。

Lùjiàn-bùpíng, bádāo-xiāngzhù,	<u>zhè</u> <u>cái</u>	shì	měirénr	lǐxiǎng	de	qíngrén.
be ready to help others for a just cause	only this	COP	beauty	ideal	SP	lover

{Only a man who is brave and righteous is the ideal lover of a beautiful lady.}

The two examples shown reveal some facts about the non-successive form "... *zhècái* ...." First, *zhè* is a pronoun referring to a matter rather than a time; therefore, it does not equal *zhèshí*. Second, *zhè* functions as the subject, and the word *cái* acts as an adverbial; thus, *zhè* and *cái* do not form a fixed language unit. Finally, what is introduced by *cái* is an adjective or a judgmental structure with the copula verb *shì* ('be') rather than an act/action.

Summary

First, all successive sentences denote the successiveness of acts/actions; that is, the acts/actions follow each other in chronological order.

Second, "*p, jiēzhe q*" is a typical successive form, which emphasizes that the acts/actions are in close succession.

Third, "*p, ránhòu q*" is another typical successive form, which stresses that the acts/actions occur in chronological order.

Fourth, "*p, zhècái q*" is a special successive form. In this form, *zhècái* and "*zhèshí cái*" are synonyms, both of which emphasize that an act/action did not occur until a certain point.

NB Some examples in this chapter are cited from literary works, political essays, articles, and so on. The sources are listed as follows:

1 *Changjiang Literature* (《长江》) 1982(3), including Examples (1), (8), (20), (23), (30), (31), and (36);
2 *Changcheng* (《长城》) 1982(3), including (52);
3 *Chinese* for Junior High School Students, Textbook 2, including (10); Book 3, including (13); Book 4, including (9) and (16); Book 5, including (41); Book 6, including (40);
4 *Chinese* for Senior High School Students, Book 1, including (15); Book 2, including (12); Book 3, including (2), (6), (7), and (11); Book 4, including (45); Book 5, including (4), (21), and (54);
5 *Chunfeng* (《春风》) 1982(1), including (46);
6 *Dangdai* (《当代》) 1982(3), including (24) and (29);

7. *Fiction Monthly* (《小说月报》) 1982(6), including (55), (56), and (57); 1982(7), including (14); 2002(2), including (47);
8. *Flower City* (《花城》) 1983(3), including (19) and (35);
9. *Harvest* (《收获》) 1983(3), including (3);
10. *October* (《十月》) 1982(4), including (53); 1983(4), including (18);
11. *Selected Works of DENG Xiaoping (1975–1982)* (《邓小平文选 (1975–1982年)》), including (26);
12. *Selected Works of Excellent Chinese Short Stories in 1980* (《1980年全国优秀短篇小说评选获奖作品集》), including (5), (27), (28), (37), (42), (43), (49), (50), and (51);
13. *Venture into the Southwest* (《闯西南》) by Buguang (不光), including (38);
14. *Zhongpian Xiaoshuo Xuankan* (《中篇小说选刊》) 1997(4), including (22); 1999(6), including (17), (25), (48);
15. *Zhongshan* (《钟山》) 1983(3), including (44).

4 "*bùdàn p, érqiě q*" and relevant forms

This chapter discusses four relevant forms of progressive complex sentences, with "*bùdàn . . . érqiě . . .*" being the typical marker for the progressive relationship.

The four progressive forms are (1) "*bùdàn p, érqiě q*"; (2) "*bùdàn . . . lián—yě . . .*" sentences; (3) "*shàngqiě p, hékuàng q*"; and (4) "*biéshuō . . . lián—yě . . .*" sentences and "*lián—yě . . . biéshuō . . .*" sentences.

4.1 "*bùdàn p, érqiě q*"

As a typical form of progressive sentences, "*bùdàn p, érqiě q*" denotes a progression from what is stated in *p* to what is stated in *q*, as is shown in the following example:

(1) <u>不但</u>应该使每个车间主任、生产队长对生产负责任、想办法、<u>而且</u>一定要使每个工人农民都对生产负责任、想办法。

<u>Bùdàn</u> yīnggāi shǐ měi gè chējiān zhǔrèn, shēngchǎnduìzhǎng
not only should make every CL workshop director production team leader
duì shēngchǎn fùzérèn, xiǎngbànfǎ, <u>érqiě</u> yīdìng
for production be responsible think of ways but also definitely
yào shǐ měi gè gōngrén nóngmín dōu duì shēngchǎn fùzérèn,
must make every CL worker farmer all for production be responsible
xiǎngbànfǎ.
think of ways

{Not only should every workshop director and production team captain, but also every worker and farmer must bear the responsibility for production and thinking of ways (to raise production).}

4.1.1 Linguistic form

In sentences in the form of "*bùdàn p, érqiě q*", *bùdàn* occurs in the anterior clause, and can either precede or follow the subject, while *érqiě* only occurs at the very beginning of the posterior clause, for example:

(2) a 不但我这么做了，而且大家都这么做了。
   <u>Bùdàn</u> wǒ zhème zuò-le, <u>érqiě</u> dàjiā dōu zhème zuò-le.
   not only I so do-PEF but also everyone all so do-PEF
   {Not only me but also everyone else has done so.}

   b 我不但这么做了，而且如实地写出来了。
   Wǒ <u>bùdàn</u> zhème zuò-le, <u>érqiě</u> rúshí de xiě-chūlái-le.
   I not only so do-PEF but also truthfully SP write out-PEF
   {Not only did I do so, but I also wrote it out truthfully.}

Synonyms of *bùdàn* that can collocate with *érqiě* include *bùjǐn*, *bùdān*, *bùzhǐ* ('不只'), *bùguāng* ('不光'), *bùdú* ('不独'), *fēidàn* ('非但'), and so on. The following are four examples:

(3) 这不仅是科学界、教育界的问题，而且是整个国家的重大政策问题。
   Zhè <u>bùjǐn</u> shì kēxuéjiè, jiàoyùjiè de wèntí, <u>érqiě</u> shì
   this not only COP scientific circles educational circles SP matter but also COP
   zhěnggè guójiā de zhòngdà zhèngcè wèntí.
   entire nation SP major policy matter
   {This matter not only concerns the scientific and educational circles but also major national policies.}

(4) 群众不只是盼望电气化，而且有力量自己搞电气化。
   Qúnzhòng <u>bùzhǐ</u> shì pànwàng diànqìhuà, <u>érqiě</u> yǒu lìliang
   masses not only COP look forward to electrification but also have strength
   zìjǐ gǎo diànqìhuà.
   oneself do electrification
   {The masses not only look forward to electrification but are also capable of achieving it themselves.}

(5) 他不单单说这支歌编了四十年，而且特别说明这支歌是全中国各族人民编的。
   Tā <u>bù-dāndān</u> shuō zhè zhī gē biān-le sìshí-nián, <u>érqiě</u>
   he not only say this CL song compose-PEF forty years but also
   tèbié shuōmíng zhè zhī gē shì quán Zhōngguó gè
   specially state this CL song COP whole China every
   zú rénmín biān de.
   ethnicity people compose MP
   {He not only said that it had taken 40 years for this song to be composed but also emphasized that the song was written by people of all ethnic groups in China.}

(6) 似乎在这之前，他连想都没想过，然而今夜，非但想，而且隐隐觉得有点恨。
   Sìhū zài zhè zhīqián, tā lián ... dōu méi xiǎng dōu méi xiǎng-guò, rán'ér
   as if at this before he not even think think-EXP but

jīn yè,   fēidàn xiǎng, érqiě yǐn-yǐn   juéde yǒudiǎn hèn.
today evening not only think but also vaguely-REDP feel a little resentful
{It seemed that he had not even thought about it before, but tonight, not only did he think about it but also felt vaguely resentful.}

Synonyms of *érqiě* that can collocate with *bùdàn* and its synonyms include *bìngqiě*, *qiě*, and *shènzhì*. The following are three examples:

(7) 下面就是首阳村，所以<u>不但</u>常有砍柴的老人和女人，<u>并且</u>有进来玩耍的孩子。

Xiàmiàn jiù shì Shǒuyáng Cūn, suǒyǐ <u>bùdàn</u> cháng yǒu kǎn
bottom Just COP Shouyang Village therefore not only often there be cut
chái   de lǎorén hé nǚrén, <u>bìngqiě</u> yǒu jìnlái wánshuǎ de háizi.
firewood SP old man and woman but also there be come in play SP child
{At the bottom (of the hill) is Shouyang Village, therefore not only old folks come here to gather firewood, but also children come to play.}

(8) 这女人<u>不单</u>开荒地多，<u>且</u>是惹不起的人物。
Zhè nǚrén <u>bùdān</u> kāi huāngdì   duō, <u>qiě</u>   shì
this woman not only   reclaim uncultivated land a lot but also COP
rě bù qǐ   de rénwù.
can't be provoked SP character
{This woman has not only reclaimed a lot of uncultivated land but is also a character that no one can afford to provoke.}

(9) 这位不速之客是谁？和韩潮记忆里的伯爵惟妙惟肖，<u>不但</u>外貌酷似，神态相仿，<u>甚至</u>那种没落衰微的贵族气息，也一模一样。
Zhè wèi bùsù-zhīkè   shì shuí? Hé Hán Cháo jìyì-lǐ   de bójué
this CL uninvited guest COP who to HAN Chao in memory SP earl
wéimiào-wéixiào, <u>bùdàn</u> wàimào kùsì,   shéntài xiāngfǎng,
very similar   not only   appearance be very alike manner roughly the same
<u>shènzhì</u> nà-zhǒng mòluò   shuāiwēi de guìzú   qìxī,
even   that kind decline wane   SP the nobility temperament
yě yīmú-yīyàng.
also entirely the same
{Who is this uninvited guest? He is very similar to the image of the earl in HAN Chao's memory. Not only are they very much alike in appearance and manner but also even in temperament of the declining nobility.}

The occurrence of *bùdàn* or its synonym is a sufficient condition for a progressive complex sentence to be formed. So long as *bùdàn* is present in the anterior clause, a progressive complex sentence can be formed even though *érqiě* or its synonym is absent in the posterior clause with or without an adverb. The following are three examples:

(10) 不但学生应该尊重教师，整个社会都应该尊重教师。
   <u>Bùdàn</u> xuésheng yīnggāi zūnzhòng jiàoshī, zhěng ge shèhuì <u>dōu</u> yīnggāi
   not only student should respect   teacher whole CL society all should
   zūnzhòng jiàoshī.
   respect teacher
   {Not only students but also the whole society should respect teachers.}

(11) 这个问题不光是铁道部门存在，其他地方和部门也同样存在。
   Zhè ge wèntí <u>bùguāng</u> shì tiědào bùmén cúnzài, qítā dìfang
   this CL problem not only COP railroad sector exist other place
   hé bùmén <u>yě</u> tóngyàng cúnzài.
   and sector also same exist
   {This problem is not only present in the railroad sector, but also in other places and sectors.}

(12) 不光是生活，是生命。
   <u>Bùguāng</u> shì shēnghuó, shì shēngmìng.
   not only COP living COP life
   {(It) is not only living but also life.}

The presence of *érqiě*, *bìngqiě*, *qiě*, or *shènzhì* is also a sufficient condition for a progressive complex sentence to be formed. If any one of them occurs between the anterior and posterior clauses, a progressive complex sentence is formed. The following are four examples:

(13) 邮局离得很远，而且不通公共汽车。
   Yóujú lí de hěn yuǎn, <u>érqiě</u> bù tōng
   post office be away from SP very far what's more NEG be connected
   gōnggòngqìchē.
   bus
   {The post office is far away, and what's more, there is no bus connection.}

(14) 母亲的眼泪，使我也想起爹的背影，并且在以后的多年，不断忆起那个背影：……
   Mǔqīn de yǎnlèi, shǐ wǒ yě xiǎng-qǐ diē de bèiyǐng,
   mother SP tear make me also think of father SP image of one's back
   <u>bìngqiě</u> zài yǐhòu de duō nián, bùduàn yì-qǐ nà ge
   what's more in after SP many year continually recall that CL
   bèiyǐng: ...
   image of one's back
   {Mother's tears also reminded me of the image of Father's back, and what's more, for many years after that, I kept thinking of that image ... }

(15) 那干部比曹光荣小几岁，且又生得面嫩、消瘦，（所以颇显年轻。）
Nà gànbu bǐ Cáo Guāngróng xiǎo jǐ-suì, qiě yòu shēng de miàn
that official than CAO Guangrong young a few years and also look SP face

nèn, xiāoshòu, (suǒyǐ pō xiǎn niánqīng.)
young thin therefore quite look young

{The official was a few years younger than CAO Guangrong, and besides, he had a young face and was thin, [therefore he looked quite young.]}

(16) 一次大风沙袭击，可以把幼苗全部打死，甚至连根拔起。
Yī cì dà fēngshā xíjī, kěyǐ bǎ yòumiáo quánbù dǎ-sǐ, shènzhì
one CL strong sandstorm attack can BA seedling all kill even

liángēnbáqǐ.
uproot

{A strong sandstorm may kill all the seedlings or can even uproot them.}

The occurrence of *bùdàn* or its synonym foreshadows a progressive momentum. Without the presence of such a word in the anterior clause, the progress in the posterior clause would appear abrupt and unexpected. Among *érqiě* and its synonyms, *shènzhì* has the strongest progressive tone, *érqiě* is less strong, and *bìngqiě* and *qiě* are the weakest. However, no matter how abrupt the progress in the posterior clause looks due to the absence of the foreshadowing in the anterior clause, it is always required by the narrative order.

There are two points worthy of attention.

First, *bùdàn* can occur more than once, and so can *érqiě*, as is shown in the following two examples:

(17) 气氛不但严肃，不但凝重，而且，简直开始凝固了！
Qìfēn bùdàn yánsù, bùdàn níngzhòng, érqiě, jiǎnzhí kāishǐ
atmosphere not only serious not only solemn but also simply start

nínggù-le!
suffocate-PEF

{The atmosphere isn't just serious or solemn but has virtually become suffocating!}

(18) （就是在这所弥漫着不祥气息的医院里，他被证实了）不仅有病，而且患的是绝症，而且到了说什么都晚了的程度。
(Jiù shì zài zhè suǒ mímàn-zhe bùxiáng qìxī de yīyuàn-lǐ, tā
just COP at this CL pervade-PRG ominous atmosphere SP in hospital he

bèi zhèngshí-le) bùjǐn yǒu bìng, érqiě huàn
PASSIVE confirmed-PEF not only have disease but also suffer from

de shì juézhèng, érqiě dào-le shuō shénme dōu wǎn-le
SP COP terminal disease but also reach-PEF say whatever all late-PEF

de chéngdù.
SP extent

{[It was in this hospital full of an ominous atmosphere that he was confirmed] not only to be ill but also terminally ill, and to the extent that it would be too late to say anything.}

Second, in some cases, *shènzhì* can occur after the subject in the posterior clause, as in the following example:

(19) 我再也不必担心有谁会拿着大棒子凶神恶煞似地追赶我，我<u>甚至</u>可以不时地抬头看看天上吱吱喳喳飞过去的小鸟，树上绽开的花儿和蓝天上白色的云朵。

wǒ	*zài yě bùbì*	*dānxīn*	*yǒu*	*shuí*	*huì*	*ná-zhe*	*dà*	*bàngzi*
I	no longer need	worry	there be	anyone	will	hold-PRG	big	stick

xiōngshén-èshà	*shìde*	*zhuīgǎn*	*wǒ,*	*wǒ*	<u>*shènzhì*</u>	*kěyǐ*	*bùshí*
evil spirit	like	chase	me	I	even	can	from time to time

de	*táitóu*	*kàn-kàn*	*tiān-shàng*	*zhīzhī-zhāzhā*	*fēi-guòqu*	*de*	*xiǎo*	*niǎo,*
SP	look up	look at	in sky	twitter	fly over	SP	little	bird

shù-shàng	*zhànkāi*	*de*	*huār*	*hé*	*lántiān-shàng*	*báisè*	*de*	*yúnduǒ.*
on tree	bloom	SP	flower	SP	in blue sky	white	SP	cloud

{No longer do I have to worry that someone will chase me with a big stick like an evil spirit; I can even look up from time to time at the twittering birds that fly across, the blooming flowers on the trees, and the white clouds in the blue sky.}

4.1.2 Semantic bases

There are multiple semantic bases for progressive sentences with "*bùdàn p, érqiě q*" being the representative form. The following four relationships form the major semantic bases for progressive sentences.

First, the typical coordinate relationship. If *p* and *q* are coordinate, then they are interchangeable; however, their positions are subject to the speaker's communicative intention. The following are three examples:

(20) 这孩子<u>不但</u>能听懂一些中国话，<u>还</u>能写不少中国字。

Zhè	*háizi*	<u>*bùdàn*</u>	*néng*	*tīng-dǒng*	*yīxiē*	*zhōngguóhuà,*	<u>*hái*</u>
this	child	not only	can	listen and understand	some	Chinese	also

néng	*xiě*	*bùshǎo*	*zhōngguózì.*
can	write	many	Chinese character

{This child not only can listen and understand some Chinese but also write quite a number of Chinese characters.}

(21) 我眼下<u>不光</u>开机子，还学修理。

wǒ	*yǎnxià*	<u>*bùguāng*</u>	*kāi*	*jīzi,*	<u>*hái*</u>	*xué*	*xiūlǐ.*
I	at present	not only	operate	machine	but also	learn	repair

{At present, I not only operate the machines but am also learning to repair them.}

(22) 这两人<u>不仅</u>胖瘦不匀，性格<u>也</u>截然不同。
Zhè liǎng rén <u>bùjǐn</u> pàngshòu-bùyún, xìnggé <u>yě</u> jiérán-bùtóng.
this two person not only different in weight personality also completely different
{These two people not only differ in weight but also very much in personality.}

In (20), "being able to understand some Chinese" and "being able to write quite a number of Chinese characters" are equal in importance. It is possible that someone who understands some Chinese may not be able to write Chinese characters if they merely practice listening and speaking. By the same token, it is not unusual for someone who can write Chinese characters to be unable to listen and understand Chinese if they are only engaged in reading and writing. Therefore, according to what the speaker needs to express and/or wants to emphasize, the positions of *p* and *q* can either be what they are in (20) or be interchanged. For the same reason, the positions of *p* and *q* in (21) and (22) can be swapped.

Second, a progressive relationship denoting a broader scope or greater degree. This progressive relationship is, in essence, a coordinate one, only that the semantic meaning of the posterior clause has a broader scope or to a greater degree than that of the anterior clause; thus, the positions of *p* and *q* cannot be swapped, as in the following two examples:

(23) 请你们出去作报告，<u>不光</u>在咱牛角沟光荣，在全公社全县都光荣。
Qǐng nǐ-men chūqu zuò bàogào, <u>bùguāng</u> zài zán Niújiǎogōu guāngróng,
invite you people go out make speech not only in our Niujiaogou honor
zài quán gōngshè quán xiàn dōu guāngróng.
in whole commune whole county both honor
{It is not only an honor for Niujiaogou, but also for the entire commune and the county, for you to be invited to deliver a speech.}

(24) <u>不光</u>她自己生在上海，长在上海，<u>而且</u>她的爸爸、妈妈、爷爷奶奶、还有爷爷奶奶的爷爷奶奶等等，等等，都是生在上海长在上海的。
<u>Bùguāng</u> tā zìjǐ shēng zài Shànghǎi, zhǎng zài Shànghǎi, <u>érqiě</u>
not only she oneself be born in Shanghai grow up in Shanghai but also
tā de bàba, māma, yéye nǎinai, háiyǒu yéye
she SP father mother paternal grandpa paternal grandma and paternal grandpa
nǎinai de yéye nǎinai děngděng, děngděng,
paternal grandma SP paternal grandpa paternal grandma and so on and so on
dōu shì shēng zài Shànghǎi zhǎng zài Shànghǎi de.
all COP be born in Shanghai grow up in Shanghai MP
{Not only was she herself born and brought up in Shanghai, but also her parents, grandparents, and great-great-grandparents were all born and brought up in Shanghai.}

In the two examples above, the semantic coverage progresses from the anterior clause to the posterior clause. In (23), "an honor for Niujiaogou" and "an honor for the entire commune and the county" are, in fact, coordinate, but the latter has a larger geographical coverage than the former, so the positions of *p* and *q* cannot be swapped. This is also true of (24). The following are two more examples:

(25) 三年工夫，<u>不仅</u>欠账还清，<u>而且</u>，在企业自有基金方面，成了临江首户，真正的百万富翁。
Sān-nián   gōngfu,   <u>bùjǐn</u>   qiànzhàng huán-qīng, <u>érqiě</u>,   zài   qǐyè
three years time   not only   debt   pay off   but also in   enterprise
zìyǒu-jījīn   fāngmiàn, chéng-le   Línjiāng   shǒuhù,   zhēnzhèng
private capital aspect   become-PEF Linjiang richest one true
de   bǎiwàn-fùwēng.
SP   millionaire
{Within three years' time, (he) not only paid off all the debts but also became the richest in Linjiang in terms of private capital—a real millionaire.}

(26) 他 …… 仿佛向我证明：他<u>不仅</u>是个人，<u>而且</u>是个很大的人。
Tā ... fǎngfú xiàng wǒ zhèngmíng: tā <u>bùjǐn</u>   shì   gè   rén,   <u>érqiě</u>
he   seem   to   me   prove   he not only   COP   CL   person but also
shì   gè   hěn   dà   de   rén.
COP   CL   very big SP   person
{He ... seemed to prove to me that he was not only a man, but a very big man.}

In each of these two examples, semantically, the posterior clause has a greater degree than the anterior clause. In (25), although "paying off all the debts" and "becoming. . . a millionaire" are in a coordinate relationship, the latter is apparently at a higher level than the former moneywise. Thus, the two clauses in (25) cannot be inverted; neither can the two clauses in (26) for the same reason.

Third, causality. In a progressive sentence on such a semantic basis, the causal relationship between *p* and *q* is marked as the progressive relationship. The following are two examples:

(27) 现在，不但许多事情都搞清楚了，<u>而且</u>许多人都觉得在精神上高大起来。
Xiànzài, <u>bùdàn</u> xǔduō shìqing dōu gǎo   qīngchǔ-le, <u>érqiě</u>   xǔduō rén
now   not only many thing   all make clear-PEF   but also many   person
dōu juéde zài jīngshén-shàng gāodà-qǐlái.
all   feel   at   in spirit   become noble
{Now, not only have many things been made clear, but also lots of people feel that they are becoming nobler.}

(28) 这个吃红苕长大的女人，<u>不仅</u>给他带来了从来没有享受过的家庭温暖，<u>并且</u>使他生命的根须更深地扎进这块土地里，……
Zhè gè   chī hóngsháo   zhǎngdà de nǚrén,   <u>bùjǐn</u>   gěi tā   dàilái-le
this CL eat sweet potato grow up   SP woman   not only   to   him   bring-PEF
cónglái méiyǒu xiǎngshòu-guò de jiātíng   wēnnuǎn, <u>bìngqiě</u> shǐ   tā
ever   NEG   enjoy-EXP   SP family   warm   but also   make his

shēngmìng	de	gēnxū	gèng	shēn	de	zhā-jìn	zhè	kuài tǔdì-lǐ, . . .
life	SP	root	more	deep	SP	go into	this	CL in land

{This woman, who grew up eating sweet potatoes, not only brought him family warmth that he had never enjoyed before but also made his life deeply rooted in this piece of land . . . }

If "*bùdàn . . . érqiě . . .*" and "*bùjǐn . . . érqiě . . .*" are removed from (27) and (28), *yīn'ér* ('therefore') can be inserted between the two clauses in either of them. This indicates that the relationship between the clauses is intrinsically causal but just marked as progressive by "*bùdàn . . . érqiě . . .*" or "*bùjǐn . . . érqiě . . .*"

In some cases, the inherent causal relationship between the clauses is made manifest by a connective, such as *yīn'ér* and *yīncǐ*, and then this causal relationship is transformed to and marked as a progressive relationship by a progressive marker. The following is an example:

(29) ……别人把这看成是一件惨事，<u>并因此而</u>可怜我，<u>甚至</u>同情我；我不需要！

. . . Biérén	bǎ	zhè	kàn-chéng	shì	yī	jiàn	cǎn	shì,	**bìng**	**yīncǐ**	**ér**
other people	BA	this	regard as	COP	one	CL	tragic	event	also	therefore	then

kělián	wǒ,	**shènzhì**	tóngqíng	wǒ;	wǒ	bù	xūyào!
pity	me	even	sympathize	with me	I	NEG	need

{ . . . others see this as a tragic event, and therefore pity me, and even sympathize with me. I don't need (anyone's pity or sympathy)!}

In the above example, *yīncǐ ér* manifests the causal relationship, and *bìng* and *shènzhì* transform this cause–effect complex sentence into a progressive one.

Fourth, the adversative relationship. In a progressive sentence with this relationship as its semantic basis, the innate adversative relationship is marked as progressive, as is illustrated by the following example:

(30) 小白同志，你看我这个团中央书记处书记，<u>不但</u>做促进工作，<u>还</u>做你的"促退"工作。

Xiǎo Bái tóngzhì,	nǐ	kàn	wǒ	zhè	gè	tuánzhōngyāng
little Bai comrade	you	see	my	this	CL	Central Committee of Communist Youth League of China

shūjìchù	shūjì,	**bùdàn**	zuò	cùjìn	gōngzuò,	**hái**	zuò	nǐ	de
secretariat	secretary	not only	do	promotion	work	also	do	you	SP

"cù tuì"		gōngzuò.
urge . . . to quit		work

{Comrade Little Bai, you see, as secretary of the Secretariat of the Central Committee of the Youth League, not only do I do the promotion work, but also the work of "urging you to quit."}

In (30), if the progressive marker "*bùdàn . . . hái . . .*" was removed and the sentence was slightly reworded, the inherent adversative relationship between the two clauses would become manifest, as can be illustrated by (31). That is to say, "*bùdàn . . . hái . . .*" marks the adversative relationship as progressive.

(31) 小白同志，你看我这个团中央书记处书记，本来应该做促进工作，可现在却做你的"促退"工作。
Xiǎo Bái tóngzhì, nǐ kàn wǒ zhè ge tuánzhōngyāng
little Bai comrade you see me this CL Central Committee of Communist Youth League of China
shūjìchù shūjì, běnlái yīnggāi zuò cùjìn gōngzuò, kě xiànzài
secretariat secretary originally should do promotion work but now
què zuò nǐ de "cù tuì" gōngzuò.
however do you SP urge. . .to quit work
{Comrade Little Bai, you see, as secretary of the Secretariat of the Central Committee of the Youth League, I should have done the promotion work, but what I am doing now is "urging you to quit."}

It should be noted that if the adversative relationship is contrastive causality, that is, *q* is hypothetically the opposite of the effect caused by *p*, then the adversative sentence cannot be transformed into a progressive one. For example:

(32) *他<u>不但</u>很瘦，<u>而且</u>精神十分饱满。
*Tā <u>bùdàn</u> hěn shòu, <u>érqiě</u> jīngshén shífēn bǎomǎn.
he not only very thin but also energy very full

The above example is grammatically incorrect because "being in high spirits" is hypothetically the opposite of the cause of "being very thin." Instead of "*bùdàn . . . érqiě . . .*," such connectives as *dàn* and *què* can be used to link the two clauses.

4.1.3 Three-level progressive sentences

"*shènzhì . . .*" can occur after "*bùdàn . . . érqiě . . .*", hence a three-level progressive sentence is formed, as is illustrated by the following example:

(33) 在五十年代和六十年代初期，它生产的多种型号的车床，<u>不仅</u>装备了大半个中国的机械生产，<u>而且</u>远销亚非拉，<u>甚至</u>竟开拓到欧罗巴。
Zài wǔshí niándài hé liùshí niándài chūqī, tā shēngchǎn de duō zhǒng
in the fifties and the sixties early stage it produce SP many kind
xínghào de chēchuáng, <u>bùjǐn</u> zhuāngbèi-le dàbàn ge zhōngguó
model SP lathe not only equip-PEF more than half CL China
de jīxiè shēngchǎn, <u>érqiě</u> yuǎn xiāo Yà-Fēi-Lā,
SP machinery production but also far sell Asia, Africa, and Latin America
<u>shènzhì</u> jìng kāituò-dào Ōuluóbā.
even unexpectedly expand to Europe
{In the 1950s and early 1960s, it produced various models of lathes, which not only equipped more than half of China's machinery factories but were also exported to Asia, Africa, Latin America, and even to Europe.}

In this sentence, "*bùjǐn . . . érqiě . . . shènzhì . . .*" indicates a three-level continuous progression.

In a three-level progressive sentence, an adverb, such as *yě* and *hái*, can be employed to introduce the second or the third level, for instance, "*bùdàn . . . yě . . . érqiě . . .*," "*bùdàn . . . hái . . . yě . . .*," and so on. The following are two examples:

(34) 大自然<u>不光</u>长栋梁材，<u>也</u>长小草，<u>而且</u>长得更多，……
Dàzìrán <u>bùguāng</u> zhǎng dòngliángcái,   <u>yě</u> zhǎng xiǎocǎo,
nature   not only   grow   trees that are used for pillars also grow   grass
<u>érqiě</u>   zhǎng de   gèng   duō, . . .
but also grow   SP   more   a lot
{In nature not only trees that can be used for pillars grows, but grasses also grow, and there are more grasses than trees.}

(35) 一场荒火，<u>不仅</u>夺去了马俊友同志的生命，<u>还</u>烧毁了我们的一片麦子，<u>也</u>烧焦了垦荒队员的心。
Yī chǎng huānghuǒ, <u>bùjǐn</u>   duóqù-le   Mǎ Jùnyǒu tóngzhì   de
one CL   wildfire   not only take away-PEF MA Junyou Comrade   SP
shēngmìng, <u>hái</u> shāohuǐ-le wǒ-men de yī   piàn màizi, <u>yě</u> shāo-jiāo-le
life   also   burn-PEF   we   SP one CL   wheat   also burn-PEF
kěnhuāng   duìyuán   de   xīn.
reclamation team member SP   heart
{A wildfire not only claimed the life of Comrade MA Junyou but also destroyed the wheat in the fields, as well as the hearts of the reclamation workers.}

Example (34) can be rephrased as (36), and (35) as (37). These sentences all denote a three-level continuous progression.

(36) 大自然不光长栋梁材，也长小草；不仅长小草，而且长得更多，……
Dàzìrán bùguāng zhǎng dòngliángcái,   yě   zhǎng xiǎocǎo;
nature   not only   grow   trees that are used for pillars also grow   grass
bùjǐn   zhǎng xiǎocǎo, érqiě   zhǎng de   gèng   duō, . . .
not only grow   grass   but also   grow   SP   more   a lot
{In nature not only trees that can be used for pillars grows, but grasses also grow, and there are more grasses than trees.}

(37) 一场荒火，不仅夺去了马俊友同志的生命，还烧毁了我们一片麦子；不仅烧毁了我们一片麦子，而且烧焦了垦荒队员的心。
Yī chǎng huānghuǒ, bùjǐn   duóqù-le   Mǎ Jùnyǒu tóngzhì   de
one CL   wildfire   not only take away-PEF Comrade MA Junyou SP
shēngmìng, hái shāohuǐ-le wǒ-men yī   piàn màizi, bùjǐn   shāohuǐ-le wǒ-men
life   also burn-PEF   we   one CL   wheat not only burn-PEF   we
yī   piàn màizi, érqiě   shāo-jiāo-le kěnhuāng   duìyuán   de   xīn.
one CL   wheat but also   burn-PEF   reclamation team member SP   heart
{A wildfire not only claimed the life of Comrade MA Junyou but also destroyed the wheat in the field, as well as the hearts of the reclamation workers.}

In a three-level progressive sentence, the presence of *bùdàn* or its synonym is not required in the first clause to foreshadow the progressive relationship, but the occurrence of such conjunctions such as *érqiě*, *bìngqiě*, and *shènzhì*, which denote progression, is indispensable in the last posterior clauses, as in the following example:

(38) 一年后，我要让两百号人有活干，有饭吃，<u>而且</u>要生活得比付出同等劳动的其他人一样好，<u>甚至</u>要更好。
Yī   nián hòu, wǒ yào ràng liǎngbǎi   hào rén   yǒu huó gàn, yǒu fàn
one year after I will let two hundred CL person have job do have food
chī, <u>érqiě</u> yào shēnghuó de bǐ fùchū tóngděng láodòng de qítā rén
eat but also will live SP as pay equivalent effort SP other person
yīyàng hǎo, <u>shènzhì</u> yào gèng hǎo.
same   good even   will more good
{In a year's time, I will let 200 people not only have jobs to do and food to eat but also live an equally good life to, or even better than, that of others who do the equivalent amount of work.}

4.1.4 *Ellipsis of the predicate in the anterior clause*

In sentences in the form of "*bùdàn p, érqiě q*," the predicate in the anterior clause can be left out provided that the predicate in the posterior clause is the same, as shown by the following example:

(39) a <u>不仅</u>文艺界，其他方面<u>也</u>有类似的问题。
<u>Bùjǐn</u> wényìjiè,   qítā fāngmiàn <u>yě</u> yǒu lèisì de wèntí.
not only literary and art circles other area   also have similar SP problem
{Not only the literary and art circles, but also other areas have similar problems.}

Without the ellipsis of the predicate in the anterior clause, (39a) would be (39b).

b 不仅文艺界有类似的问题，其他方面也有类似的问题。
Bùjǐn   wényìjiè   yǒu lèisì   de wèntí, qítā fāngmiàn
not only literary and art circles have similar SP problem other area
yě   yǒu lèisì   de wèntí.
also have similar SP problem
{Not only do the literary and art circles have similar problems, but other areas also do.}

In some cases of predicate ellipsis, what is omitted is only the main part of the predicate, and what remains is the auxiliary and the prepositional phrase acting as an adverbial, as well as the subject, as shown in (40a) and (41a). Without the ellipsis, (40a) would be (40b), and (41a) would be (41b).

(40) a 我们<u>不仅</u>要从思想上，<u>而且</u>要从工作制度上创造有利于杰出人才涌现和成长的必要条件。

Wǒ-men bùjǐn yào cóng sīxiǎng-shàng, érqiě yào cóng
we not only must from in ideology but also must from
gōngzuò zhìdù-shàng chuàngzào yǒulì yú jiéchū réncái yǒngxiàn
in working system create be conducive to outstanding talent emerge
hé chéngzhǎng de bìyào tiáojiàn.
and grow SP necessary condition
{We must not only ideologically but also institutionally create necessary conditions conducive to the emergence and growth of outstanding talents.}

b 我们不仅要从思想上创造有利于杰出人材涌现和成长的条件，而且……

Wǒ-men bùjǐn yào cóng sīxiǎng-shàng chuàngzào yǒulì yú
we not only must from in ideology create be conducive to
jiéchū réncái yǒngxiàn hé chéngzhǎng de tiáojiàn, érqiě…
outstanding talent emerge and grow SP condition but also
{We must not only ideologically create necessary conditions conducive to the emergence and growth of outstanding talents, but also…}

(41) a 只要我们党的领导是正确的，那就<u>不仅</u>能够把全党的力量，<u>而且</u>能够把全国人民的力量集合起来，干出轰轰烈烈的事业。

Zhǐyào…jiù wǒ-men dǎng de lǐngdǎo shì zhèngquè de, nà jiù bùjǐn
as long as… our party SP leadership COP correct MP then not only
nénggòu bǎ quán dǎng de lìliang, érqiě nénggòu bǎ quán guó rénmín
can BA whole party SP strength but also can BA whole nation people
de lìliang, jíhé-qǐlái, gàn-chū hōnghōng-lièliè de shìyè.
SP strength bring together accomplish powerful and dynamic SP cause
{As long as our Party's leadership is correct, then (we) will be able to bring together the strength of not only the whole Party but also the whole nation, so as to accomplish a magnificent cause.}

b …… 不仅能够把全党的力量集合起来，干出轰轰烈烈的事业，而且……

…Bùjǐn nénggòu bǎ quán dǎng de lìliang jíhé-qǐlái, gànchū
not only can BA whole party SP strength bring together accomplish
hōnghōng-lièliè de shìyè, érqiě…
powerful and dynamic SP cause but also
{…will not only be able to bring together the strength of the whole Party so as to accomplish a magnificent cause, but also…}

4.2 "bùdàn…lián—yě…" sentences

As a subtype of "bùdàn…érqiě…" sentences, "bùdàn…lián—yě…" sentences also denote a progression from what is stated in *p* to what is stated in *q*. However, these sentences have some special features.

4.2.1 Linguistic form

In "*bùdàn . . . lián—yě . . .*" sentences, *bùdàn*, *bùjǐn* or *bùguāng*, and so on, can be present in the anterior clause, and "*lián—yě*" can occur in the posterior clause. The word *lián* can be replaced by "*jiù lián*" or *jiùshì*, and *yě* can be substituted by *dōu*. In some cases, *yě* or *dōu* can be absent. The following are three examples:

(42) 他<u>不但</u>没有到过外省，<u>连</u>县界<u>也</u>没出过。
Tā <u>**bùdàn**</u> méiyǒu dào-guò wàishěng, <u>lián</u> xiànjiè <u>yě</u>
he not only NEG be-EXP other provinces even county borders
méi chū-guò.
NEG exit-EXP
{Not only has he not been to other provinces, but he has also never been outside the county boundary.}

(43) 可是又不巧，踏上红石崖，<u>不但</u>"百中"老人没有来，<u>就连</u>董昆<u>也</u>到县城领火药去了。
Kěshì yòu bùqiǎo, tà-shàng Hóngshíyá, <u>**bùdàn**</u> "bǎizhòng" lǎorén
but just unluckily get to Hongshiya not only a hundred hits old man
méiyǒu lái, <u>jiù lián</u> Dǒng Kūn <u>yě</u> dào xiànchéng lǐng
NEG come even DONG Kun go to county town collect
huǒyào qù-le.
gunpowder go-PEF
{But unluckily, when (we) got to Hongshiya, not only did the old "sharpshooter" not come, but even DONG Kun went to the county town to collect gunpowder.}

(44) <u>不单</u>是尖端武器、常规武器有科研问题，<u>就</u>是减轻战士身上带的东西的重量，同样有科研问题。
<u>**Bùdān**</u> shì jiānduān-wǔqì, chángguī-wǔqì yǒu
not only COP cutting-edge weapon conventional weapon there be
kēyán wèntí, <u>jiùshì</u> jiǎnqīng zhànshi shēn-shàng dài de dōngxi de
scientific research issue even reduce soldier on body carry SP stuff SP
zhòngliàng, tóngyàng yǒu kēyán wèntí.
weight similarly there be scientific research issue
{Scientific research is not only necessary for making cutting-edge and conventional weaponry but even for reducing the weight of soldiers' baggage.}

The word *érqiě* can precede "*lián—yě*," i.e., "*bùdàn . . . érqiě lián—yě . . .*," as in the following example:

(45) 时间一天一天过去了，他<u>不但</u>未按期回贵阳，<u>而且连</u>一封信<u>也</u>没写给我。
Shíjiān yītiān yītiān guòqu-le, tā <u>**bùdàn**</u> wèi ànqī huí Guìyáng,
time day by day pass-PEF he not only NEG on time return Guiyang
érqiě <u>lián</u> yī fēng xìn <u>yě</u> méi xiě gěi wǒ.
but also even one CL letter NEG write to me
{As time went by, not only did he not return to Guiyang as scheduled, but he didn't even write a letter to me.}

In "*bùdàn . . . érqiě lián—yě . . .*" sentences, "*lián—yě*" is used to highlight an extreme or exaggerated situation, for example:

(46) 不但深翻不了一丈，就连一层地皮也揭不下来。
Bùdàn shēn fān bù liǎo yī zhàng, jiù lián yě yī céng dìpí yě
not only deep dig NEG succeed one CL just even one CL ground
jiē bù xiàlái.
uncover NEG complete
{Not only can't (the farmland) be plowed deep, but it is even hard to remove a layer of dirt.}

If *lián*, "*jiù lián*," or *jiùshì* was removed, the extreme situation stated in the posterior clause would become implied, and the original sentence would become a general "*bùdàn . . . érqiě . . .*" sentence. However, not all "*bùdàn . . . érqiě . . .*" sentences imply a progression to an extreme situation. Compare the following two examples:

(47) 不但我辞职，我们老一代的都不兼职了。
Bùdàn wǒ cízhí, wǒ-men lǎoyīdài de dōu bù
not only I resign we older generation SP all NEG
jiānzhí-le.
hold two or more posts concurrently-PEF
{Not only am I quitting, but no one else in us older generation will hold more than one post any longer.}

(48) 不但我不干，最听他指挥的那几个人都不干了！
Bùdàn wǒ bù gàn, zuì tīng tā zhǐhuī de nà jǐ gè rén dōu
not only I NEG do most listen his order SP that several CL person all
bù gàn le!
NEG do MP
{Not only am I quitting, but those who listen to him most are also quitting.}

The word *lián* is absent in both examples above, which are general progressive sentences. Between them, (47) does not denote a progression to an extreme situation; thus, *érqiě*, rather than *lián*, can be inserted between the two clauses, whereas (48) expresses a progression to an extreme situation; therefore, *lián* can occur between the two clauses, hence a "*bùdàn . . . lián—yě . . .*" sentence.

4.2.2 Semantic basis for "*bùdàn . . . lián—yě . . .*" sentences

The semantic basis for all "*bùdàn . . . lián—yě . . .*" sentences is the coordinate relationship, which is characterized by progression and similarity. In terms of scope and degree, the posterior clause is a progression from the anterior clause. In terms of the nature, the situation referred to by the predicate in the anterior clause is the same as or similar to the situation referred to by the predicate in the posterior clause. The following are two examples:

(49) 阿雪的铺子前门庭若市，<u>不光</u>年轻人挤，<u>连</u>上了年纪的<u>也</u>来瞧新鲜，……
Ā Xuě de pùzi-qián méntíng-ruòshì, bùguāng niánqīngrén jǐ,
A Xue SP in front of store swarm with customers not only young people crowd
<u>lián</u> ... <u>yě</u> shàng-le niánjì de <u>yě</u> lái qiáo xīnxian, ...
even   get old-PEF SP come see novelty
{Not only young people crowded in front of A Xue's store, but even old folks came to see the novelty . . . }

(50) 从此以后，陈奂生的身份显著提高了，<u>不但</u>村上的人要听他讲，<u>连</u>大队干部对他的态度<u>也</u>友好得多……
Cóngcǐ yǐhòu, Chén Huànshēng de shēnfèn xiǎnzhù tígāo-le, bùdàn
from now on CHEN Huansheng SP status significantly improve-PEF not only
cūn-shàng de rén yào tīng tā jiǎng, lián ... yě dàduì gānbù
in village SP person need listen him speak even   village committee cadre
duì tā de tàidù yě yǒuhǎo de duō...
to he SP attitude friendly SP more
{Since then, CHEN Huansheng's status has improved significantly. Not only do his fellow villagers must listen to him, even the cadres of the village are much friendlier to him . . . }

In (49), what the young men did and what the old ones did were similar. However, from the anterior clause to the posterior clause is a progression in degree and scope. "Crowding" and "coming to see the novelty" are the same type of actions and could be unified, the sentence could be rewritten as "Not only young people, but also old folks crowded (in front of A Xue's store)." The relationship between the two clauses in (50) is the same as in (49).

4.2.3 Predicate ellipsis in "bùdàn . . . lián—yě . . ." sentences

In a "*bùdàn . . . lián—yě . . .*" sentence, if the anterior and posterior clauses have different subjects but the same predicate, the predicate in the anterior clause can be omitted to avoid redundancy, as in (51a) and (52a). If the predicate in the anterior clause is present, (51a) will become (51b), and (52a) will become (52b).

(51) a <u>不但</u>她，<u>连</u>学贯中外古今的毕部长<u>也</u>说不出。
Bùdàn tā, lián ... yě xuéguàn zhōngwài-gǔjīn
not only her even   well versed in both Chinese and Western learning in ancient and modern times
de Bì bùzhǎng yě shuō bù chū.
SP Minister BI cannot tell
{Not only she, but even Minister BI, who is well versed in both Chinese and Western learning in ancient and modern times, can't tell.}

b 不但她说不出，连学贯中外古今的毕部长也说不出。
Bùdàn tā shuō bù chū, lián ... yě
not only she cannot tell even
xuéguàn zhōngwài-gǔjīn
well versed in both Chinese and Western learning in ancient and modern times

de   Bì bùzhǎng   yě   shuō bù chū.
SP   Minister BI   cannot tell
{Not only can't she tell, but even Minister BI, who is well versed in both Chinese and Western learning in ancient and modern times, can't tell.}

(52) a 咳，这些天，<u>不光</u>孩子，连大人<u>都</u>乏呀。

Hāi,   zhèxiē   tiān,   <u>bùguāng</u>   háizi,   lián ... <u>dōu</u>   dàrén   dōu   fá   ya.
alas   these   day   not only   child   even   adult   tired MP
{Alas, not only children but also adults are tired these days.}

b 不光孩子乏，连大人都乏。

Bùguāng   háizi   fá,   lián ... <u>dōu</u>   dàrén   dōu   fá.
not only   child   tired   even   adult   tired
{Not only are children tired, but adults are also tired.}

4.3 "shàngqiě p, hékuàng q"

As a progressive sentence form, "*shàngqiě p, hékuàng q*" means that compared with what is stated in *p*, what is stated in *q* is not worth mentioning. The following is an example:

(53) 爹去世已经整整十年了，当年的县劳模<u>尚且</u>被人淡忘，<u>何况</u>他撇下的孤儿呢？

Diē   qùshì   yǐjīng   zhěng-zhěng   shí   nián   le,   dāngnián
dad   pass away already exactly-REDP   ten   year   MP   then
de   xiàn   láomó   <u>shàngqiě</u>   bèi   rén   dànwàng,
SP   county model worker even   PASSIVE   person   fade from the memory
<u>hékuàng</u>   tā   piē-xià   de   gū'ér   ne?
let alone   he   leave behind   SP   orphan   MP
{It has been exactly ten years since Dad passed away. Over time people have even forgotten the then county model worker, let alone the orphans he left behind.}

The above example starts with the fact that people have even forgotten the then county model worker and then progresses to emphasize that the orphans being forgotten is natural and therefore not worth mentioning.

4.3.1 Linguistic form

In terms of linguistic form, sentences in the form of "*shàngqiě p, hékuàng q*" have three aspects meriting attention.

First, *shàngqiě* usually occurs in the anterior clause as the typical marker. In some cases, only *dōu*, *hái*, *yě*, or *lián—yě* (*dōu*) and the like occurs in the anterior clause, but all of them can be replaced by *shàngqiě*, as in the following three examples:

(54) 这浑浊的空气，好人都受不了，<u>何况</u>肺病患者。
Zhè húnzhuó de kōngqì, hǎorén dōu shòu bù liǎo, hékuàng
this dirty SP air healthy person even cannot stand let alone
fèibìng huànzhě.
lung disease patient
{The foul air is even too much for healthy people, let alone those with lung diseases.}

(55) 一头骡子有时<u>还</u>尥蹶子呢，<u>何况</u>车！
Yī tóu luózi yǒushí hái liàojuězi ne, hékuàng chē!
one CL mule sometimes even kick the hind legs MP let alone vehicle
{Even a mule sometimes kicks, let alone a vehicle!}

(56) <u>连</u>土地<u>都</u>难以做到旱涝保收，<u>何况</u>人？
Lián ... dōu tǔdì dōu nányǐ zuò-dào
even land be difficult achieve
hànlào-bǎoshōu, hékuàng rén?
ensure stable yields despite drought or excessive rain let alone person
{It is difficult even for land to produce stable yields, let alone people.}

In some sentences, no conjunction is present in the anterior clause, but *shàngqiě* can be present, for example:

(57) 常言说：望山跑死马，<u>何况</u>行人是在饥饿疲乏中步行呢。
Chángyán shuō: wàngshānpǎosǐmǎ,
saying go although the mountain doesn't look far, even a horse would be exhausted after running there
hékuàng xíngrén shì zài jī'è pífá zhōng bùxíng ne.
let alone pedestrian COP at hungry weary LOC walk MP
{As the saying goes, running to a mountain that doesn't look far exhausts horses, not to mention hungry and tired walkers.}

Second, the posterior clause uses *hékuàng* as the typical marker, and the adverb *gèng* usually precedes *hékuàng*. The following are two examples:

(58) 据我所知，就连北大那几位死去的名教授的书画古玩，<u>尚且</u>在劫难逃，<u>更何况</u>苏伯伯那区区几柜书呢？
Jù wǒ suǒ zhī, jiù lián ... shàngqiě běidà nà jǐ
according to I PAP know just even Peking University that several
wèi sǐqù de míng jiàoshòu de shūhuà gǔwán. shàngqiě
CL die SP famous professor SP painting and calligraphy work antique
zàijié-nántáo, gèng hékuàng Sū bóbo nà qūqū jǐ
impossible to escape the fate not to mention SU uncle that only several
guì shū ne?
cabinet book MP
{As far as I know, it was even impossible for the paintings, calligraphy works, and antiques owned by those deceased famous professors at Peking University to

(59) 连草原上的乳牛都知道爱护自己的犊子，更何况你打的是自己的儿子！
Lián ... dōu cǎoyuán-shàng de rǔniú dōu zhīdào àihù zìjǐ de
even   on grassland SP cow   know love and care for oneself SP
dúzi, gèng hékuàng nǐ dǎ de shì zìjǐ de érzi!
calf let alone   you beat SP COP oneself SP son
{Even the cows on the grassland love and care for their calves, let alone human beings. How can you beat your own son?!}

If *hékuàng* or *gèng-hékuàng* is used in the posterior clause, the sentence is a rhetorical question. If *gèng-bùyòngshuō* or *gèng-bùbìshuō* is used in the posterior clause, the sentence is a declarative one. The following example is a declarative sentence:

(60) 见面尚且怕，更不必说敢有托付了。
Jiànmiàn shàngqiě pà, gèng bùbìshuō gǎn yǒu tuōfù le.
meet   even   be afraid needless to say dare have request MP
{(I) was even afraid to meet (them), needless to say that (I) dared request (them) to do anything).}

In some cases, as long as *shàngqiě* or one of its synonyms is present in the anterior clause, *hékuàng* or *gèng-bùyòngshuō* can be absent in the posterior clauses, as can be seen in the following example:

(61) 对梁倩尚且如此这般，对别人又该如何呢？
Duì Liáng Qiàn shàngqiě rúcǐ zhèbān, duì biérén yòu gāi rúhé ne?
treat LIANG Qian even such such   treat others then should how MP
{If (you) treat LIANG Qian this way, how should (you) treat others?}

Third, if there are two progressions in a row, "*shàngqiě . . . hékuàng . . . gèng hékuàng . . .*" or "*shàngqiě . . . hékuàng . . . yòu hékuàng . . .*" can be used, as in the following two examples:

(62) 结婚？谈何容易。现在黄花闺女还嫁不出去，何况她这离婚的四十岁的女人，更何况她还有一个儿子。
Jiéhūn? Tánhéróngyì. Xiànzài huánghuāguīnǚ hái jià bù chūqu,
marry   by no means easy now virgin girl   even cannot be married
hékuàng tā zhè líhūn de sìshí-suì de nǚrén, gèng hékuàng tā hái yǒu
let alone she this divorce SP forty years SP woman let alone   she even have
yī gè érzi.
one CL son
{Marry someone? Easier said than done. Now no one even wants to marry a virgin girl, let alone a 40-year-old divorcee like her, particularly with a son.}

(63) 连北京都有那么多人迷 "参考片"，<u>何况</u>在这大西北的兰州！<u>又何况</u>陆老师这种难得搞到一张 "内部参考片" 票的中学老师！
<u>Lián</u> ... <u>dōu</u> Běijīng <u>dōu</u> yǒu nàme duō rén mí "cānkǎopiān",
even　　　Beijing　　have that　many person be fascinated reference film
<u>hékuàng</u> zài zhè dàxīběi　　de Lánzhōu! <u>Yòu</u> <u>hékuàng</u> Lù lǎoshī zhè-zhǒng
let alone in this Northwest China SP Lanzhou again let alone teacher LU this kind
nándé　gǎo-dào yī　zhāng "nèibù cānkǎopiān"　piào de zhōngxué lǎoshī!
difficult get　　one CL　　internal reference film ticket SP high school teacher
{Even Beijing has so many people who are fascinated by the "reference films," let alone people in Lanzhou in Northwest China, particularly those who have difficulty getting an "internal reference film" ticket like LU, a high school teacher!}

4.3.2 Formation of "hékuàng q"

In sentences in the form of "shàngqiě p, hékuàng q," hékuàng is generally followed by words referring to the counterpart in the anterior clause. This counterpart can be the subject (person or matter) or an adverbial (location, time, or matter). In short, what follows hékuàng is what is not worth mentioning. Compare the following examples:

(64) 他<u>尚且</u>搬不动，<u>何况</u>你我！
Tā　<u>shàngqiě</u>　bān bù dòng,　　　<u>hékuàng</u>　　nǐ　　wǒ!
he　　even　　　be unable to move　let alone　you　　Me
{He can't even move (it), let alone you or me.}

(65) 他在这儿<u>尚且</u>如此放肆，<u>何况</u>在别的场合！
Tā zài zhèr <u>shàngqiě</u> rúcǐ fàngsì,　<u>hékuàng</u> zài bié　de chǎnghé!
he at here　even　　such take liberties let alone on other SP occasion
{Even at here he takes liberties like this, let alone on other occasions!}

(66) 他在这时候<u>尚且</u>如此放肆，<u>何况</u>在别的时候！
Tā zài zhè shíhou <u>shàngqiě</u> rúcǐ fàngsì,　<u>hékuàng</u> zài bié　de shíhòu!
he at this time　even　　such take liberties let alone at other SP time
{Even at this time he takes liberties like this, let alone at other times!}

(67) 他对你<u>尚且</u>如此<u>放肆</u>，<u>何况</u>对我们！
Tā duì　nǐ　<u>shàngqiě</u>　rúcǐ　fàngsì,　　<u>hékuàng</u>　duì　　wǒ-men!
he with you　even　　such take liberties let alone with　us
{Even with you he takes liberties like this, let alone with us!}

In (64), after hékuàng, "nǐ wǒ" ('you and me') is a counterpart of the subject tā ('he') in the anterior clause. Similarly, "zài biéde chǎnghé" ('on other occasions') in (65), "zài biéde shíhòu" ('at other times') in (66), and "duì wǒmen" ('with us') in (67) referring to location, time, and object respectively, are counterparts of the adverbials in the anterior clauses.

In some cases, *hékuàng* can introduce an independent component clause acted by a subject–predicate structure. There are two different situations that require the use of a subject–predicate structure: first, what needs to be introduced is the matter to be emphasized as well as the characteristic of a certain aspect of the matter, and second, what needs to be introduced is the matter to be emphasized as well as the relationship between the matter and its counterpart in the anterior clause. Compare the following examples:

(68) 煤渣<u>尚且</u>有用，<u>何况</u>人呢！
    Méizhā   <u>*shàngqiě*</u>   *yǒuyòng,*   <u>*hékuàng*</u>   *rén*   *ne!*
    coal cinder   even   be useful   let alone   human   MP
    {Even coal cinders are useful, let alone people!}

(69) 煤渣<u>尚且</u>有用，<u>何况</u>人还有两只手呢！
    Méizhā   <u>*shàngqiě*</u>   *yǒuyòng,*   <u>*hékuàng*</u>   *rén*   *hái yǒu liǎng zhī shǒu ne!*
    coal cinder   even   be useful   let alone   human   and have two CL hand MP
    {Even coal cinders are useful, let alone people, who have two hands!}

(70) 煤渣<u>尚且</u>有用，<u>何况</u>你还是个人呢！
    Méizhā   <u>*shàngqiě*</u>   *yǒuyòng,*   <u>*hékuàng*</u>   *nǐ*   *hái*   *shì*   *gè*   *rén*   *ne!*
    coal cinder   even   be useful   let alone   you   moreover   COP   CL   human   MP
    {Even coal cinders are useful, let alone you, who are a human being!}

(71) 煤渣<u>尚且</u>有用，<u>何况</u>你所唾弃的还是人呢！
    Méizhā   <u>*shàngqiě*</u>   *yǒuyòng,*   <u>*hékuàng*</u>   *nǐ*   *suǒ*   *tuòqì*   *de*   *hái*   *shì*
    coal cinder   even   be useful   let alone   you   PAP   despise   SP   moreover   COP
    rén   *ne!*
    human   MP
    {Even coal cinders are useful (therefore they shouldn't be despised), let alone a person, who you despise!}

In (68), *hékuàng* only introduces the highlighted *rén* ('human being'), the counterpart of the subject *méizhā* ('coal cinder') in the anterior clause. In (69), *hékuàng* introduces a subject–predicate structure, in which *rén* is the emphasis, and "*hái yǒu liǎng zhī shǒu*" ('and have two hands') indicates the characteristics of a human being. In (70) and (71), *hékuàng* also introduces a subject–predicate structure; that is, *rén* is the emphasis, and both *nǐ* ('you') and "*nǐ suǒ tuòqì de*" ('who you despise') refer to the matters that are related to human beings.

4.3.3 Differences between "*shàngqiě . . . hékuàng . . .*" and "*bùdàn . . . lián—yě . . .*"

First, "*shàngqiě . . . hékuàng . . .*" sentences and "*bùdàn . . . lián—yě . . .*" sentences are opposite in terms of the direction of the progression.

All progressive sentences in the form of "*shàngqiě p, hékuàng q*" can be rewritten as "*bùdàn . . . lián—yě . . .*" sentences, but what is stated in *p* and what is stated in *q* need to be swapped; i.e., "*shàngqiě B, hékuàng A*" needs to be rewritten as "*bùdàn A, jiù lián B*." Compare the following two examples:

(72) a 大风浪尚且经得住，何况小风浪！
    Dà fēnglàng   shàngqiě jīng de zhù,   hékuàng xiǎo   fēnglàng!
    big wind and wave   even   can be withstood let alone small wind and wave
    {Even strong winds and huge waves can be withstood, let alone gentle winds and small waves!}

    b 不但小风浪经得住，就是大风浪也经得住！
    Bùdàn xiǎo fēnglàng   jīng de zhù,   jiù shì   dà   fēnglàng
    not only small wind and wave can be withstood even COP big wind and wave
    yě   jīng de zhù!
    also can be withstood
    {Not only gentle winds and small waves, but also strong winds and huge waves can be withstood!}

(73) a 小风浪尚且经不住，何况大风浪！
    Xiǎo fēnglàng   shàngqiě jīng bù zhù,   hékuàng dà   fēnglàng!
    small wind and wave   even   cannot be withstood let alone big wind and wave
    {Even gentle winds and small waves can't be withstood, not to mention strong winds and huge waves!}

    b 不但大风浪经不住，就连小风浪也经不住！
    Bùdàn   dà   fēnglàng   jīng bù zhù,   jiù lián . . . yě   xiǎo
    not only big wind and wave cannot be withstood even   small
    fēnglàng   yě jīng bù zhù!
    wind and wave cannot be withstood
    {Not only can't strong winds and huge waves be withstood, but also gentle winds and small waves!}

In some cases, if a sentence in the form of "*shàngqiě p, hékuàng q*" needs to be rewritten as a "*bùdàn . . . lián—yě . . .*" sentence, the wording of the original sentence should be modified, as in the following two examples:

(74) a 见面尚且怕，更不必说敢有托付了。
    Jiànmiàn shàngqiě pà,   gèng bùbìshuō   gǎn yǒu tuōfù le.
    meet   even   be afraid more needlessly to say dare make request MP
    {(I was) even afraid to meet (them), let alone request (them to do anything).}

    →b 不但害怕有所托付，就连见面也害怕。
    Bùdàn hàipà   yǒu suǒ tuōfù, jiù lián . . . yě jiànmiàn yě hàipà.
    not only be afraid make PAP request just even   meet   be afraid
    {Not only (was I) afraid to request (them to do anything), but even meet (them).}

(75)　a 煤炭渣尚且可以铺路，何况她还是个人呢！
　　　Méitànzhā shàngqiě kěyǐ pūlù,　hékuàng tā hái　shì gè rén ne!
　　　coal cinder even　　can pave road let alone she moreover COP CL person MP
　　　{Even coal cinders are useful, such as paving roads, let alone her, a human being!}

　→b 不仅人有用，就连煤炭渣也有用。
　　　Bùjǐn　　rén　　yǒuyòng,　jiù　lián　　yě　méitànzhā　yě　yǒuyòng.
　　　not only　person　be useful　just　even　　　coal cinder　　be useful
　　　{Not only are people useful, but even coal cinders.}

With respect to the direction of the progression, "*bùdàn . . . lián—yě . . .*" sentences are upward and sentences in the form of "*shàngqiě p, hékuàng q*" are downward. If "A" stands for the lower level and B for the higher level, A progresses upward to "B" in "*bùdàn . . . lián—yě . . .*" sentences and B progresses downward to A in "*shàngqiě p, hékuàng q*" sentences, as is illustrated by Diagram 4.1:

$$A \quad \frac{bùdàn \quad \rightarrow \quad lián—yě}{shàngqiě \quad \leftarrow \quad hékuàng} \quad B$$

Diagram 4.1

Next, the two forms have different semantic bases. In "*bùdàn . . . lián—yě . . .*" sentences, the progression is in degree or scope; therefore, the relationship between the clauses is coordinate in essence. Nevertheless, "*shàngqiě . . . hékuàng . . .*" sentences are based on an inferential relationship; hence, they are sentences of the causal type. Compare the following two examples:

(76)　a 大风浪尚且经得住，何况小风浪！
　　　Dà　fēnglàng　shàngqiě　jīng de zhù,　hékuàng　xiǎo　fēnglàng!
　　　big　wind and wave　even　　can withstand　let alone　small　wind and wave
　　　{Even strong winds and huge waves can be withstood, let alone gentle winds and small waves!}

　　b 既然大风浪经得住，小风浪当然也经得住！
　　　Jìrán　　dà　fēnglàng　jīng de zhù,　xiǎo　fēnglàng　dāngrán
　　　now that　big　wind and wave　can be withstood　small　wind and wave　of course
　　　yě　jīng de zhù!
　　　also　can be withstood
　　　{Now that strong winds and huge waves can be withstood, gentle winds and small waves can, of course, be withstood!}

Since "*shàngqiě . . . hékuàng . . .*" sentences are based on an inferential relationship, they can be rewritten as inferential sentences, thus (76a) can be rewritten as (76b). Compare another two examples:

(77) a 不但小风浪经得住，连大风浪也经得住！

<u>Bùdàn</u> xiǎo   fēnglàng   jīng de zhù,   <u>lián</u> . . . <u>yě</u>   dà
not only small wind and wave can be withstood even   big
fēnglàng   yě   jīng de zhù!
wind and wave also can be withstood

{Not only can gentle winds and small waves be withstood, but even strong winds and huge waves!}

b* 既然小风浪经得住，大风浪当然也经得住！

*<u>Jìrán</u>   xiǎo   fēnglàng   jīng de zhù,   dà   fēnglàng   <u>dāngrán</u>
now that small wind and wave can be withstood big wind and wave of course
<u>yě</u>   jīng de zhù!
also can be withstood

As demonstrated by (77a) and (77b), a "*bùdàn* . . . *lián—yě* . . ." sentence is not inferential; therefore, it cannot be rewritten as an inferential one.

In summary, "*shàngqiě* . . . *hékuàng* . . ." sentences are progressive in form and causal in essence. From the anterior clause to the posterior clause is a downward progression, which highlights such meanings as "not a problem" and "not worth mentioning."

4.3.4 Two sentence forms similar to "*shàngqiě p, hékuàng q*"

There are two sentence forms similar to "*shàngqiě p, hékuàng q*."

First, "*p, hékuàng q*."

In sentences in the form of "*p, hékuàng q*," *shàngqiě* is not and cannot be present in the anterior clause. What is stated in the anterior clause is a reason or a judgment, and what *hékuàng* introduces in the posterior clause is an additional reason, which refers to something difficult to accomplish or something unusual. The following are three examples:

(78) 场上爆发了一阵热烈的掌声。因为五发四中已经是优秀了，何况这个五发四中是从虎穴里掏得的虎子！

Cháng-shàng   bàofā-le   yī   zhèn rèliè de zhǎngshēng. Yīnwèi
on range   burst-PEF one   CL   warm   SP applause   because
wǔfā-sìzhòng   yǐjīng shì yōuxiù   le,
hitting the target with four shots out of five already COP excellent MP
hékuàng   zhè   gè   wǔfā-sìzhòng   shì cóng
let alone this CL   hitting the target with four shots out of five COP from
huxué-lǐ   tāo-dé de huzǐ!
in tiger's lair get   SP tiger cub

{There was a burst of warm applause on the shooting range, because four out of five shots were already excellent, not to mention that this hit rate was achieved in extremely bad weather conditions!}

(79) 如果一切从新开始，她会找到一个比大亮更好的，<u>何况</u>还有一个 "山盟虽在，锦书难托" 的人呢。

Rúguǒ yīqiè cóngxīn kāishǐ, tā huì zhǎo-dào yī gè bǐ Dàliàng
if everything again begin she will find one CL than Daliang
gèng hǎo de, <u>hékuàng</u> hái yǒu yī gè
more good MP let alone still there be one CL
"*shānméng-suīzài, jǐnshū-nántuō*"
the vows of eternal love are still kept, but the love letters are nowhere to be sent to
de rén ne.
SP person MP
{If everything started anew, she would find a better husband than Daliang, let alone someone who once swore a vow to her but is now out of touch with.}

(80) 不消说，这是个苦差事，<u>更何况</u>还是远离林场，单独作业。

Bùxiāoshuō, zhè shì gè kǔ chāishi, <u>gèng hékuàng</u> hái shì
needless to say this COP CL hard job let alone moreover COP
yuǎnlí línchǎng, dāndú zuòyè.
be far away tree farm by oneself work
{Needless to say, it's a hard job, not to mention working alone in a place far away from the tree farm.}

Such words as *hékuàng* in (78) and (79) and *gèng-hékuàng* in (80) can all be replaced by *kuàngqiě*. The anterior and posterior clauses in each example are in a coordinate relationship rather than inferential. What *hékuàng* introduces is an additional piece of evidence that reinforces the reason or judgement made in the anterior clause. Therefore, "...*hékuàng*..." sentences can also be regarded as downward progressive sentences.

Second, "*shàngqiě p, fǎndào* (反倒) *q*."

In sentences in the form of "*shàngqiě p, fǎndào q,*" *shàngqiě*, rather than *hékuàng*, is present in the anterior clause and what is used in the posterior clause is *fǎndào*, *dàofǎn*, *jìngrán*, or *jūrán*, among others. In terms of meaning, the fact stated in the anterior clause is taken as a starting point of the discussion, and the fact stated in the posterior clause contrasts with the starting point and has a tone of dissatisfaction or appreciation. The following are three examples:

(81) 看不上眼的王胡<u>尚且</u>那么多，自己<u>倒反</u>这么少，这是怎样的大失体面的事呵！

Kànbùshàngyǎn de Wáng Hú <u>shàngqiě</u> nàme duō, zìjǐ <u>dǎofǎn</u>
despise SP WANG Hu even that many oneself on the contrary
zhème shǎo, zhè shì zěnyàng de dà shī tǐmiàn de shì he!
so few this COP how SP greatly lose face SP thing MP
{What a shame that even WANG Hu, whom he looked down upon, had so many (lice), but (he) himself had so few!}

(82) 如此重大的事情厂长<u>尚且</u>不能个人决定，他竟然违背原则，擅自作主！

Rúcǐ zhòngdà de shìqing chǎngzhǎng <u>shàngqiě</u> bù néng gèrén juédìng,
such important SP matter factory director even NEG can personal decide

	tā	*jìngrán*	*wéibèi*	*yuánzé,*	*shànzì*		*zuòzhǔ!*
	he	unexpectedly	violate	principle	without authorization		decide

{Even the factory director can't make a personal decision on such an important matter, but he has gone so far as to violate the principle and make the decision without authorization!}

(83) 父亲对我们讲话<u>尚且</u>采取商量的口吻，你在我面前<u>居然</u>如此放肆！
Fùqin duì wǒ-men jiǎnghuà <u>shàngqiě</u> cǎiqǔ shāngliang de kǒuwěn, nǐ zài wǒ
father to us speak even adopt discuss SP tone you at my
miànqián <u>jūrán</u> rúcǐ fàngsì!
before face unexpectedly such presumptuous
{Even Father spoke to us in a consultative manner, how dare you be so arrogant in front of me!}

The basis for "*shàngqiě . . . fǎndào . . .*" sentences is the adversative relationship between the clauses, which is just opposite to the relationship between the clauses in "*shàngqiě . . . hékuàng . . .*" sentences. Compare the two following two examples:

(84) 这么大的石头，大人们<u>尚且</u>搬不动，<u>何况</u>他只是个十二三岁的小孩子！
Zhème dà de shítou, dàrén-men <u>shàngqiě</u> bān bù dòng, <u>hékuàng</u> tā zhǐ
so big SP stone adult-PL even be unable to move let alone ta only
shì gè shí'èrsān-suì de xiǎoháizi!
COP CL twelve or three years SP child
{Even an adult wouldn't be able to move such a big stone, not to mention him, a kid of only 12 or 13.}

(85) 这么大的石头，大人们<u>尚且</u>搬不动，他这个十二三岁的小孩子<u>反倒</u>搬动了。(真了不起！)
Zhème dà de shítou, dàrén-men <u>shàngqiě</u> bān bù dòng, tā zhè ge
so big SP stone adult-PL even be unable to move he this CL
shí'èr-sān suì de xiǎoháizi <u>fǎndào</u> bān-dòng le. (Zhēn liǎobùqǐ!)
twelve or thirteen CL SP child on the contrary move PEF Really great
{Even an adult wouldn't be able to move such a big stone, but this 12- or 13-year-old kid moved it. [It's amazing!]}

Example (84) means that an adult cannot move such a big stone and that it is even more unlikely for a kid to move it; thus, the two clauses are not opposites. However, what (85) means is that an adult cannot move such a big stone but the kid can; therefore, the two clauses contrast with each other in meaning.

The word *fǎndào* and its synonyms emphasize the contrast between what the anterior clause means and what the posterior clause does. The word *què* can be added and placed before *fǎndào* or simply replace *fǎndào* in some cases. For example, (81) can be rewritten as (86):

110　*"bùdàn p, érqiě q" and relevant forms*

(86) 看不上眼的王胡尚且那么多，自己却（倒反）这么少……

Kànbùshàngyǎn	de	Wáng Hú	shàngqiě	nàme	duō,	zìjǐ	què
despise	SP	WANG Hu	even	that	many	oneself	however

(dǎofǎn)　　　zhème　shǎo . . .
on the contrary　so　few

{What a shame that even WANG Hu, who he looked down upon, had so many (lice), but (he) himself had so few . . . }

Thus, "*shàngqiě . . . fǎndào . . .*" sentences should be classified as adversative complex sentences. The occurrence of *shàngqiě* in the anterior clause does not suffice to prove that they are progressive sentences.

4.4 Progressive sentences with *biéshuō*

There are two progressive sentence forms with *biéshuō*: "*biéshuō . . . lián—yě . . .*" sentences and "*lián—yě . . . biéshuō . . .*" sentences, both of which are special in a certain sense.

4.4.1 "*biéshuō . . . lián—yě . . .*" sentences and "*bùdàn . . . lián—yě . . .*" sentences

A "*biéshuō . . . lián—yě . . .*" sentence is basically equivalent to a "*bùdàn . . . lián—yě . . .*" sentence, as *biéshuō* can be replaced by *bùdàn*, or *bùjǐn*, among others. The following are four examples:

(87) 别说人，连双眼睛都挤不进去。

Biéshuō　rén, 　lián . . . dōu　shuāng yǎnjing　dōu　jǐ bù jìnqu.
not to mention　body　even　　　　pair　eye　　　be unable to squeeze . . . in

{You can't even get a glimpse from the outside, not to mention squeezing yourself in.}

(88) 别说姑娘们，连与他同年龄的小伙子，他都从不敢主动与他们搭讪。

Biéshuō　gūniang-men, lián . . . dōu　yǔ tā　tóng　niánlíng de xiǎohuǒzi,
not to mention　girl-PL　　even　　　as him　same　age　　SP young man
tā　dōu　cóng　bù　gǎn　zhǔdòng　yǔ　tā-men　dāshàn.
he　never　NEG　dare　active　　with　them　　chat

{He never dared to strike up a conversation with young men of his own age, let alone girls.}

(89) 别说羊角垴的这位军烈属，就连被撂在一边的伊汝，也至少半信半疑看待她的来访。

Biéshuō　Yángjiǎonǎo　de　zhè　wèi　jūnlièshǔ,
not to mention　Yangjiaonao　SP　this　CL　family of martyrs or servicemen
jiù lián . . . yě　bèi　　liào　zài　yībiān　de　Yīrǔ, 　yě　zhìshǎo
even　　　PASSIVE　leave　on　one side　SP　Yiru　　　at least

bànxìn-bànyí		*kàndài*	*tā*	*de*	*láifǎng.*
half believe and half doubt		regard	she	SP	visit

{Even Yiru, who was left aside, regarded her visit with at least some suspicion, let alone the one whose family members were remembered as martyrs.}

(90) 没上过山的人，<u>别说</u>扛着百十斤的水泥袋，<u>就是</u>空手往上爬，<u>也</u>会感到十分吃力。

Méi shàng-guò shān de rén, biéshuō káng-zhe bǎi-shí-jīn
NEG climb-EXP mountain SP person not to mention carry-PRG about 50 kilos
de shuǐnídài, jiùshì kōngshǒu wǎngshàng pá, yě huì gǎndào
SP cement sack even if empty-handed climb up will feel
shífēn chīlì.
very hard

{Anyone who has never climbed a mountain would find it very difficult to climb up even if they were empty-handed, let alone carrying a sack of 50 kilos or so of cement on their shoulders.}

In "*biéshuō . . . lián—yě . . .*" sentences, *biéshuō* can be replaced by *béngshuō, mànshuō, bùyàoshuō*, and so on, as in the following four examples:

(91) <u>甭说</u>人的手艺不如前，<u>就连</u>这红砖<u>也</u>不比早先，好像是豆腐渣捏出来的，……

Béngshuō rén de shǒuyì bùrú qián, jiù lián yě zhè hóng
not to mention person SP craftsmanship be worse than before even this red
zhuān yě bùbǐ zǎoxiān, hǎoxiàng shì dòufuzhā niē-chūlái de, . . .
brick be worse than before as if COP soybean dregs make MP

{Even the red bricks are not as good as before—as if they were made of soybean dregs—not to mention that people's craftsmanship (in handmade articles) isn't as good as before . . . }

(92) 山高皇帝远，解放以来，<u>慢说</u>省、地、县的工作人员从未来过这穷乡僻壤，<u>就是</u>公社的干部<u>也</u>是一年半载不着边儿。

Shān'gāo huángdì yuǎn, jiěfàng yǐlái,
if the mountains are high, then the emperor is far away liberate since
mànshuō shěng, dì, xiàn de gōngzuòrényuán cóngwèi
not to mention province prefecture county SP government official never
lái-guò zhè qióngxiāng-pìrǎng, jiùshì yě gōngshè de gànbu yě
come-EXP this remote and backward place even commune SP cadre
shì yīnián-bànzǎi bù zháo biānr.
COP about a year not show up

{If the mountains are high, then the emperor is far away. Being remote and undeveloped, this village, since liberation (the overthrow of the Kuomintang regime in 1949), has only been sporadically visited by commune cadres, not to mention that the province-, prefecture-, or county-level government officials have never been here.}

112 *"bùdàn p, érqiě q" and relevant forms*

(93) 华丽的服装只有演员演戏的时候穿，平时<u>不要说</u>穿，<u>就连</u>看着<u>也</u>觉得碍眼。
     Huálì   de fúzhuāng zhǐyǒu yǎnyuán yǎnxì de shíhou chuān,   píngshí
     gorgeous SP costume only actor act SP time wear at normal times
     <u>*bùyàoshuō*</u>   *chuān,   <u>jiù lián</u> … <u>yě</u> kàn-zhe   <u>yě</u> juéde àiyǎn.*
     not to mention wear   even   look-PRG   feel   unpleasant to the eye
     {Gorgeous costumes are only worn by actors when they are acting. At ordinary times, they even look unpleasant, not to mention wearing them.}

(94) <u>不要讲</u>这使裘干事大感意外，<u>就连</u>我们其他人<u>也</u>吃了一惊。
     <u>*Bùyàojiǎng*</u> *zhè shǐ   Qiú gànshi   dà   gǎn yìwài,   <u>jiù lián</u> … <u>yě</u>*
     not to mention this make QIU secretary greatly feel unexpected even
     wǒ-men   qítā   rén   <u>yě</u> chī-le yī jīng.
     we   other   person   be surprised-PEF
     {This even surprised us, let alone Secretary QIU.}

If *biéshuō* or its synonym is present in the anterior clause, *lián* or *jiù-lián* is optional in the posterior clause as long as an adverb—such as *yě* or *hái*—is present. The following are three examples:

(95) （虽然穷得当当响，可是小成旺却在双亲温暖的手掌中长到七八岁。）好家伙，<u>不用说</u>讲话，乡村里流行的时曲小调<u>也</u>会唱好一摞哪。
     (Suīrán qióng de dāng-dāng xiǎng, kěshì xiǎo Chéngwàng què   zài
     although extremely poor   but   little Chengwang   however at
     shuāngqīn wēnnuǎn de shǒuzhǎng-zhōng zhǎng-dào qī-bā-suì.)
     parents   warm   SP   in palm   grow up to   seven or eight years of age
     Hǎojiāhuo, <u>bùyòngshuō</u>   jiǎnghuà, xiāngcūn-li   liúxíng   de
     oh boy   not to mention   speak   in the countryside   spread widely   SP
     shíqǔ-xiǎodiào   <u>yě</u>   huì   chàng   hǎo   yī   luò   na.
     popular and folk song   also   can   sing   quite   one   pile   MP
     {[Although the family was extremely poor, Little Chengwang grew up in the warm hands of his parents until he was seven or eight years old.] Oh boy, he was able to sing lots of songs that were popular in the countryside then, let alone speaking (well).}

(96) 要是抓不住，<u>别说</u>官儿做不成，<u>还要</u>押进京城治罪。
     Yàoshi zhuā bù zhù, <u>biéshuō</u>   guānr zuò bù chéng, <u>hái</u>   <u>yào</u>   yā-jìn
     if   fail to catch   not to mention official cannot work as   even   need   escort to
     jīngchéng   zhìzuì.
     national capital   punish
     {If (he) fails to catch (the criminal), (he) will be escorted to the capital city for punishment, not to mention that (he) couldn't continue to work as a government official.}

(97) <u>别说</u>教他们，教你<u>也</u>成！
     <u>*Biéshuō*</u>   *jiāo   tā-men,   jiāo   nǐ   <u>yě</u>   chéng!*
     not to mention   teach   them   teach   you   even   okay
     {(Someone) can even teach you, let alone them!}

Compared with the "*bùdàn . . . lián—yě . . .*" sentences, "*biéshuō . . . lián—yě . . .*" sentences have some semantic particularities; that is, *biéshuō* and its synonyms can show the speaker's disdain or contempt, or commendation of a matter followed by the exclusion of that matter. If the progression is upward, namely, from an inferior matter to a superior matter of the same type, the sentence comments on the latter by disdaining or despising the former. On the other hand, if the progression is downward, that is, from a superior matter to an inferior matter of the same type, the sentence highlights the latter by commending and then excluding the former. Compare the following two examples:

(98) <u>别说</u>同事讲话他不听,<u>就是</u>院长讲话他<u>也</u>敢反驳。

<u>Biéshuō</u>　　 tóngshì 　jiǎnghuà tā bù 　tīng, <u>jiùshì</u> . . . <u>yě</u> yuànzhǎng
not to mention colleague 　speak　 he NEG listen 　even 　　　　　　 dean
jiǎnghuà tā <u>yě</u> gǎn 　fǎnbó.
speak 　 he 　　 dare 　refute

{He was even bold enough to talk back to the dean, not to mention that he wouldn't listen to his colleagues.}

(99) <u>别说</u>院长讲话他不敢反驳,<u>就是</u>同事讲话他<u>也</u>不敢不听。

<u>Biéshuō</u>　　 yuànzhǎng jiǎnghuà tā bù 　gǎn fǎnbó, <u>jiùshì</u> . . . <u>yě</u> tóngshì
not to mention dean 　　　　 speak　 he NEG dare refute 　even 　　　　　 colleague
jiǎnghuà tā <u>yě</u> bù 　gǎn bù 　tīng.
speak 　 he 　　 NEG dare NEG listen

{He didn't even have the guts not to listen to his colleagues, not to mention that he would not be bold enough to talk back to the dean.}

The progression in (98) is upward, with *biéshuō* indicating the inferior status of the colleagues' opinions. The sentence emphasizes that the dean's opinion was no more important than the colleagues' opinions. On the contrary, the progression in (99) is downward, with *biéshuō* exalting the dean's opinion and then excluding it. The sentence emphasizes that the colleagues' opinions are no less powerful than the dean's opinion. In each of these two sentences, *biéshuō* can be replaced by *bùdàn*, *bùjǐn* and so on, but the replacement will remove all the implications of *biéshuō*.

4.4.2 "*lián—yě . . . biéshuō . . .*" sentences and "*biéshuō . . . lián—yě . . .*" sentences

Often "*biéshuō . . . lián—yě . . .*" sentences can be rewritten as "*lián—yě . . . biéshuō . . .*" sentences. Compare the following two examples, between which (100) is an original one from a short story and (101) is a rewritten sentence.

(100) <u>别说</u>是嫁妆,<u>连</u>一双草鞋<u>都</u>没穿出来。

<u>Biéshuō</u>　　　 shì 　jiàzhuang, <u>lián</u> . . . <u>dōu</u> yī-shuāng cǎoxié 　　<u>dōu</u>
not to mention COP dowry 　　　even 　　　　 a pair 　　straw sandals
méi chuān-chūlái.
NEG bring

{How can a dowry be expected, as (she) didn't even bring a pair of straw sandals?}

(101) 连一双草鞋<u>都</u>没穿出来，<u>别说</u>是嫁妆！

<u>Lián</u> . . . <u>dōu</u> yī-shuāng cǎoxié <u>dōu</u> méi chuān-chūlái, <u>biéshuō</u>
even   a pair   straw sandals   NEG bring   not to mention
shì   jiàzhuang.
COP dowry

{(She) didn't even bring a pair of straw sandals, let alone a dowry!}

However, there are differences between "*lián—yě . . . biéshuō . . .*" sentences and "*biéshuō . . . lián—yě . . .*" sentences.

First, in terms of the progressive direction, "*biéshuō . . . lián—yě . . .*" sentences are the same as "*búdàn . . . lián—yě . . .*" sentences, whereas "*lián—yě . . . biéshuō . . .*" sentences are the same as sentences in the form of "*shàngqiě p, hékuàng q.*" For instance, (100) and (101) can be respectively rewritten as (102) and (103).

(102) <u>不但</u>没有什么<u>嫁妆</u>，连一双草鞋<u>都</u>没有穿出来！

<u>Bùdàn</u> méiyǒu shénme jiàzhuang, <u>lián</u> . . . <u>dōu</u> yī-shuāng cǎoxié   <u>dōu</u>
not only not have any   dowry   even   a pair   straw sandals
méiyǒu chuān-chūlái!
NEG   bring

{She not only had no dowry but she didn't even bring a pair of straw sandals!}

(103) 草鞋<u>尚且</u>没穿出来，<u>何况</u>是嫁妆！

Cǎoxié   <u>shàngqiě</u> méi chuān-chūlái, <u>hékuàng</u> shì   jiàzhuang!
straw sandals even   NEG bring   let alone   COP dowry

{(She) didn't even bring straw sandals, let alone a dowry.}

In other words, in "*lián—yě . . . biéshuō . . .*" sentences there exists an inferential relationship between the clauses. The anterior clause is where the progression starts, which is actually the basis for the inference, and the posterior clause is where the progression ends, which is also the conclusion of the inference. Obviously, "*lián—yě . . . biéshuō . . .*" sentences differ from "*shàngqiě . . . hékuàng . . .*" ones in that the section of "*hékuàng . . .*" is acted by a rhetorical question whereas the section of "*biéshuō . . .*" is acted by a declarative clause.

Second, in terms of linguistic form, *gèng* can be added and placed before *biéshuō* in "*lián—yě . . . biéshuō . . .*", and the particle *le* can be present at the end of "*biéshuō . . .*," i.e., "*lián—yě . . . gèng biéshuō . . . le.*" However, this does not hold for "*biéshuō . . . lián—yě . . .*" For instance, (103) can be rewritten as (104).

(104) 连一双草鞋都没穿出来，更别说是嫁妆了！

<u>Lián</u> . . . <u>dōu</u> yī-shuāng cǎoxié   dōu méi chuān-chūlái, gèng biéshuō
even   a pair   straw sandals   NEG bring   not to mention
shì   jiàzhuang le!
COP dowry   MP

{(She) didn't even bring a pair of straw sandals, let alone a dowry!}

The following are another two examples:

(105) ……他连科室那几个坐办公室的姑娘都分不清楚，更别说别的姑娘。
…Tā <u>lián</u> … <u>dōu</u> kēshì nà jǐ gè zuò bàngōngshì
he even administrative office that several CL work in the office
de gūniang <u>dōu</u> fēn bù qīngchǔ, <u>gèng biéshuō</u> biéde gūniang.
SP girl cannot clearly distinguish not to mention other girl
{…He can't even tell the girls who work in the office apart, let alone other girls.}

(106) ……连动物都不会有，更不要说会有男人出现。
…<u>lián</u> … <u>dōu</u> dòngwù <u>dōu</u> bù huì yǒu, <u>gèng bùyàoshuō</u> huì yǒu
even animal NEG will there be not to mention will there be
nánrén chūxiàn.
man appear
{…there will not even be any animals, let alone men.}

In both (105) and (106), *gèng* is present before *biéshuō* and *bùyàoshuō*, and *le* can be used and placed at the end of the sentences.

Summary

First, "*bùdàn p, érqiě q*" is a typical progressive complex sentence form, which denotes an upward progression from the anterior clause to the posterior clause.

As a subtype of "*bùdàn…érqiě…*" sentences, "*bùdàn…lián—yě…*" sentences use "*lián—yě*" to introduce an extreme situation, which is an exaggerated one in some cases. Not all "*bùdàn…érqiě…*" sentences can be rewritten as "*bùdàn…lián—yě…*" sentences.

Third, "*shàngqiě p, hékuàng q*" is a form of downward progressive sentences emphasizing that the matter in the posterior clause is not worth mentioning compared with the matter in the anterior clause. In terms of the direction of the progression, "*shàngqiě…hékuàng…*" sentences are just opposite "*bùdàn…lián—yě…*" sentences.

Fourth, there are two forms of progressive sentences with *biéshuō*: "*biéshuō…lián—yě…*" sentences and "*lián—yě…biéshuō…*" sentences, between which the former are basically equivalent to "*bùdàn…lián—yě…*" sentences, and the latter are similar to sentences in the form of "*shàngqiě p, hékuàng q.*"

In addition, "*bùdànbù p, fǎn'ér q*" is a form of reversed progressive sentences, which can be referred to in Chapter 8, Volume III.

NB Some examples in this chapter are cited from literary works, political essays, articles, and so on. The sources are listed as follows:

1 *Baihuazhou* (《百花洲》) 1998(3), including Example (33);
2 *Changjiang Literature* (《长江》) 1982(3), including (34);

3. *Changcheng* (《长城》) 1982(1), including (15), (22), (23), (54), (90), (92) and (95);
4. *Chinese for Junior High School Students*, Book 1, including (5) and (14); Book 2, including (19) and (26); Book 3, including (16); Book 4, including (93);
5. *Chinese for Senior High School Students*, Book 2, including (43);
6. *Chunfeng* (《春风》) 1982(1), including (21);
7. *Dangdai* (《当代》) 1982(3), including (79), (94) and (96);
8. *Eight Hundred Words in Modern Chinese* (《现代汉语八百词》), including (82) and (83);
9. *Fiction Monthly* (《小说月报》) 1982(2), including (49), (52a), and (53); 1982(3), including (24); 1982(5), including (13) and (80);
10. *Flower City* (《花城》) 1983(4), including (29), (38), and (106);
11. *Harvest* (《收获》) 1982(2), including (61) and (62); 1982(4), including (45); 1983(4), including (35);
12. *In Memory of the Forgotten* (《为了忘却的纪念》) by LU Xun (鲁迅), including (60);
13. *October* (《十月》) 1982(1), including (12), (30), and (59); 1982(2), including (46); 1982(3), including (20) and (27); 1982(4), including (97); 1983(4), including (9), (25), (56), (58), and (91);
14. *People's Literature* (《人民文学》) 1982(2), including (6), (8) and (63);
15. *Living on Vetch* (《采薇》) by LU Xun (鲁迅), including (7);
16. *Selected Works of DENG Xiaoping* (1975–1982) (《邓小平文选 (1975-1982年)》), including (1), (3), (10), (11), (39a), (40a), (41a), (44), and (47);
17. *Selected Works of Excellent Chinese Short Stories in 1980* (《1980年全国优秀短篇小说评选获奖作品集》), including (28), (42), (50), (51a), (55), (87), and (89);
18. *Short Stories Since the Foundation of People's Republic of China* (《建国以来短篇小说》), including (4), (57), (78), and (100);
19. *The True Story of Ah Q* (《阿Q正传》) by LU Xun (鲁迅), including (81);
20. *Works* (《作品》) 1999(4), including (18);
21. *Zhongpian Xiaoshuo Xuankan* (《中篇小说选刊》) 1999(6), including (17);
22. *Zhongshan* (《钟山》) 1983(4), including (88) and (105).

5 "*(huòzhě) p, huòzhě q*" and relevant forms

This chapter deals with alternative complex sentences in various forms with "*(huòzhě) . . . huòzhě . . .*" as a typical marker. The discussion in this chapter consists of two parts: (1) sentences in the form of "*huòzhě p, huòzhě q*" and (2) sentences in the form of "*bùshì p, jiùshì q.*"

Although the form of "*yàome p, yàome q*" functions practically the same as "*bùshì p, jiùshì q,*" its uniqueness deserves a detailed description, which can be found in Chapter 6, Volume II.

5.1 "*(huòzhě) p, huòzhě q*"

As a typical marker for alternative complex sentences, "*(huòzhě) . . . huòzhě . . .*" conjoins two or more options, indicating disjunction or alternation. The following is an example:

(1) （有的背着光线，）<u>或者</u>斜倚在书桌旁边，<u>或者</u>蹲在阴暗的角落里，（埋头看书、做习题。）

(Yŏude bèi-zhe guāngxiàn,) <u>huòzhě</u> . . . <u>huòzhě</u> . . . xiéyǐ zài
some have the back to-PRG light either . . . or . . . recline at
shūzhuō-pángbiān, <u>huòzhě</u> dūn zài yīn'àn de jiǎoluò-lǐ, (máitóu kàn
beside desk squat at dark SP in corner concentrate on read
shū, zuò xítí.)
book do exercise
{[Some have their backs to the light,] recline back (in their seats) at the desks, or squat in a dark corner, [concentrating on reading or doing schoolwork.]}

5.1.1 Linguistic form

In some cases, the conjunction *huòzhě* occurs in pairs as a collocation, i.e., forming "*huòzhě . . . huòzhě . . .*", as in the following example:

(2) <u>或者</u>是无产阶级世界观，<u>或者</u>是资产阶级世界观。

<u>*Huòzhě*</u> . . . <u>*huòzhě*</u> . . . *shì wúchǎnjiējí shìjièguān, <u>huòzhě</u> shì zīchǎnjiējí shìjièguān.*
either . . . or . . . COP proletariat worldview COP bourgeoisie worldview
{(It is) either the proletarian worldview or the bourgeois worldview.}

DOI: 10.4324/9781003362166-5

118   *"(huòzhě) p, huòzhě q" and relevant forms*

More often than not, *huòzhě* only occurs in the posterior clause rather than in both clauses. Below are two examples:

(3)   有些人从地方上拿东西，<u>或者</u>低价购买。
      Yǒuxiē   rén   cóng   dìfāng-shàng   ná   dōngxi,   <u>huòzhě</u>
      some   person   from   in nonmilitary department take stuff   or
      dījià   gòumǎi.
      lower price   buy
      {Some (military personnel) either take things from nonmilitary sources at will or buy them cheaply.}

(4)   她可能在这个岗位上工作了三个月五个月，<u>或者</u>是三年五载了。
      Tā   kěnéng   zài   zhègè gǎngwèi-shàng   gōngzuò-le sān   gè   yuè   wǔ
      she   probably at   this   in post   work-PEF   three CL   month five
      gè   yuè,   <u>huòzhě</u>   shì   sānnián-wǔzǎi   le.
      CL   month   or   COP   three years five years   MP
      {She has been in this post for a while, perhaps a few months or even a few years.}

If there are three options in a sentence, there can be three occurrences of *huòzhě*, that is, "*huòzhě* . . . *huòzhě* . . . *huòzhě* . . . ," as in the following two examples:

(5)   （她渴望立即参加到他的生活中去，）<u>或者</u>主宰他的生活，<u>或者</u>依附于他的生活，<u>或者</u>两样都有，矛盾而又合理地同时存在；（只要是两个人的生活融汇在一起，怎么都行。）
      (Tā   kěwàng   lìjí   cānjiā-dào   tā   de   shēnghuó-zhōng   qù,)
      she   be eager   immediately participate in   he   SP   in life   go
      <u>*huòzhě*</u> . . . <u>*huòzhě*</u> . . . <u>*huòzhě*</u> . . .   *zhǔzǎi   tā   de   shēnghuó,   <u>huòzhě</u>*
      either . . . or . . . or . . .   dominate   he   SP   life   or
      yīfù-yú   tā   de   shēnghuó,   <u>huòzhě</u>   liǎng-yàng   dōu   yǒu,   máodùn
      depend on   he   SP   life   two kinds   both exist   contradictory
      ér   yòu   hélǐ   de   tóngshí   cúnzài;   (zhǐyào   shì   liǎng   gè
      but   also reasonable SP   at the same time exist   as long as COP   two   CL
      rén   de   shēnghuó   rónghuì   zài   yīqǐ,   zěnme   dōu   xíng.
      person SP   life   integrate be   together   however   all   okay
      {[She longed to be part of his life right away,] either dominating or depending on his life, or both. (She understood that) it would be contradictory but reasonable for them to live together; [however, it would be all right as long as their lives were to be integrated.]}

(6)   <u>或者</u>有个强盗要来抢，<u>或者</u>这个已经一十有八的女儿会惹出一笔风流债，<u>或者</u>与落难秀才私定终身。反正是这个套路。
      <u>*Huòzhě*</u> . . . *huòzhě* . . . *huòzhě* . . .   *yǒu   gè   qiángdào   yào   lái   qiǎng,   <u>huòzhě</u>*
      either . . . or . . . or . . .   there be CL   robber   will   come   rob
      zhègè   yǐjīng   yīshí-yǒu-bā   de   nǚ'ér   huì   rě-chū   yī   bǐ   fēngliúzhài,
      this   already   eighteen   SP   daughter   will   have   one   CL   romantic entanglement

huòzhě   *yǔ*   *luònàn*   *xiùcai*   *sīdìng-zhōngshēn*.
           with   be in distress scholar   pledge to marry without parental permission
Fǎnzhèng shì zhègè tàolù.
anyway   COP this norm
{Perhaps a robber will come to rob (the daughter), or perhaps the 18-year-old daughter will have a romantic entanglement, or perhaps she will pledge to marry a troubled scholar without her parents' permission. (The story) will be commonplace, anyway.}

In some cases, *huòzhě* can be used interchangeably with *huòshì*, *huòzé*, or *huò*, as in the following three examples:

(7) 就他的志向来说，他更愿意教化学、物理，或是当一个治疗克山病的医生。
Jiù ... láishuō   *tā de zhìxiàng láishuō, tā gèng yuànyì   jiāo*
as far as ... be concerned   he SP ideal   he more be willing teach
huàxué,   wùlǐ,   huòshì dāng yī   gè zhìliáo kèshānbìng   de yīshēng.
chemistry physics or   be one CL treat   Keshan disease SP doctor
{As far as his ideals are concerned, he would rather teach chemistry or physics, or be a doctor treating Keshan disease.}

(8) 至今还有一些干部，所到之处，或则迎送吃喝，或则封锁交通，或则大肆宣扬，很不妥当。
Zhìjīn   hái   yǒu   yīxiē   gànbù,   suǒdàozhīchù,
till now still there be some   cadre   places where someone has been
huòzé ... huòzé ... huòzé ... yíngsòng-chīhē,   huòzé fēngsuǒ
either ... or ... or   welcome, entertain, and see someone off block
jiāotōng, huòzé dàsì   xuānyáng, hěn   bù   tuǒdàng.
traffic   excessively publicize very NEG   appropriate
{Up to now, there are still some cadres who, wherever they go, are treated with warm and considerate hospitality, have traffic blocked, or have their visit excessively publicized. Such behavior is quite inappropriate.}

(9) 那些来自全球各个角落的新闻、轶事，常使他激动不已，或愤慨，或讪笑，或惊讶，或焦虑。
Nàxiē láizì   quánqiú   gè gè jiǎoluò de xīnwén, yìshì,   cháng
those come from the whole world every CL corner SP news   anecdote often
shǐ tā jīdòng-bùyǐ,   huò ... huò ... huò ... fēnkǎi,   huò shànxiào, huò
make him thrilled   either ... or ... or   indignant   ridicule
jīngyà,   huò jiāolǜ.
surprised   anxious
{The news and anecdotes from all corners of the world often make him thrilled, indignant, mocking, surprised, or anxious.}

If a sentence in the form of "(*huòzhě*) *p*, *huòzhě q*" needs to be rewritten as an interrogative sentence with the person remaining unchanged, "(*huòzhě*) ... *huòzhě* ..." needs to be replaced by "(*shì*) *p*, *háishì q*," as in the following examples:

(10) 现在，你面临着两条道儿的选择：<u>或者</u>往好里走，<u>或者</u>破罐破摔！
Xiànzài, nǐ miànlín-zhe liǎng tiáo dàor de xuǎnzé: <u>huòzhě</u>... <u>huòzě</u>
now   you   be faced with-PRG two CL road SP choose either...or...
wǎng hǎo-lǐ zǒu,   <u>huòzhě</u> pòguàn-pòshuāi!
go for the better   smash a pot to pieces just because it's cracked
{Now, you are faced with two choices: change for the better, or write yourself off!}

(11) 现在，你面临着两条道儿的选择，<u>是</u>往好里走，<u>还是</u>破罐破摔？
Xiànzài, nǐ miànlín-zhe liǎng tiáo dàor de xuǎnzé, shì... <u>háishì</u>...
now   you   be faced with-PRG two CL road SP choose either...or...
wǎng hǎo-lǐ zǒu, <u>háishì</u> pòguàn-pòshuāi?
go for the better   smash a pot to pieces just because it's cracked
{Now, you are faced with two choices: will you change for the better, or write yourself off?}

If there are two options in the anterior clause of an unconditional concessive sentence, either *háishì* or *huòzhě* can be used. However, "*háishì* . . . *háishì* . . ." can be rewritten as "*shì* . . . *háishì* . . . ," but ". . . *huòzhě* . . ." cannot be rewritten as "*huòzhě* . . . *huòzhě* . . ." Compare the following examples:

(12) a 无论教语文，<u>还是</u>教历史，他都能行。
Wúlùn   jiāo   yǔwén, <u>háishì</u> jiāo   lìshǐ,   tā   dōu   néng   xíng.
whether teach Chinese or   teach history he   both can   capable
{He can teach Chinese or history.}

b 无论教语文，<u>或者</u>教历史，他都能行。
Wúlùn   jiāo   yǔwén, <u>huòzhě</u> jiāo lìshǐ,   tā   dōu   néng   xíng.
whether teach Chinese or   teach history he   both can   capable
{He can teach Chinese or history.}

c 无论<u>是</u>教语文，<u>还是</u>教历史，他都能行。
Wúlùn   <u>shì</u> jiāo   yǔwén,   <u>háishì</u> jiāo lìshǐ,   tā   dōu   néng   xíng.
whether COP   teach Chinese   or   teach history he   both can   capable
{He can teach Chinese or history.}

*d 无论<u>或者</u>教语文，<u>或者</u>教历史，他都能行。
Wúlùn   <u>huòzhě</u>... <u>huòzhě</u>   jiāo   yǔwén, <u>huòzhě</u> jiāo   lìshǐ,   tā   dōu
whether either...or...   teach Chinese   teach history he   both
néng   xíng.
can   capable

5.1.2 Options indicated by "*huòzhě p, huòzhě q*"

Sentences in the form of "*huòzhě p, huòzhě q*" can indicate three types of options.
    First, irrealis options, which refer to those situations that have not occurred yet and that are available to be chosen from.

In some cases, the list of the options is exhaustive. In other cases, only important options are listed, with other possibilities unmentioned. The following are two examples:

(13) 这样，就只有两条路走，<u>或是</u>袁沛文跟陶慧贞走，<u>或是</u>袁沛文跟陶慧贞断，这都是佟英所不愿意的。

Zhèyàng, jiù zhǐ yǒu liǎng tiáo lù zǒu, <u>huòshì</u> <u>huòshì</u> Yuán Pèiwén
so just only there be two CL road walk either...or... YUAN Peiwen
gēn Táo Huìzhēn zǒu, <u>huòshì</u> Yuán Pèiwén gēn Táo Huìzhēn duàn, zhè
follow TAO Huizhen walk YUAN Peiwen with TAO Huizhen break up this
dōu shì Tóng Yīng suǒ bù yuànyì de.
both COP TONG Ying PAP NEG be willing SP
{So, there are only two possibilities: either YUAN Peiwen follows TAO Huizhen or YUAN Peiwen breaks up with Tao Huizhen, neither of which is what TONG Ying wants (to be the case).}

(14) 抬回去<u>或者</u>当儿子，<u>或者</u>做女婿……

Tái-huíqu <u>huòzhě</u> <u>huòzhě</u> dāng érzi, <u>huòzhě</u> zuò nǚxu...
carry back either...or... be son be son-in-law
{Carry (the wounded soldier) back (home); he could be your son or son-in-law, (or anything else as you see fit)...}

In (13), the list of the options is exhaustive, indicated by "there are only two possibilities." In (14), only the two important options are listed, and the ellipsis points at the end of the sentence imply that there might exist a third or even a fourth option.

The irrealis options can be mutually exclusive; for instance, "YUAN Peiwen follows TAO Huizhen" and "YUAN Peiwen breaks up with Tao Huizhen" in (13), and "be your son" and "be your son-in-law" in (14). However, in some cases, the listed irrealis options are not mutually exclusive, as in the following example:

(15) （这样郁郁闷闷地呆下去，）<u>或者</u>是发神经病，<u>或者</u>是重进国民党的监狱，<u>或者</u>是受到左翼学生的怀疑、冷落、孤立乃至难以设想的残酷打击，（没有一条活路。）

(Zhèyàng yùyù-mènmèn de dāi-xiàqu,) <u>huòzhě</u> <u>huòzhě</u> <u>huòzhě</u> shì
so depressed SP continue to wait either...or...or COP
fā shénjīngbìng, <u>huòzhě</u> shì chóng jìn guómíndǎng de jiānyù, <u>huòzhě</u>
have mental illness COP again go Kuomintang SP prison
shì shòudào zuǒyì xuéshēng de huáiyí, lěngluò, gūlì nǎizhì nányǐ
COP receive left wing student SP suspect neglect isolate even be difficult
shèxiǎng de cánkù dǎjī, (méiyǒu yī tiáo huólù.)
imagine SP cruel attack there not be one CL way to survive
{[If (I) continue to wait in such depression,] (I) may get mentally ill or be put in prison again by the Kuomintang or be treated with suspicion, neglect, isolation by leftwing students or even be attacked by them with imaginable cruelty, [there is no single way to survive.]}

Among the three possibilities listed in (15), one, or two, or all three will occur.

Second, realis options, which refer to situations that have occurred. The situations may occur to different people at the same time or alternately to one person. The following are two examples:

(16) 这些客人都穿着不怕泥水的翻毛马靴，<u>或者</u>打着绑腿。
Zhèxiē kèrén dōu chuān-zhe bù pà níshuǐ de fānmáo mǎxuē, <u>huòzhě</u>
these guest all wear-PRG mud-proof SP suede riding boots or
dǎ-zhe bǎngtuǐ.
wear-PRG leg wrappings
{These guests are all wearing mud-proof suede boots or leg wrappings.}

(17) 尹影一回家就埋头在书堆里，<u>或者</u>咬着笔杆苦思冥想，对着稿纸沉吟发愣。
Yǐn Yǐng yī jiù huíjiā jiù máitóu zài shūduī-lǐ, <u>huòzhě</u>
YIN Ying as soon as get home immerse oneself at in stack of books sometimes
yǎo-zhe bǐgǎn kǔsī-míngxiǎng, duì-zhe gǎozhǐ chényín fālèng.
bite-PRG pen think hard face-PRG manuscript ponder be in a daze
{As soon as YIN Ying got home, she would bury herself in the books, or would think hard while gnawing a pen and gazing at her manuscript in a daze.}

If the listed situations occur to different people at the same time, *huòzhě* is synonymous with *yǒude* ('some'), as is in (18). In cases where *huòzhě* means "some", there are usually two or more occurrences of *huòzhě*, as in the following example:

(18) 我就认识几个这样的，<u>或是</u>为了进大学抱铁饭碗，<u>或是</u>为了出国一去不回，<u>或是</u>满脑子个人的功名利禄。
Wǒ jiù rènshi jǐ gè zhèyàng de, <u>huòshì</u> wèile jìn dàxué
I just know several CL such MP some for enter university
bào tiěfànwǎn, <u>huòshì</u> wèile chūguó yīqùbùhuí, <u>huòshì</u> mǎnnǎozi
hold iron rice bowl some for go abroad be gone for ever some head (full of)
gèrén de gōngmíng-lìlù.
personal SP fame and fortune
{I know a few of such people. Some go to college in order to get a secure job (after graduation), some to go overseas permanently (after graduation), and others to seek personal fame and fortune.}

In the above example, there is one occurrence of *huòzhě* and two occurrences of *huòshì*, which can all be replaced by *yǒude*.

The word *huòzhě* is a conjunction, whereas *yǒude* is a pronominal phrasal word functioning as a noun. However, they are synonymous and can occur in both clauses in the same sentence in some cases. The following is an example:

(19) 有男有女，有老有少，......<u>或者</u>诉说自身的不幸，<u>或者</u>请他们给自己的孩子命名；<u>有的</u>索性跪在马车前不起来，拍胸大叫，要求伯爵率领回到俄国去打布尔什维克。

Yǒu   nán yǒu   nǚ,   yǒu   lǎo yǒu   shào, ... huòzhě sùshuō zìshēn
there be male there be female there be old there be young   some   recount oneself
de bùxìng;   huòzhě qǐng tā-men gěi zìjǐ   de háizi mìngmíng; yǒude suǒxìng
SP misfortune some   ask them for oneself SP child name   some   simply
guì zài   mǎchē-qián   bù qǐlái,   pāi xiōng dàjiào, yāoqiú
kneel at   before carriage cannot stand up thump chest   yell   ask
bójué shuàilǐng huí-dào   Éguó   qù dǎ   bù'ěrshíwéikè.
count lead   return to Russia go fight Bolshevik
{There were men and women, old and young . . . some recounted their own misfortunes; some asked them to give a name to their child; some simply knelt in front of the carriage and wouldn't stand up, thumping their chest and shouting, asking the count to lead them back to Russia to fight the Bolsheviks.}

If the situations occur to one person alternately, *huòzhě* means *yǒushí* ('sometimes'), as is in (17). In some sentences, *huòzhě* occurs twice or more, as in the following example:

(20)   （张铁匠）不时地转向每一个发问者，古铜色的四方脸庞上露出庄重的微笑，或颔首认可，或笑着辟谣，或婉言解释，或郑重说明。
(Zhāng tiějiàng)   bùshí   de zhuǎn-xiàng měi yī gè fāwènzhě,
ZHANG Blacksmith from time to time SP turn to   every one CL questioner
gǔtóngsè   de sìfāng liánpáng-shàng lù-chū zhuāngzhòng de wēixiào,
bronze-colored SP square on face   appear serious   SP smile
huò   hànshǒu rènkě,   huò   xiào-zhe pìyáo,   huò
sometimes   nod   acknowledge sometimes laugh-PRG refute a rumor sometimes
wǎnyán   jiěshì,   huò   zhèngzhòng   shuōmíng.
tactful expression explain   or   solemn   declare
{[Blacksmith ZHANG] turned to every questioner from time to time, with a serious smile on his bronze-colored square face. He sometimes acknowledged something with a nod, sometimes laughed to refute a rumor, sometimes provided an explanation politely, and other times made a statement solemnly.}

In (20), there are four occurrences of *huò*, and each of them can be replaced by *yǒushí* or *yīhuìr* (for a moment).

Third, wording options, which refer to two different expressions. For wording options, *huòzhě* is usually followed by *shuō*. The following are two examples:

(21)   他刚回国，对我们的生活还不够了解，或者说还不习惯。
Tā gāng huíguó,   duì   wǒ-men de shēnghuó hái bùgòu
he Just return to one's country about we SP life still insufficiently
liǎojiě, huòzhě shuō hái bù   xíguàn.
know   or   say still NEG be used to
{He has just returned to the country, (so he) doesn't have enough knowledge about our life, or in other words, isn't used to it yet.}

(22) 我感到画家像突然惊异地发现了什么，<u>或者说</u>作画时忍不住某种情绪的流露。

  Wǒ gǎndào huàjiā xiàng tūrán jīngyì de fāxiàn-le shénme, <u>*huòzhě*</u>
  I feel painter as if suddenly surprised SP discover-PEF something or
  <u>*shuō*</u> *zuòhuà shí rěn bù zhù mǒu zhǒng qíngxù de liúlù.*
  say paint time can't help doing something certain type mood SP reveal
  {I felt that the artist had suddenly discovered something in surprise, or to put it another way, the artist could not help but reveal some mood as he was painting.}

The two options linked by "*huòzhě shuō*" describe the matter from two different perspectives of equal importance, and in some cases, the second expression is greater than the first one in degree. The following is an example:

(23) 这个人，对党还是有意见，<u>或者说</u>，有不少意见。

  Zhè gè rén, duì dǎng háishi yǒu yìjiàn, <u>*huòzhě shuō*</u>*, yǒu*
  this CL person about party still have negative opinion or say have
  bùshǎo yìjiàn.
  quite a lot negative opinion
  {This person still has some or even many negative opinions about the Party.}

If *huòzhě-shuō* indicates that the expression that follows is greater in degree, it can be rewritten as "*huòzhě shènzhì*" ('or even'). For example, *huòzhě-shuō* in (23) can be replaced by "*huòzhě shènzhì*." The following are another two examples:

(24) 莲莲却一切依然如故，<u>或其至</u>比过去更狭隘更平庸。

  Liánlián què yīqiè yīrán rúgù, <u>*huò shènzhì*</u> *bǐ guòqù gèng*
  Lianlian however all still be the same as before or even than past more
  xiá'ài gèng píngyōng.
  narrow more mediocre
  {Lianlian, however, remains the same or is even more narrow-minded and mediocre than before.}

(25) 假如他坚持的意见不那么正确，<u>或者其至</u>是错误的，那么结果会是——我不敢想了，低下头去看稿。

  Jiǎrú tā jiānchí de yìjiàn bù náme zhèngquè, <u>*huòzhě shènzhì*</u> *shì cuòwù de,*
  if he Insist SP idea NEG so correct or even COP wrong MP
  náme jiéguǒ huì shì— wǒ bù gǎn xiǎng le, dī-xià tóu qù kàn gǎo.
  then consequences will COP I NEG dare think MP lower the head look manuscript
  {If what he insists on is not so true, or even untrue, what will the consequences be—I dare not think of them, so I look down at the manuscript.}

Without *huò* in (24) or *huòzhě* in (25), the sentences would be progressive ones. However, with those words, both are alternative complex sentences implying wording options.

5.2 "*Bùshì p, jiùshì q*"

As another form of alternative complex sentences, "*bùshì p, jiùshì q*" also indicates disjunction or alternation, emphasizing that one of the two options or alternatives must be taken, for example:

(26) 他怎么被撸掉了呢？<u>不是</u>没本事，<u>就是</u>犯了错误，二者必居其一！
Tā zěnme bèi lū-diào le ne? <u>Bùshì</u> ... <u>jiùshì</u> ... méi
he how PASSIVE remove from the position PEF MP if not...then not have
běnshi, jiùshì fàn-le cuòwù, èrzhě bìjū-qíyī!
ability make-PEF mistake must be one or the other
{Why was he removed from his post? It must be because he had done something wrong, if not because he was incapable. It must be one or the other!}

In sentences in the form of "*huòzhě p, huòzhě q*," the selection between the two options is free with flexibility, thus this form can be called as a form of open alternative sentences. On the contrary, in sentences in the form of "*bùshì p, jiùshì q*," the selection is strictly limited to the two options with no flexibility; thus, this form can be called as a form of closed alternative sentences.

5.2.1 Linguistic form

In sentences in the form of "*bùshì p, jiùshì q*," *bùshì* and *jiùshì* always cooccur and collocate with each other, as in the following two examples:

(27) 一般庙宇的塑像，往往<u>不是</u>平板，<u>就是</u>怪诞，……
Yībān miàoyǔ de sùxiàng, wǎng-wǎng <u>bùshì</u> ... <u>jiùshì</u> ... píngbǎn, jiùshì
general temple SP statue Usually if not...then plain and rigid
guàidàn, ...
absurd
{In general, the statues in temples are absurd if not plain and rigid ... }

(28) 最近，只要一丢饭碗，她站起来就走。<u>不是</u>给这个或者那个打电话，<u>就是</u>在房间里写东西。
Zuìjìn, zhǐyào yī ... jiù ... diūfànwǎn, tā zhàn-qǐlái jiù zǒu.
recently so long as as soon as put down bowl she stand up leave
<u>Bùshì</u> ... <u>jiùshì</u> ... gěi zhè gè huòzhě nà gè dǎdiànhuà, jiùshì zài fángjiān-lǐ
if not...then to this CL or that CL call at in room
xiě dōngxi.
write something
{Recently, as soon as she finished eating, she would stand up and leave for her room to write something if not to make a phone call to someone.}

What "*bùshì* ... *jiùshì* ..." conjoins is often two options. If there are three options, another conjunction can be added to introduce the third one, for instance, "*zài jiùshì*" ('otherwise, then'), "*zàibù jiùshì*" ('otherwise, then'), and "*yàobù jiùshì*" ('otherwise, then'), as in the following three examples:

(29) 然而在排练时却遭到了不少麻烦，<u>不是</u>场地安排不过来，<u>就是</u>学生没有时间唱，<u>再就是</u>乐队不凑手。

Rán'ér zài páiliàn shí què zāodào-le bùshǎo máfan,
however at rehearse time however encounter-PEF many trouble
<u>*bùshì*</u> ... <u>*jiùshì*</u> ... <u>*zài jiùshì*</u> ... *chǎngdì ānpái bù guòlái,* <u>*jiùshì*</u> *xuéshēng*
if not ... then ... otherwise, then venue cannot be arranged student
méiyǒu shíjiān chàng, <u>*zài jiùshì*</u> *yuèduì bù cǒushǒu.*
not have time sing band NEG handy
{However, a lot of trouble was encountered during the rehearsals. If it wasn't that the venue could not be arranged, then the students did not have time to practice singing, or the band happened to be unavailable.}

(30) 这些日子来，他夜里常常出去。<u>不是</u>借口开会，<u>就是</u>借口去同志家坐坐，<u>要不就</u>干脆什么也不说，吃罢晚饭就匆匆走了。

Zhèxiē rìzi lái, tā yèlǐ cháng-cháng chū-qu. <u>*Bùshì*</u> ... <u>*jiùshì*</u> ... <u>*yàobù jiù*</u> ...
these day during he night often-REDP go out if not ... then ... otherwise, then
jièkǒu kāihuì, <u>*jiùshì*</u> *jièkǒu qù tóngzhì jiā*
use ... as an excuse have a meeting use ... as an excuse go comrade home
zuò-zuò, <u>*yàobù jiù*</u> *gāncuì shénme yě bù shuō, chī-bà wǎnfàn jiù cōngcōng*
sit-REDP simply whatever NEG say finish eating dinner then hurried
zǒu le.
leave MP
{He often goes out at night these days. He leaves hurriedly after dinner, if not with the excuse of attending a meeting then visiting a comrade or simply saying nothing.}

(31) 这样大的孩子在驾驶室里没个老实劲，<u>不是</u>摸摸变速杆，<u>就是</u>动动仪表盘，<u>要不就</u>瞅着窗外乱喊乱叫。

Zhèyàng dà de háizi zài jiàshǐshì-lǐ méi gè lǎoshíjìn,
so old SP child at in driver's cab not have CL good behavior
<u>*bùshì*</u> ... <u>*jiùshì*</u> ... <u>*yàobù jiù*</u> ... *mō-mō biànsùgān,* <u>*jiùshì*</u> *dòng-dòng*
if not ... then ... otherwise, then touch-REDP gear lever touch-REDP
yíbiǎopán, <u>*yàobù jiù*</u> *chǒu-zhe chuāng-wài luànhǎn-luànjiào.*
dashboard look-PRG outside of the window shout and yell for no reason
{Children of this age don't behave themselves in the driver's cab. They would feel the gear lever or play with the dashboard or look out the window shouting and yelling.}

In the form of "*bùshì p, jiùshì q,*" *p* and *q* are usually acted by predicative words or phrases but sometimes by nouns or nominal words or phrases, as in the following example:

(32) 其必然的结果，<u>不是</u>机会主义，<u>就是</u>盲动主义。
 Qí   birán de jiéguǒ,   <u>bùshì</u>...<u>jiùshì</u>...   jīhuìzhǔyì,   <u>jiùshì</u>
 its inevitable SP consequences if not...then   opportunism
 mángdòngzhǔyì.
 putschism
 {The inevitable consequences are putschism if not opportunism.}

Regardless of whether *p* and *q* are acted by predicative or nominal words, "*bùshì . . . jiùshì . . .*" marks an alternative relationship. However, when it comes to syntactic constituent analysis, "*bùshì . . . jiùshì . . .*" needs to be treated on a case-by-case basis. Compare the following two examples:

(33) a 他不是出了事，就是害了病。
 Tā   bùshì...<u>jiùshì</u>...   chū-le   shì,   jiùshì   hài-le   bìng.
 He   if not...then   be-PEF   trouble have-PEF illness
 {He must be sick if not in trouble.}

 b 他不是董事长，就是总经理。
 Tā   bùshì...<u>jiùshì</u>...   dǒngshìzhǎng,   jiùshì   zǒngjīnglǐ.
 He   if not...then   chair of the board   general manager
 {He must be the General Manager if not the Chair of the Board.}

In (33a), "*bùshì . . . jiùshì . . .*" is only a marker for alternative complex sentences. However, apart from being a marker, "*bùshì . . . jiùshì . . .*" in (33b) also includes a judgmental verb *shì*. In this sentence, *tā* acts as the subject, *shì* as the verb, *bù* and *jiù* as adverbials, and *dǒngshìzhǎng* and *zǒngjīnglǐ* as the judgmental complements.

In some cases, "*bùshì . . . jiùshì . . .*" is interchangeable with "*chúle . . . jiùshì . . .*". If *chúle* means "if not," "*chúle p, jiùshì q*" is a complex sentence form rather than a simple sentence form. The following is an example:

(34) (万秀芳)心灵好学，一天<u>除了</u>写，<u>就是</u>看。
 (Wàn Xiùfāng) xīnlíng hàoxué, yītiān <u>chúle</u>...<u>jiùshì</u>... xiě, <u>jiùshì</u> kàn.
 WAN Xiufang smart   studious all day if not...then   write   read
 {WAN Xiufang is smart and studious. All day long she reads or writes.}

5.2.2 Options indicated by "*bùshì p, jiùshì q*"

Sentences in the form of "*bùshì p, jiùshì q*" can indicate two types of options.

First, irrealis options, which refer to two situations that have not occurred or not have been proved. Between the two options, one or the other needs to be selected. The following are two examples:

(35) 积四十年和二十八年的经验，中国人<u>不是</u>倒向帝国主义一边，<u>就是</u>倒向社会主义一边，绝无例外。

Jī   sìshí   nián   hé   èrshíbā   nián   de   jīngyàn,
accumulate forty   year   and   twenty-eight year   SP   experience
Zhōngguórén   <u>bùshì</u>... <u>jiùshì</u>... dǎo-xiàng dìguózhǔyì yībiān,   <u>jiùshì</u>
Chinese people if not...then   turn to   imperialism one side   then
dǎo-xiàng   shèhuìzhǔyì   yībiān,   jué   wú   lìwài.
turn to   socialism   one side   absolutely there not be   exception
{Based on the 40 years and 28 years of experiences respectively, the Chinese either turned to the socialist camp or to the imperialist camp, without any exception.}

(36) 按本地的习惯，女人用彩色丝线绣鞋垫，<u>不是</u>为自己准备嫁妆，<u>就是</u>为未来的女婿准备礼品。爱爱都是为了谁呢？

Àn   běndì   de   xíguàn,   nǚrén   yòng   cǎisè   sīxiàn   xiù
according to this locality SP custom   woman   use   multicolor silk thread embroider
xiédiàn,   <u>bùshì</u>...<u>jiùshì</u>... wèi zìjǐ   zhǔnbèi jiàzhuang, <u>jiùshì</u> wèi   wèilái de
insole   if not...then   for oneself prepare dowry   for   future SP
nǚxu   zhǔnbèi lǐpǐn.   Àiài   dōu   shì   wèile   shuí   ne?
husband   prepare Gift   Aiai   all   COP   for   who   MP
{According to local custom, women embroider insoles with colored silk threads, as a gift for their future husbands if not as a dowry for themselves. Who is Aiai doing all this for?}

Second, realis options, which refer to two situations that alternately occur in different places or at different times. The two options are situations that have occurred or matters that should be the cases. Between the two options, one or the other needs to be selected. The following are two examples:

(37) 每回她来，都是匆匆忙忙的。<u>不是</u>开会晚了，<u>就是</u>要赶去干什么。

Měi-huí   tā   lái,   dōu shì   cōngcōng-mángmáng de. <u>Bùshì</u>...<u>jiùshì</u>...
every time she   come   all COP   hurried   SP   if not...then
kāihuì   wǎn-le, <u>jiùshì</u> yào   gǎn   qù   gàn shénme.
have a meeting late-PEF   must   rush   go   do   something
{She always came back late or left in a hurry. She either came from a meeting that ended late or rushed to leave to get something done.}

(38) 路西边<u>不是</u>丝茅夹阻，<u>便是</u>榛蔓拥塞。

Lù   xībiān   <u>bùshì</u>...<u>biànshì</u>... sīmáo   jiāzǔ,   <u>biànshì</u> zhēnmàn   yōngsè.
road west   if not...then   silk grass   block   hazel tree congest
{The west side of the road is congested with hazel trees if not blocked by silk grass.}

Summary

First, "(huòzhě) p, huòzhě q" is a typical alternative complex sentence form, which conjoins two or more options and indicates selection or alternation. The selection between/among the options is relatively free with flexibility; thus, it can be termed as a form of open alternative sentences.

Second, if an alternative complex sentence in the form of "(*huòzhě*) *p, huòzhě q*" is to be transformed into an interrogative sentence with the person remaining unchanged, "(*huòzhě*) . . . *huòzhě* . . ." needs to be replaced by "(*shì*) . . . *háishì* . . ."

Third, "*bùshì p, jiùshì q*" is also a commonly used form of alternative complex sentences. This form emphasizes that between the two options, one or the other needs to be selected; thus, it can be regarded as a form of closed alternative sentences. If a third option needs to be introduced, there can be another conjunction, for instance, "*zài jiùshì*," "*zàibu jiùshì*," "*yàobù jiùshì*," and so on.

NB Some examples in this chapter are cited from literary works, political essays, articles, and so on. The sources are listed as follows:

1 *Changcheng* (《长城》) 1982(1), including Examples (21) and (29);
2 *Chinese* for Junior High School Students, Book 2, including (1); Book 5, including (4);
3 *Chinese* for Senior High School Students, Book 1, including (27); Book 3, including (32);
4 *Chunfeng* (《春风》) 1982(1), including (34);
5 *Dangdai* (《当代》) 1982(3), including (30); 1983(4), including (36);
6 *Fiction Monthly* (《小说月报》) 1982(5), including (25); 1982(6), including (24);
7 *Harvest* (《收获》) 1982(2), including (9);
8 *October* (《十月》) 1982(1), including (7), (16), (20), and (22); 1982(2), including (15); 1982(4), including (5) and (18); 1983(4), including (11), (19), (28), and (31);
9 *People's Literature* (《人民文学》) 1982(3), including (17); 1982(4), including (37);
10 *Qingming* (《清明》) 1983(3), including (13);
11 *Selected Works of DENG Xiaoping* (1975–1982) (《邓小平文选(1975–1982年)》), including (3) and (8);
12 *Selected Works of Excellent Chinese Short Stories in 1980* (《1980年全国优秀短篇小说评选获奖作品集》), including (14) and (38);
13 *Selected Works of MAO Tse-tung* (《毛泽东选集》), including (2) and (35);
14 *Works* (《作品》) 1999(4), including (6);
15 *Youth* (《青春》) 1982(1), including (23).

6 "*yàome p, yàome q*" and relevant forms

Yàome is an important connective that indicates an alternative relationship in modern Chinese, but it has been rarely discussed in grammar textbooks. This chapter consists of three sections: (1) the function of "*yàome p, yàome q*"; (2) the usage of *yàome*; (3) comparisons between "*yàome p, yàome q*" and such relevant forms as "*bùshì p, jiùshì q*"; "*yàobù p, yàobù q*"; and "*huòzhě p, huòzhě q*."

6.1 Functions of "*yàome p, yàome q*"

As a form of alternative complex sentences, the function of "*yàome p, yàome q*" is basically the same as that of "*bùshì p, jiùshì q*." In this form, between the two options, one or the other needs to be taken. The following are two examples:

(1) 男女之间的关系<u>要么</u>无爱无缘如同路人，<u>要么</u>有爱有缘灵与肉二者完全结合，非此即彼。

Nánnǚ   zhījiān   de guānxi   yàome . . . yàome . . . wú   ài
man and woman between SP relationship either . . . or . . .   there not be love
wú   yuán   rútóng lùrén,   yàome   yǒu   ài   yǒu
there not be predestined relationship be like passer-by   there be love there be
yuán   líng yǔ ròu èrzhě wánquán   jiéhé, fēicǐ-jíbǐ.
predestined relationship soul and flesh both completely unite   either this or that
{The relationship between a man and a woman is either like two passersby, or a complete union of flesh and soul of the two, whose love for each other was predestined. It is either the former or the latter.}

(2) 邹达海自认为是养蛐蛐的行家，决心在这小小的躯体上孤注一掷，<u>要么</u>发家，<u>要么</u>成为抱瓢要饭的花子。

Zōu Dáhǎi   zì   rènwéi shì yǎng qūqu de hángjiā, juéxīn   zài zhè
ZOU Dahai oneself think COP raise cricket SP expert   determine at this
xiǎo-xiǎo   de   qūtǐ-shàng gūzhù-yīzhì,   yàome . . . yàome . . .
small-REDP   SP   on body   put all the eggs in one basket either . . . or . . .
fājiā,   yàome   chéngwéi bào   piáo   yàofàn de   huāzi.
become rich   become   hold   gourd ladle beg   SP   beggar
{ZOU Dahai considered himself an expert in raising crickets, so he determined to put all his eggs in one basket and bet on those small creatures, either to make a fortune or become a penniless beggar.}

In a sentence in the form of *"yàome p, yàome q,"* there are two—and only two—options, between which one or the other needs to be taken. The two options can be irrealis situations or alternating ones. For example, the options listed in (1) and (2) are all irrealis situations. The following are four examples:

(3) 要么杀人，要么被杀，假如二者供你选择呢？
<u>Yàome</u> ... <u>yàome</u> ... shā rén, <u>yàome</u> bèi shā, jiǎrú èrzhě gōng nǐ
either ... or ... kill person PASSIVE kill if both offer you
xuǎnzé ne?
choose MP
{Either kill or be killed, which would you choose between the two?}

(4) 他不知这是怎样造成的，<u>要么</u>是自己想得太多了，<u>要么</u>就是宋丹身上的一种什么东西征服了他。
Tā bù zhī zhè shì zěnyàng zàochéng de, <u>yàome</u> ... <u>yàome</u> ... shì zìjǐ
he NEG know this COP how cause MP either ... or ... COP oneself
xiǎng de tài duō le, <u>yàome</u> jiù shì Sòng Dān shēn-shàng de yī
think SP too much MP just COP SONG Dan on body SP a
zhǒng shénmedōngxi zhēngfú-le tā.
kind something overwhelm-PEF him
{He did not know what caused this. (He thought) it was either (because) he had thought too much, or (because) something about SONG Dan had somehow overwhelmed him.}

(5) 是么！人家<u>要么</u>神气十足，<u>要么</u>高深莫测的，咱们还是远着点走吧！
Shì me! Rénjia <u>yàome</u> shénqì-shízú, <u>yàome</u> gāoshēn-mòcè de, zán-men
COP MP other people some arrogant some enigmatic MP we
háishi yuǎn-zhe diǎn zǒu ba!
had better far-PRG a bit walk MP
{Indeed! They are either arrogant or enigmatic, so we'd better stay away from them!}

(6) 那些不了解他的人，<u>要么</u>对他产生误解，<u>要么</u>被他的才华惊倒。
Nàxie bù liǎojiě tā de rén, <u>yàome</u> duì tā chǎnshēng wùjiě,
those NEG know him SP person some about him occur misunderstanding
<u>yàome</u> bèi tā de cáihuá jīng-dǎo.
some PASSIVE he SP talent stun
{Those who don't know him very well either misunderstand him or are stunned by his talent.}

In (3) and (4), respectively, the two options are irrealis situations to be proved. In (5) and (6), respectively, the options are two different realis situations that occur to different people; therefore, *"yàome p, yàome q"* is synonymous with *"yǒude p, yǒude q."*

6.2 Usage of *yàome*

In complex sentences, the conjunction *yàome* can occur singly, in pairs, or more than twice. It is pointed out in *Chinese Knowledge*, whose editor-in-chief is ZHANG Zhigong,[1] that complex sentences using "*bùshì* . . . *jiùshì* . . ." or "*yàome* . . . *yàome* . . ." to link the two options indicate one or the other must be taken and that these conjunctions must occur in pairs. However, with respect to *yàome*, Zhang's opinion is somewhat arbitrary.

6.2.1 *yàome occurring in pairs*

Often *yàome* occurs in pairs, each acting as a marker for the option it introduces, that is, "*yàome p, yàome q*."

The following are two examples:

(7) 要么拒绝治疗（后果是他的部队继续陷于瘫痪）；要么接受治疗（后果是他和他的部属无论其肉体还是精神都将浸泡在中国人臊臭尿液中）。这种选择对堂堂大日本帝国的一名将领来说不能不说是十分艰难的。

<u>Yàome</u> . . . <u>yàome</u> . . . jùjué zhìliáo (hòuguǒ shì tā de bùduì jìxù
either . . . or . . . refuse treat consequence COP he SP troop continue
xiànyú tānhuàn); <u>yàome</u> jiēshòu zhìliáo (hòuguǒ shì tā hé tā de
fall into paralyze accept Treat consequence COP he and he SP
bùshǔ wúlùn qi ròutǐ háishi jīngshén dōu jiāng jìnpào zài Zhōngguórén
subordinate whether his body or spirit both will soak at Chinese
sāochòu niàoyè-zhōng). Zhè zhǒng xuǎnzé duì . . . <u>láishuō</u> táng-táng dà Rìběn dìguó
stinky in urine this type choose for dignified Japanese Empire
de yī míng jiànglǐng láishuō bùnéngbù shuō shì shífēn
SP one CL high-ranking military officer have to say COP very
jiānnán de.
difficult MP
{(He) will either refuse the medical treatment [the consequence is that his troops will continue to be paralyzed]; or accept the medical treatment [the consequence is that he and his subordinates will be soaked in the Chinese guys' stinky urine both physically and mentally]. This type of choice is extremely difficult for a high-ranking military officer of the dignified Japanese Empire.}

(8) 终有一天，<u>要么</u>因它而阻碍社会的健康发展，<u>要么</u>有健康发展的社会来战胜它，别无他途。

Zhōng yǒu yī tiān, <u>yàome</u> . . . <u>yàome</u> . . . yīn tā ér zǔ'ài shèhuì
finally there be one day either . . . or . . . because it therefore hinder society
de jiànkāng fāzhǎn, <u>yàome</u> yǒu jiànkāng fāzhǎn de shèhuì lái zhànshèng
SP healthy develop there be healthy develop SP society come defeat
tā, biéwútātú.
it there is no other way
{Eventually, it will either hinder the healthy development of society or be defeated by a healthily developing society, without any other possibilities.}

A synonymous form of "*yàome p, yàome q*" is "*yào jiùshì p, yào jiùshì q*." The following is an example:

(9) 处在今天的国际环境中，殖民地半殖民地的任何英雄好汉们，<u>要就是</u>站在帝国主义战线方面，变成世界反革命力量的一部分；<u>要就是</u>站在反帝国主义战线方面，变成世界革命力量的一部分。

> Chǔzài jīntiān de guójì huánjìng-zhōng, zhímíndì bànzhímíndì de rènhé
> be in today SP international in environment colony semi-colony SP any
> yīngxiónghǎohàn-men, <u>yào jiùshì</u> … <u>yào jiùshì</u> … zhàn zài dìguózhǔyì zhànxiàn
> hero-PL either … or … stand on imperialism camp
> fāngmiàn, biàn-chéng shìjiè fǎn'gwémíng lìliàng de yī bùfèn;
> side become world counter revolutionary force SP one part
> <u>yào jiùshì</u> zhàn zài fǎndìguózhǔyì zhànxiàn fāngmiàn, biàn-chéng shìjiè
> stand on anti-imperialism camp side become world
> gémìng lìliàng de yī bùfèn.
> revolutionary force SP one part
> {In today's international environment, any heroes in colonies and semi-colonies have to take sides, either join the imperialist camp and become part of the world's counterrevolutionary forces or join the anti-imperialist camp and become part of the world's revolutionary forces.}

6.2.2 Multiple occurrences of *yàome*

Regardless of whether the options are irrealis or alternating situations, the number of the options connected by *yàome* in a complex sentence is not always limited to two. In some cases, there are three or even four options; thus, *yàome* needs to occur three or four times accordingly, that is, "*yàome p, yàome q, yàome r, yàome s*."

The following are two examples, and in each of them, *yàome* occurs three times.

(10) 县委领导在研究善后处理此事时，曾经有过几种打算，把一应家具变卖了，连同银行存款，<u>要么</u>一起寄交环珲河北老家的家属，<u>要么</u>全部交作党费，<u>要么</u>充作县委机关的职工福利。

> Xiànwěi lǐngdǎo zài … shí yánjiū shànhòu chǔlǐ cǐ
> county party committee leader when study cope with the aftermath deal this
> shì shí, céngjīng yǒu-guò jǐ zhǒng dǎsuàn, bǎ yīyīng jiājù
> matter once have-EXP several CL plan BA all furniture
> biànmài le, liántóng yínháng cúnkuǎn, <u>yàome</u> … <u>yàome</u> … <u>yàome</u> …
> sell MP and bank savings either … or … or …
> yīqǐ jì-jiāo Huánhuī Héběi lǎojiā de jiāshǔ, <u>yàome</u> quánbù
> together send to Huanhui Hebei hometown SP family member all
> jiāo-zuò dǎngfèi, <u>yàome</u> chōng-zuò xiànwěi jīguān de
> pay as party membership dues be as county party committee office SP
> zhígōng fúlì.
> staff welfare
> {When the leaders of the County Party Committee studied how to deal with the aftermath, they had several plans. After all the furniture was sold, the proceeds and Huanhui's savings could be sent to his family in his hometown in Hebei, be paid as his party membership dues, or be used as the County Party Committee's staff welfare.}

(11) 这一刻，家属院里的老夫老妻、少夫少妻破天荒地没有了甜言蜜语，儿女情长，感情不合的也没有斗嘴。<u>要么</u>相对无言，<u>要么</u>少言寡语，<u>要么</u>低声合计着今后的日子。

Zhè yī kè,   jiāshǔyuàn-lǐ   de lǎofū-lǎoqī,   shàofū-shàoqī
this a moment in residential compound SP old married couple young married couple
pòtiānhuāng   de méiyǒu-le   tiányán-mìyǔ,   érnǚ-qíngcháng,
for the first time SP not have-PEF honeyed words lasting affection between a couple
gǎnqíng bù   hé de yě   méiyǒu dòuzuǐ. <u>Yàome</u> xiāngduì   wúyán,
feeling NEG join SP also NEG argue some face each other have nothing to say
<u>yàome</u>   shǎoyán-guǎyǔ, <u>yàome</u>   dīshēng   héjì-zhe   jīnhòu de   rìzi.
some speak little some low voice discuss-PRG future SP life
{At this moment, in the residential compounds, the couples—old or young—for the first time do not have sweet talk or expressions of affection or arguments between those who don't get along. Some couples are just sitting silently, some are very quiet, and some are discussing their future life in a low voice.}

In (10), the options are irrealis situations, whereas in (11) they are alternating situations.

In the following example with four occurrences of *yàome*, the listed options are alternating situations.

(12) 人们<u>要么</u>尊他孙老，<u>要么</u>唤他老孙，<u>要么</u>称他孙猴，<u>要么</u>就叫孙会计。

Rén-men   <u>yàome</u> zūn   tā   Sūn lǎo, <u>yàome</u>   huàn tā   lǎo Sūn,   <u>yàome</u>
person-PL some respect him SUN old some call him old SUN some
chēng tā   Sūn hóu,   <u>yàome</u> jiù   jiào Sūn kuàijì.
call him SUN monkey some just call SUN accountant
{Some people address him by SUN Old as a respectful term, some call him Old Sun, some refer to him as Monkey King (as he has the same last name as Monkey King's), and others use Accountant SUN.}

6.2.3 Single occurrence of *yàome*

In some alternative sentences, there is only one occurrence of *yàome*, as it does not introduce or mark the options.

In some cases, *yàome* only occurs in the anterior clause, and the posterior clause is in the form of "*yào* VP *jiù* VP" or "*jì* (*rán*) VP *jiù* VP"; therefore, the whole sentence is in the form of "*yàome p, q* (*yào/jì* VP *jiù* VP)." The following are two examples:

(13) 四辈儿<u>要么</u>不哭，<u>要</u>哭<u>就</u>哭得声泪俱下，……

Sìbèir <u>yàome</u> bù   kū, <u>yào</u>   <u>jiù</u> kū <u>jiù</u> kū de shēnglèi-jùxià, ...
Sibeir either NEG cry or cry cry SP cry loudly and shed many tears
{Sibeir usually doesn't cry, but when he does, he cries loudly and is in floods of tears.}

(14) 要么不来，既然来到长沙做官就一定要把旧游之地岳麓书院振兴起来，……
Yàome bù lái, jìrán jiù lái-dào Chángshā zuòguān jiù yīdìng
either NEG come now that come to Changsha be an official certainly
yào bǎ jiùyóu zhī dì Yuèlùshūyuàn zhènxīng-qǐlái, …
must BA place one visited before Yuelu Academy start to revitalize
{Now that (I) have chosen to come to Changsha as a local official, (I) must revitalize Yuelu Academy, which (I) visited before; or (I) would not have chosen to come.}

In these two examples, the options in the posterior clauses are, respectively, marked by "*yào* VP *jiù* VP" and "*jì (rán)* VP *jiù* VP."

It is worthy of note that *yàome* can occur singly in the posterior clause in some cases, where there is a slot for *yàome* in the anterior clause, that is, "Ø *p, yàome q*."

The following are two examples in which *yàome* occurs singly in the posterior clause:

(15) 我想回油田去，要么就提前退休，回老家，放放牛。
Wǒ xiǎng huí yóutián qù, yàome jiù tíqián tuìxiū, huí
I want to return oil field go otherwise then bring forward retire return
lǎojiā, fàng-fàng niú.
hometown raise cattle
{I want to return to the oil field or, if not, I will retire early and go back to my hometown to raise some farm cattle.}

(16) 你赶快拍个电报通知他，要么打个长途电话，可以说得详细些。
Nǐ gǎnkuài pāi gè diànbào tōngzhī tā, yàome dǎ gè
you quickly send CL telegram inform him otherwise make CL
chángtúdiànhuà, kěyǐ shuō de xiángxì xiē.
long-distance phone call can say SP detailed some
{You should quickly send him a telegram, or make a long-distance call so that you can give him more details.}

In (15) and (16), *yàome* is used to introduce a supplementary option, meaning "if not *p*, then …". The absence of *yàome* before *p* implies that *p* is the speaker's preference or inclination, and the presence of *yàome* before *q* indicates that the speaker, after raising *p*, realizes that it might not be viable and therefore comes up with a supplementary option, which is *q*. Consequently, the presence of *yàome* before *q* not only marks it as an option but also justifies *p* as another option. Take (15) for example, the hearer will not realize that "returning to the oil field" is an option until they hear "otherwise retiring early and going back to my hometown to raise some farm cattle." If *yàome* was present before "returning to the oil field," the hearer would be aware that "returning to the oil field" was an option from the outset. Sentence (16) is the same case.

In sentences in the form of "Ø *p, yàome q*," there are two types of relations between *p* and *q*.

First, juxtaposition of the options. In (15), "returning to the oil field" is juxtaposed with "going back to hometown." By the same token, in (16), "sending a telegram" is juxtaposed with "making a long-distance phone call."

Second, antithesis between condition and result. Option *p* is a condition for Option *q*. Since *q* denotes an unfavorable result of *p*, *yàome* is used to emphasize *q* will be an unfavorable choice if *p* is given up. The following are two examples:

(17) 今夜晚，你们把这饭菜拿过去，明日就多待几席，<u>要么</u>剩下也吃不完。
Jīnyèwǎn, nǐ-men bǎ zhè fàncài ná-guòqu, míngrì jiù duō dài
tonight you-PL BA this food take tomorrow then more entertain
jǐ xí, <u>yàome</u> shèngxià yě chī bù wán.
several tables otherwise remain also cannot eat all
{Take this food (to your place) tonight so that you can entertain more guests tomorrow, otherwise (we) won't be able to finish it if it remains here.}

(18) 公社能看上叫我去迎接，咱便要知趣，<u>要么</u>，就失礼了。
Gōngshè néng kàn-shàng jiào wǒ qù yíngjiē, zán biàn yào zhīqù,
commune can see...as suitable ask me go welcome I then must sensible
<u>yàome</u>, jiù shīlǐ le.
otherwise then be impolite MP
{The commune (leadership) regarded that I was suitable and asked me to go and welcome (the guest), so I should be sensible (and go), otherwise I would be rude.}

In the above examples, *yàome* occurs only once and introduces an unfavorable result as an option, which proves the importance of taking Option *p*. However, if *yàome* occurs in pairs, (17) and (18) will respectively become (19) and (20) in which *p* and *q* are in juxtaposition.

(19) 要么多待几席，要么剩下吃不完。
Yàome... yàome... duō dài jǐ xí, yàome shèngxià
either...or... more entertain several tables remain
chī bù wán.
cannot finish eating
{Either (we) entertain more guests, or (we) won't be able to finish it if it remains here.}

(20) 要么知趣去迎接，要么不知趣而失礼。
Yàome... yàome... zhīqù qù yíngjiē, yàome bù zhīqù ér
either...or... sensible go welcome or NEG sensible therefore
shīlǐ.
be impolite
{Either (I) go and welcome (the guest), or (I) would be rude (if I didn't).}

If *yàome* occurs singly, the two options that it relates to can be located in different complex sentences. In other words, "Ø *p*" can be included in one complex sentence and "*yàome q*" in another one, as in the following two examples:

(21) 到乡下的第一天，我们在庄上转了整整一个上午，也没找到厕所。后来看到房子后边有一个玉米秆子搭的小棚子，心想，<u>要么</u>到那里去吧。

Dào xiāngxià de dìyī tiān, wǒ-men zài zhuāng-shàng zhuàn-le
arrive countryside SP first day we at in village walk around-PEF
zhěng-zhěng yī gè shàngwǔ, yě méi zhǎodào cèsuǒ. Hòulái kàn-dào
entirely one CL morning still NEG find toilet after see
fángzi-hòubiān yǒu yī gè yùmǐ gǎnzi dā de xiǎo péngzi, xīnxiǎng,
rear of house there be one CL corn stalk make SP small shed think
<u>yàome</u> dào nàli qù ba.
or go to there go MP

{On the first day in the country, we spent the whole morning walking around in the village but did not see any toilets. Later, when we saw a small shed made of cornstalks behind a house, we thought that we could go there (to relieve ourselves).}

(22) "我还是那句话，到上海去。……" 圣荃说得简简单单。不过句句实在。翠翠摇着头只是不响。……"<u>要么</u>到乡下去？" 奶奶另找了办法。

"Wǒ háishì nà jù huà, dào Shànghǎi qù..." Shèngquán shuō de
I still that CL words go to Shanghai go Shengquan say SP
jiǎnjiǎn-dāndān. Bùguò jù-jù shízài. Cuìcuì yáo-zhe tóu zhǐshì
simple however every sentence honest Cuicui shake-PRG head but
bù xiǎng.... "<u>Yàome</u> dào xiāngxià qù?" Nǎinai lìng
NEG reply or go to countryside go grandma additionally
zhǎo-le bànfǎ.
find-PEF way

{"I insist on my idea of going to Shanghai..." Shengquan spoke briefly but honestly. Cuicui shook her head without saying anything. "Or alternatively we could go to the countryside?" Grandma came up with another option.}

Example (21) includes two options: "using a toilet" and "using the small shed." In this example, "Ø *p*" is implied in the first sentence, and "*yàome q*" is present in the second sentence. Example (22) also includes two options, that is, "going to Shanghai" and "going to the countryside," which are located in different sentences as well.

On occasions where different speakers put forward different opinions, a speaker's "Ø *p*" and "*yàome q*" can be separated by what other speakers say, as the following example:

(23) 班级要成立红卫兵战斗队了，红五类们聚在一起，讨论着应该给战斗队起什么名字。

Bānjí yào chénglì Hóngwèibīng Zhàndòuduì le, hóngwǔlèi-men
class be going to form Red Guard combat team MP five red categories-PL
jù zài yīqǐ, tǎolùn-zhe yīnggāi gěi zhàndòuduì qǐ shénme míngzi.
gather at together discuss-PRG should to combat team give what name

{The class was going to form a Red Guard combat team. Those in the Five Red Categories were gathering to discuss what name to give to the combat team.}

姜爱国说："叫作董存瑞战斗队。"
Jiāng Àiguó   shuō: "Jiàozuò   Dǒng Cúnruì Zhàndòuduì."
JIANG Aiguo say   be called   DONG Cunrui combat team
{JIANG Aiguo said, "It should be called DONG Cunrui Combat Team."}

雯雯说："叫作海燕战斗队。"
Wénwén   shuō: "Jiàozuò   Hǎiyàn Zhàndòuduì."
Wenwen say   be called   petrel combat team
{"It should be called Petrel Combat Team," Wenwen said.}

王彧说："叫作海燕战斗队。"
Wáng Yù   shuō: "Jiàozuò   Hǎiyàn Zhàndòuduì."
WANG Yu say   be called   petrel combat team
{WANG Yu agreed, "Yes, Petrel Combat Team"}

魏玉娥说："叫作雄鹰战斗队。"
Wèi Yù'é   shuō: "Jiàozuò   Xióngyīng Zhàndòuduì."
WEI Yu'e say   be called   eagle combat team
{WEI Yu'e said, "Let's call it Eagle Combat Team."}

谁也不听谁的，吵个不休……
Shuí   yě   bù   tīng   shuíde,   chǎo   gè   bù   xiū...
everyone also   NEG   listen whose   argue   CL   NEG   stop
{No one would listen to anyone else, so they kept arguing...}

"要么干脆叫代代红战斗队。" 姜爱国……又多出了一种意见。
"Yàome   gāncuì   jiào   Dàidàihóng Zhàndòuduì."   Jiāng Àiguó...   yòu
or   simply   be called everlasting red combat team JIANG Aiguo   again
duō-chū-le   yī   zhǒng   yìjiàn.
more-PEF   a   type   opinion
{"How about simply calling it Everlasting Red Fighters?" JIANG Aiguo... made another suggestion.}

"要么叫遵义战斗队。"雯雯也提出了一条。
"Yàome   jiào   Zūnyì Zhàndòuduì."   Wénwén   yě   tíchū-le   yī tiáo.
or   be called Zunyi combat team   Wenwen   also   put forward-PEF   a CL
{"Or it can be called Zunyi Combat Team." Wenwen also had a new idea.}

"要么叫破旧立新。"
"Yàome   jiào   pòjiù-lìxīn."
or   be called destroy the old and establish the new
{"Or Iconoclastic Combat Team."}

没完没了了。
Méiwán-méiliǎo le.
be endless   MP
{The argument went on and on.}

Example (23) tells a story about four people arguing about what their combat team should be called. For JIANG Aiguo, the combat team can be called either DONG Cunrui Combat Team or Everlasting Red Fighters, and for Wenwen, either Petrel Combat Team or Zunyi Combat Team . . . Since *yàome* is absent before *p*, the occurrence of "*yàome q*" can be in a separate sentence from *p*. Nonetheless, however far apart they are, relevance always exists between *p* and *q* thanks to "*yàome q*."

6.3 "*yàome p, yàome q*" and relevant forms

Generally, *yàome* is used in "*yàome p, yàome q*" most often. For a better understanding of "*yàome p, yàome q*," it is necessary to discuss its synonymous forms, such as "*bùshì p, jiùshì q*"; "*yàobù p, yàobù q*"; and "*huòzhě p, huòzhě q*."

6.3.1 "*yàome p, yàome q*" and "*bùshì p, jiùshì q*"

The two forms, "*yàome p, yàome q*" and "*bùshì p, jiùshì q*," are both used for closed alternative complex sentences, seemingly without any differences. Compare the following two examples:

(24) a 他肯定会提升：不是当主任，就是当处长。
Tā kěndìng huì tíshēng: bùshì . . . jiùshì . . . dāng zhǔrèn, jiùshì
He definitely will promote if not . . . then . . . be director
dāng chùzhǎng.
be section chief
{He is certain to be promoted to section chief if not director.}

b 他肯定会提升：要么当主任，要么当处长。
Tā kěndìng huì tíshēng: Yàome . . . yàome . . . dāng zhǔrèn, yàome
he definitely will promote either . . . or . . . be director
dāng chùzhǎng.
be section chief
{He is certain to be promoted to section chief if not director.}

However, the two forms differ in the following two aspects.
First, in terms of structure, "*yàome p, yàome q*" is looser, whereas "*bùshì p, jiùshì q*" is tighter.
Proof 1: in sentences in the form of "*yàome p, yàome q*," a phonetic pause can occur between *yàome* and *p* or between *yàome* and *q* in speech, and a comma can be used to signify the pause in written language. However, this does not hold for "*bùshì p, jiùshì q*." The following are two examples:

140 *"yàome p, yàome q" and relevant forms*

(25) 问明了情况后，他皱紧了眉头，最后提出：<u>要么</u>，让张宗昌入赘；<u>要么</u>，让张宗昌立即滚蛋。

Wèn   míng le   qíngkuàng hòu, tā zhòujǐn-le méitóu, zuìhòu tíchū:
inquire clear PEF situation after he frown-PEF   final put forward
<u>yàome</u> . . . <u>yàome</u> . . . , ràng Zhāng Zōngchāng   rùzhuì;
either . . . or . . .   make ZHANG Zongchang   marry into and live with
                                                        the bride's family
<u>yàome</u>, ràng Zhāng Zōngchāng   lìjí   gǔndàn.
        make ZHANG Zongchang   immediately get lost
{After inquiring about the situation, he first frowned and finally said: Either make ZHANG Zongchang a live-in son-in-law (who lives in the wife's home with her family) or ask him to get lost right away.}

(26) 我的意思是说，<u>要么</u>，你骆大胡子连你儿子一起，统统"枪毙"，<u>要么</u>，就连我一起批！

Wǒ de yìsi   shì shuō, <u>yàome</u>   <u>yàome</u> . . . , nǐ Luò dàhúzi   lián nǐ
I   SP meaning COP say   either . . . or . . .   you LUO moustache with your
érzi yīqǐ,   tǒngtǒng "qiāngbì", <u>yàome</u>, jiù lián wǒ yīqǐ   pī!
son together both   reject   just with me together approve
{I mean, either, you, bearded LUO, will be rejected along with your son or you will be approved along with me!}

Proof 2: annotated expressions or clauses can be inserted in "*yàome p, yàome q*" but not in "*bùshì p, jiùshì q*." The following are two examples:

(27) 反正这两年，书记段长都不在段上，<u>要么</u>在局里开会—如今有的是会要开，也都要负责人参加；<u>要么</u>在省城休病假，一休就是一、二个月......

Fǎnzhèng zhè liǎng nián, shūjì   duànzhǎng   dōu bù zài duàn-shàng,
anyway   This two   year secretary section chief both NEG be at in section
<u>yàome</u>   <u>yàome</u> . . . zài jú-lǐ   kāihuì   —rújīn   yǒudeshì   huì
either . . . or . . .   at in bureau attend meetings nowadays there be a lot meeting
yào kāi, yě dōu yào fùzérén   cānjiā; yàome zài shěngchéng
must attend also all must person in charge attend   in provincial capital
xiū bìngjià, yī   xiū   jiù shì yī, èr   gè yuè...
be on sick leave once be on leave then COP one or two CL month
{In the past couple of years, neither the Party secretary nor the head of the section has been in the section in any case. They either attend meetings in the bureau—there are numerous meetings nowadays and they all require the people in charge to attend—or they are on sick leave in the provincial capital, always for one or two months . . . }

(28) "那你为什么要选择这种工作呢？" "我又没有什么特长，<u>要么</u>当小学教员，可我不喜欢孩子；<u>要么</u>到服务行业去；<u>要么</u>干这个。"

"Nà nǐ wèishénme yào xuǎnzé zhè zhǒng gōngzuò ne?" "Wǒ yòu méiyǒu
then you why   want choose this type work   MP I   really not have
shénme tècháng, <u>yàome</u> <u>yàome</u> <u>yàome</u> dāng xiǎoxué   jiàoyuán,
any   special skill either . . . or . . . or . . .   be   elementary school teacher

"yàome p, yàome q" and relevant forms

kě wǒ bù   xǐhuān háizi; <u>yàome</u> dào fúwù hángyè qù; <u>yàome</u> gàn zhè gè."
but I   NEG like   child   go to service industry go   do this CL

{"Then why do you want to choose this type of work?"

"(Because) I don't really have any special skills. I could be an elementary school teacher, but I don't like children, or I could be employed in the service industry, or I could take this up."}

Proof 3: "*yàome p, yàome q*" has some varieties, such as "*yàome p, yàome q, yàome r, yàome s*", "Ø *p, yàome q*" and so on, whereas "*bùshì p, jiùshì q*" does not. In the following examples, (29a) is in the form of "*yàome p, yàome q*," which can be rewritten as (29b) in the form of "*yàome p, yàome q, yàome r*" and (29c) in the form of "Ø *p, yàome q*." However, (30) is in the form of "*bùshì p, jiùshì q*," and it cannot be rewritten as any other form.

(29) a 要么考美院，要么考音专。

<u>Yàome</u> . . . <u>yàome</u> . . . kǎo   měiyuàn, yàome kǎo   yīnzhuān.
either . . . or . . .   apply for art school apply for music school

{Either apply for an art school or apply for a music school.}

b 要么考美院，要么考音专，要么干脆呆在文化馆。

<u>Yàome</u> . . . <u>yàome</u> . . . <u>yàome</u> . . . kǎo měiyuàn, yàome kǎo   yīnzhuān,
either . . . or . . .   apply for art school apply for music school
yàome gāncuì dāi zài wénhuàguǎn.
        simply stay at cultural center

{Either apply for an art school or a music school or just stay in the culture center.}

c 我想考美院。要么考音专！

Wǒ xiǎng   kǎo   měiyuàn. Yàome kǎo   yīnzhuān!
I   want to apply for art school or   apply for music school

{I want to apply for an art school, or a music school!}

(30) 不是考美院，就是考音专。

Bùshì . . . jiùshì . . . kǎo   měiyuàn, jiùshì kǎo   yīnzhuān.
if not . . . then . . . apply for art school   apply for music school

{Apply for a music school if not an art school.}

Second, with respect to collocation, there is more variety in "*bùshì p, jiùshì q*" than in "*yàome p, yàome q*."

To begin with, certain words indicating a hypothetical situation can occur before "*bùshì p, jiùshì q*," such as *ruò* ('if') and *yào* ('if'); thus, alternative complex sentences can be transformed into hypothetical complex sentences with those words. On the contrary, no such words can precede "*yàome p, yàome q*." The following are two examples:

(31) 对于一个自知丑陋的人讲漂亮之类的奉承话，<u>若不</u>是挪揄，<u>就</u>是出于恶毒的用心。

Duìyú yī gè zìzhī-chǒulòu de rén jiǎng piàoliang zhī
to a CL be self-conscious about one's ugly looks SP person say pretty SP
lèi de fèngchéng huà, <u>ruòbùshì</u> yéyú, <u>jiùshì</u> chūyú èdú de yòngxīn.
kind SP flatter words if not ridicule then come from malicious SP intention
{Such flattery as "you are pretty" to someone who is self-conscious about her unattractiveness is malicious if not sarcastic.}

(32) 他常常白天跑这儿，跑那儿，一刻不停地进行摄影采访，晚上<u>要不</u>是埋头写图片说明，采访纪实，<u>就</u>是在暗房一干就是大半夜，……

Tā cháng-cháng báitiān pǎo zhèr, pǎo nàr, yīkè bù tíng de jìnxíng
he often daytime run here run there a moment NEG stop SP do
shèyǐng cǎifǎng, wǎnshàng <u>yàobùshì</u> máitóu xiě túpiàn shuōmíng,
photograph interview nighttime if not concentrate on write photo caption
cǎifǎng jìshí, <u>jiùshì</u> zài ànfáng yī gān jiù shì dàbàn yè, …
interview record then in darkroom sometime work just COP more than half night
{He often ran around during the day, taking pictures and interviewing, and at night, he would work late into the night in the darkroom if not busy with writing photo captions and documenting interviews … }

Then, *p* and *q* in "*bùshì p, jiùshì q*" can be acted by verbs or predicative phrases, or even nouns, whereas *p* and *q* in "*yàome p, yàome q*" are usually acted by verbs or predicative phrases but not typical nouns that refer to people. Compare the following examples:

(33) a 我<u>不是</u>当编辑，<u>就是</u>当记者。

Wǒ <u>bù</u> <u>shì</u> dāng biānji, <u>jiù</u> <u>shì</u> dāng jìzhě.
I NEG COP be editor then COP be reporter
{I will be a reporter if not an editor.}

b 我<u>要么</u>当编辑，<u>要么</u>当记者。

Wǒ <u>yàome</u> … <u>yàome</u> … dāng biānji, <u>yàome</u> dāng jìzhě.
I either … or … be editor be reporter
{I will either be an editor or a reporter.}

(34) a 他<u>不是</u>编辑，<u>就是</u>记者。

Tā <u>bùshì</u> … <u>jiùshì</u> … biānji, <u>jiùshì</u> jìzhě.
he if not … then editor reporter
{He is either an editor or a reporter.}

*b 他要么编辑，<u>要么</u>记者。

Tā <u>yàome</u> … <u>yàome</u> … biānji, <u>yàome</u> jìzhě.
he either … or … editor reporter

If "*bùshì . . . jiùshì . . .*" links two nouns, the word *shì* is a typical judgmental verb. For this reason, if "*bùshì p, jiùshì q*" is to be transformed into "*yàome p, yàome q*," the verb *shì* needs to remain, that is, "*yàome shì . . . yàome shì . . . ,*" as illustrated by the following examples:

(35) a 他不是编辑，就是记者。
　　　Tā　　bùshì . . . jiùshì . . .　　biānji,　　jiùshì　　jìzhě.
　　　he　　if not . . . then . . .　　editor　　　　　　　reporter
　　　{He is either an editor or a reporter.}

　　　b 他要么是编辑，要么是记者。
　　　Tā　　yàome . . . yàome . . .　　shì　　biānji,　　yàome　　shì　　jìzhě.
　　　he　　either . . . or . . .　　　　COP　　editor　　　　　　　COP　　reporter
　　　{He is either an editor or a reporter.}

Third, "*yàome p, yàome q*" and "*bùshì p, jiùshì q*" have different scopes and semantic focuses.

To begin with, the options in "*yàome p, yàome q*" can be either objective or subjective. In other words, *p* and *q* can be objective descriptions of facts or subjective intentions or desires. However, the options in "*bùshì p, jiùshì q*" can only be objective. Among the following four examples, options in (36a) and (36b) are objective, whereas options in (37a) and (37b) are subjective.

(36) a 她的成绩要么第一，要么第二。
　　　Tā　　de　　chéngji　　yàome . . . yàome . . .　　dìyī,　　yàome　　dì'èr.
　　　she　　SP　　score　　either . . . or . . .　　　　 first　　　　　　 second
　　　{Her score is ranked either first or second.}

　　　b 她的成绩不是第一，就是第二。
　　　Tā　　de　　chéngji　　bùshì . . . jiùshì . . .　　dìyī,　　jiùshì　　dì'èr.
　　　she　　SP　　performance　either . . . or . . .　　first　　　　　　 second
　　　{Her score is ranked second if not first.}

(37) a 要么把我排第一，要么干脆别排！
　　　Yàome . . . yàome . . .　　bǎ　　wǒ　　pái　　dìyī,　　yàome　　gāncuì　　bié　　pái!
　　　either . . . or . . .　　　　BA　　me　　rank　first　　　　　　　simply　　 do not　rank
　　　{Either rank me first, or simply don't rank me.}

　　　*b 不是把我排第一，就是干脆别排！
　　　Bùshì . . . jiùshì . . .　　bǎ　　wǒ　　pái　　dìyī,　　jiùshì　　gāncuì　　bié　　pái!
　　　if not . . . then . . .　　　BA　　me　　rank　first　　　　　　　simply　　 do not　rank

In some cases, it seems possible for a sentence in the form of "*yàome p, yàome q*" involving subjective options to be rewritten as the one in the form of "*bùshì p, jiùshì q.*" However, once the sentence is rewritten, the subjective options will become objective ones. The following is an example:

(38)　（刘钊）"你<u>要么</u>答应，<u>要么</u>拒绝—"（丁晓）"你真是一只狼！"
(Liú Zhāo) "Nĭ <u>yàome</u>... <u>yàome</u>... dāying, <u>yàome</u> jùjué—" *(Dīng Xiăo)* "Nĭ
LIU Zhao   you   either...or...   accept   refuse   DING Xiao   you
zhēn   shì   yī   zhī   láng!"
really   COP   one   CL   wolf
{[LIU Zhao] "You either accept or refuse..."
[DING Xiao] "You are a real wolf!"}

The options in the above example are subjective. LIU Zhao urges DING Xiao to make a fast choice between *dāying* ('accepting') and *jùjué* ('refusing') with "*yàome...yàome...*" Thus, "*yàome...yàome...*" is unlikely to be replaced by "*bùshì...jiùshì...*" Even if it was replaced, the meaning and tone of urging would disappear, and the sentence would, accordingly, become one that states the advantage and disadvantage objectively.

Next, even when the options are objective, "*yàome p, yàome q*" and "*bùshì p, jiùshì q*" differ slightly in tone.

"*bùshì p, jiùshì q*" sounds more assertive and rigid than "*yàome p, yàome q.*" For example, (39b) is more assertive than (39a).

(39)　a 要么当主任，要么当处长。
Yàome...*yàome*...   dāng   zhŭrèn,   yàome   dāng   chùzhăng.
either...or...   be   director   be   section chief
{Either be director or section chief.}

b 不是当主任，就是当处长。
Bùshì...*jiùshì*...   dāng   zhŭrèn,   jiùshì   dāng   chùzhăng
if not...then...   be   dean   be   section chief
{Be section chief if not director.}

Between the following two examples, (40a) sounds more certain, and (40b) takes on a tone of speculation.

(40)　a 候选人不是张辉，就是李良。
Hòuxuănrén   *bùshì*...*jiùshì*...   Zhāng Huī,   jiùshì   Lĭ Liáng.
candidate   either...or...   ZHANG Hui   LI Liang
{The candidate must be LI Liang if not ZHANG Hui.}

b 候选人要么是张辉，要么是李良。
Hòuxuănrén   *yàome*...*yàome*...   shì   Zhāng Huī,   yàome   shì   Lĭ Liáng.
candidate   either...or...   COP   ZHANG Hui   COP   LI Liang
{The candidate is either ZHANG Hui or LI Liang.}

If the speaker chooses not to sound very certain, they are likely to use "*yàome p, yàome q*," for instance, Example (6). The following is another example:

(41) 她就是她，<u>要么</u>是火，<u>要么</u>是冰。
Tā jiù shì tā, <u>yàome</u> ... <u>yàome</u> ... shì huǒ, <u>yàome</u> shì bīng.
she just COP her either...or... COP fire COP ice
{She is who she is, sometimes as warm as the sun, but other times as cold as ice.}

6.3.2 "*yàome p, yàome q*" and "*yàobù p, yàobù q*"

Sentences in the form of "*yàobù p, yàobù q*" can be rephrased as the ones in the form of "*yàome p, yàome q*." The following are two examples:

(42) 我<u>要不</u>就留在家给她带孩子，当保姆；<u>要不</u>，就搬出去。
Wǒ <u>yàobù</u> ... <u>yàobù</u> ... jiù liú zài jiā gěi tā dài háizi, dāng
I either...or... just stay at home for her look after child be
bǎomǔ; <u>yàobù</u>, jiù bān-chūqu.
nanny either...or... just move out
{I'll either stay home and look after the kid for her as a nanny, or otherwise, just move out.}

(43) 怎么办？<u>要不</u>认栽赔人家，<u>要不</u>找管理处去，交税就得受保护！
Zěnmebàn? <u>Yàobù</u> ... <u>yàobù</u> ... rènzāi péi
what to do either...or... accept bad luck compensate
rénjia, <u>yàobù</u> zhǎo guǎnlǐchù qù, jiāo shuì
the other person involved turn to administrate office go pay tax
jiù děi shòu bǎohù!
just must PASSIVE protect
{What to do? Either accept the bad luck and compensate the other party or turn to the Administrative Office (for protection), (because you) will be protected since (you) have paid taxes!}

However, "*yàobù p, yàobù q*" and "*yàome p, yàome q*" differ from each other in the following two aspects.

First, the options in "*yàome p, yàome q*" can be either objective or subjective, whereas the options in "*yàobù p, yàobù q*" are generally subjective rather than objective. In this regard, "*yàobù p, yàobù q*" and "*bùshì p, jiùshì q*" are just the opposite. Comparisons among the sentences of (44a-c) and (45a-c) present a clear picture of the difference between "*yàobù p, yàobù q*" and "*bùshì p, jiùshì q*" as well as their interrelationships with "*yàome p, yàome q*," thus showing that (44c) and (45b) are ill-formed sentences.

146 *"yàome p, yàome q" and relevant forms*

(44) a 要么你留下，要么你赶快走。(subjective)
Yàome . . . yàome . . .   nǐ   liú-xià,   yàome   nǐ   gǎnkuài   zǒu.
either . . . or . . .   you   stay   you   quickly   leave
{You either stay or leave quickly.}

b 要不你留下，要不你赶快走。(subjective)
Yàobù . . . yàobù . . .   nǐ   liú-xià,   yàobù   nǐ   gǎnkuài   zǒu.
either . . . or . . .   you   stay   you   quickly   leave
{You either stay or leave quickly.}

*c 不是你留下，就是你赶快走。(subjective)
Bùshì . . . jiùshì . . . nǐ   liú-xià,   jiùshì nǐ   gǎnkuài   zǒu.
if not . . . then   you   stay   you   quickly   leave

(45) a 这一向他要么满不在乎，要么斤斤计较。(objective)
Zhè   yīxiàng   tā   yàome . . . yàome . . .   mǎnbùzàihu,   yàome   jīnjīn-jìjiào.
this past   he   either . . . or . . .   not care at all   fussy

*b 这一向他要不满不在乎，要不斤斤计较。(objective)
Zhè   yīxiàng   tā   yàobù . . . yàobù . . .   mǎnbùzàihu,   yàobù   jīnjīn-jìjiào.
this past   he   either . . . or . . .   not care at all   fussy

c 这一向他不是满不在乎，就是斤斤计较。(objective)
Zhè   yīxiàng   tā   bùshì . . . jiùshì . . . mǎnbùzàihu,   jiùshì jīnjīn-jìjiào.
this past   he   if not . . . then . . .   not care at all   fussy
{Recently he has been either indifferent or fussy.}

Nevertheless, it does not mean that the options in sentences in the form of "*yàobù p, yàobù q*" cannot be objective. If *yàobù* is followed by *jiùshì*, that is, "*yàobù jiùshì p, yàobù jiùshì q,*" then the options can be objective. Example (46) is a rewrite of (45b).

(46) 这一向他要不就是满不在乎，要不就是斤斤计较。
Zhè   yīxiàng   tā   yàobù jiùshì . . . yàobù jiùshì . . .   mǎnbùzàihu,   yàobù jiùshì
this past   he   if not . . . then   not care at all
jīnjīn-jìjiào.
fussy
{Recently he has been either fussy or indifferent.}

The following is another example:

(47) 可是找了一个，两个，三个，四个，赵艮皆未看中，要不就是家境不富裕，要不就是模样丑陋或一派委琐，……
Kěshì zhǎo-le yī   gè,   liǎng gè,   sān gè,   sì   gè,   Zhào Gèn   jiē   wèi
but   find-PEF one CL   two   CL   three CL   four CL   ZHAO Gen   all   NEG
kànzhòng,   yàobù jiùshì . . . yàobù jiùshì . . .   jiājìng bù   fùyù,   yàobù jiùshì   múyàng
be satisfied either . . . or . . .   family NEG rich   looks

chǒulòu   huò   yī   pài   wěisuǒ,...
ugly   or   one   CL   indecent
{(Her brother-in-law) found four (young men for her), but ZHAO Gen was not satisfied with any of them, either (because of) poor family background, or (because of) ugly or indecent looks ... }

In (47), *yàobù* is present and immediately followed by *jiùshì*. The following is another example:

(48) 老镇长 ······ 喜欢讲话。要么是几条合理化建议，要么是几句顺口溜的 "喜歌"，倒也惹人发笑。
Lǎo zhènzhǎng ... xǐhuān jiǎnghuà. Yàome   yàome ... shì   jǐ   tiáo
old town mayor   like   talk   either ... or ...   COP   several   CL
hélǐhuà   jiànyì,   yàome   shì   jǐ   jù   shùnkǒuliū   de
rationalization proposal   yàome   COP   several sentence   doggerel   SP
"xǐgē",   dào   yě   rě   rén   fāxiào.
well-wishing song unexpectedly also   make   person   start to laugh
{The old town mayor liked talking. (He) would sometimes make some rationalization proposals, and sometimes create a few lyrics of "well-wishing songs" of the doggerel style, which were funny.}

In the above example, *yàome* is followed by *shì*. If *yàome* is to be replaced by *yàobù*, *jiù* still needs to be present and follow *yàobù*. Example (49) is a rewrite of (48).

(49) 要不就是几条合理化建议，要不就是几句顺口溜的 "喜歌" ······
Yàobù jiùshì ... yàobù jiùshì ... jǐ   tiáo   hélǐhuà   jiànyì,   yàobù jiùshì
either ... or ...   several CL   rationalization proposal
jǐ   jù   shùnkǒuliū   de   "xǐgē" ...
several   sentence doggerel   SP   well-wishing song
{Either some rationalization proposals, or a few lyrics of "well-wishing songs" of the doggerel style ... }

Second, when the options are subjective, "*yàome p, yàome q*" means almost the same as "*yàobù p, yàobù q.*" However, *yàome* is firmer than *yàobù* in tone.

Because *yàome* is relatively firm in tone, it is a better choice for expressing determination. The following is an example:

(50) 要么随波逐流，要么撞得头破血流滚下台！
Yàome   yàome ...   suíbō-zhúliú,   yàome   zhuàng   de
either ... or ...   go with the flow   bump   SP
tóupò-xuèliú   gǔnxiàtái!
head is broken and blood is flowing   step down
{(I) will either go with the flow, or I'll fail completely and step down!}

In this example, it would be inappropriate to replace *yàome* with *yàobù* because *yàobù* is not firm enough in tone.

148 *"yàome p, yàome q" and relevant forms*

To force someone to make a choice, *"yàome p, yàomeù q"* is more appropriate, whereas to offer advice or having a discussion, *"yàobù p, yàobù q"* is more suitable. Compare the following two examples, between which (51) carries a threatening tone, while (52) has a tone of tactful advice.

(51) 要么答应我立即结婚，要么你我今后别再相见！
<u>Yàome</u> . . . <u>yàome</u> . . . dāying wǒ lìjí jiéhūn, <u>yàome</u> nǐ wǒ
either . . . or . . . agree me immediately marry you I
jīnhòu bié zài xiāngjiàn!
from now on do not again see each other
{Either you agree to marry me right away, or you and I will never see each other again!}

(52) 要不你写封信让我带去，要不你去找他当面谈谈。
<u>Yàobù</u> . . . <u>yàobù</u> . . . nǐ xiě fēng xìn ràng wǒ dài-qù, <u>yàobù</u> nǐ qù
either . . . or . . . you write CL letter let me take you go
zhǎo tā dāngmiàn tán-tán.
look for him face to face talk-REDP
{You can either write a letter and let me take it to him, or you can talk to him face to face.}

In addition, if *yàome* only occurs in the posterior clause, it can always be replaced by *yàobù*, as has been attested by all the examples above. However, it does not mean that any *yàobù* occurring singly in the posterior clause can be replaced by *yàome*, as in the following example:

(53) 幸亏他没当评委，要不我很难评上。
Xìngkuī tā méi dāng píngwěi, <u>yàobù</u> wǒ hěn nán píng-shàng.
fortunately he NEG be judge otherwise I very difficult be selected
{Fortunately, he wasn't on the selection committee; otherwise, it would be very difficult for me to be selected.}

In general, *yàobù* can be used interchangeably with *fǒuzé* ('otherwise'), and it can occur in a few types of non-alternative complex sentences.

6.3.3 *"yàome p, yàome q" and "huòzhě p, huòzhě q"*

In some cases, *"huòzhě p, huòzhě q"* means "between the two options, one or the other needs to be taken", which is almost the same as what *"yàome p, yàome q"* means. The following is an example:

(54) 这样，就只有两条路走，或是袁沛文跟陶慧贞走，或是袁沛文跟陶慧贞断，这都是佟英所不愿意的。
Zhèyàng, jiù zhǐ yǒu liǎng tiáo lù zǒu, <u>huòshì</u> . . . <u>huòshì</u> . . .
so just only there be two CL road walk either . . . or . . .
Yuán Pèiwén gēn Táo Huìzhēn zǒu, <u>huòshì</u> Yuán Pèiwén gēn
YUAN Peiwen follow TAO Huizhen leave YUAN Peiwen with

Táo Huìzhēn duàn, zhè dōu shì Tóng Yīng suǒ bù yuànyì de.
TAO Huizhen break up this both COP TONG Ying PAP NEG want SP
{So, there are only two possibilities: either YUAN Peiwen follows TAO Huizhen or YUAN Peiwen breaks up with Tao Huizhen, neither of which is what TONG Ying wants (to be the case).}

In (54), *huòshì* can be replaced by *yàome*.

However, there are still some minor differences between "*huòzhě p, huòzhě q*" and "*yàome p, yàome q*", even though both can be used to mean "either-or".

First, "*huòzhě p, huòzhě q*" has an impression of the speaker being objective with a firm and calm tone, whereas the speaker using "*yàome p, yàome q*" sounds as if they were making an overstatement and speaking emotionally. For instance, the options in Example (2) are subjective, and therefore, *yàome* is better than *huòzhě* as the former can reflect the speaker's unwavering determination. The following is an example:

(55) 我就像丢了魂，干哪样不像哪样！下午，我把饭煮糊了，糊得像焦炭！炒的菜，<u>要么</u>咸得要死，<u>要么</u>没盐味儿！
Wǒ jiù xiàng diū-le hún, gàn nǎ yàng bù xiàng nǎ yàng!
I just like lose-PEF soul do whichever CL NEG be like whichever CL
Xiàwǔ, wǒ bǎ fàn zhǔ hú le, hú de xiàng jiāotàn! Chǎo
afternoon I BA rice boil burn PEF burn SP like coke stir fry
de cài, yàome ...... yàome ...... xián de yàosǐ, yàome méi yán wèir!
SP dish either... or... salty SP extremely NEG salt taste
{My mind wandered, and I couldn't do anything! In the afternoon, I overcooked the rice, and it was burned like coke! The dishes that I cooked were either terribly salty or bland as if there was no salt in them at all!}

The options in this example are objective, and the use of *yàome* vividly reflects the consequences resulted from the speaker's bad mood; nevertheless, the use of *huòzhě* would not be as effective.

The use of "*huòzhě ... huòzhě ...*" in Example (54) gives an impression of the speaker explaining the situation objectively. The following is an example:

(56) 大家要是同意，我去找地方党组织，动员群众抬你们。抬回去<u>或者</u>当儿子，<u>或者</u>做女婿。
Dàjiā yàoshi tóngyì, wǒ qù zhǎo dìfāng dǎng zǔzhī, dòngyuán
everyone if agree I go look for locality party organization mobilize
qúnzhòng tái nǐ-men. Tái-huíqu huòzhě ...... huòzhě ...... dāng érzi, huòzhě zuò
masses carry you-PL carry back either... or... be son be
nǚxu.
son-in-law
{If everybody agrees, I will go and look for the local Party organization and mobilize the masses to carry you (to their homes), where you could be their son or son-in-law.}

In (56), the speaker only needs to advise the listeners of the two possibilities, so *yàome . . . yàome . . .* is unnecessary.

Second, with respect to the connectives, *jiù* can occur in the posterior clause in sentences in the form of *"yàome p, yàome q"* to indicate an inferential relationship between the two clauses. However, *jiù* usually cannot occur in the posterior clause with *"huòzhě p, huòzhě q."* The following is an example:

(57) 自视甚高的人，往往容易走极端，<u>要么</u>对任何人的褒贬都不在意，<u>要么</u><u>就</u>恰恰相反。

Zìshìshènggāo de rén, wǎngwǎng róngyì zǒu jíduān,
think highly of oneself SP person often easy go extremes
*<u>yàome</u> . . . <u>yàome</u> . . . duì rènhé rén de bāobiǎn dōu bù zàiyì, <u>yàome</u> **jiù***
either . . . or . . . to any person SP judge all NEG care just
qià-qià xiāngfǎn.
exactly opposite
{People with high self-esteem tend to go to extremes easily—they either don't care about anybody else's appraisal or just the other way around.}

If *yàome* occurs three times in a row in an alternative complex sentence, *jiù* can be present in the third clause, as in the following example:

(58) 以前，我总觉得，你们的心都很简单，<u>要么</u>是一团火，<u>要么</u>是一块石头，<u>要么</u><u>就</u>是摊稀脏的烂泥。

Yǐqián, wǒ zǒng juéde, nǐ-men de xīn dōu hěn jiǎndān,
before I always feel you-PL SP heart all very simple
<u>yàome</u> . . . <u>yàome</u> . . . <u>yàome</u> . . . shì yī tuán huǒ, yàome shì yī kuài
either . . . or . . . or . . . COP one CL fire COP one CL
*shítou, <u>yàome</u> **jiù** shì tān xīzāng de lànní.*
stone just COP pool dirty SP mud
{I used to think that your hearts were all simple: like a fire, or a stone, or a pool of mud.}

Summary

First, *"yàome p, yàome q"* is a form of closed alternative complex sentences and emphasizes between the two listed options one or the other needs to be taken. The listed options in *"yàome p, yàome q"* can be irrealis or alternating situations.

Second, *yàome* often occurs in pairs, introducing two clauses and acting as a marker for the two options. However, *yàome* can also occur more than twice or only singly in the anterior or posterior clause in some cases.

Third, there are similarities and differences between *"yàome p, yàome q"* and the other three forms: *"bùshì p, jiùshì q"*; *"yàobù p, yàobù q"*; and *"huòzhě p, huòzhě q."* Knowledge about the subtle differences between them will facilitate the understanding of relevant language facts in Chinese.

NB Some examples in this chapter are cited from literary works, political essays, articles, and so on. The sources are listed as follows:

1. *Changcheng* (《长城》) 1985(3), including Example (12);
2. *Dangdai* (《当代》) 1982(2), including (42) and (43); 1982(3), including (6); 1985(1), including (41);
3. *Flower City* (《花城》) 1984(2), including (15);
4. *Fragments of Civilization* (《文明的碎片》) by YU Qiuyu (余秋雨), including (14);
5. *Harvest* (《收获》) 1982(4), including (22); 1984(3), including (23); 1984(4), including (5), (21), and (57);
6. *Mengya* (《萌芽》) 1983(3) (supplement), including (31);
7. *Modern Chinese Dictionary* (《现代汉语词典》), including (16);
8. *October* (《十月》) 1982(1), including (2); 1983(3), including (50); 1983(4), including (38); 1983(5), including (58); 1984(4), including (17), (18), (26), (27), and (55); 1987(1), including (28); 1987(2), including (47); 1987(3), including (4), (32), and (48);
9. *Popular Stories* (《大众小说》) 1987(2), including (25);
10. *Qingming* (《清明》) 1983(3), including (54);
11. *Selected Works of Excellent Chinese Short Stories in 1980* (《1980年全国优秀短篇小说评选获奖作品集》), including (56);
12. *Selected Works of MAO Tse-tung* (《毛泽东选集》), including (9);
13. *Ten Thousand Jinshi* (《十万进士》) by YU Qiuyu (余秋雨), including (8);
14. *Xiao Shuo Jia* (《小说家》) 1987(2), including (11);
15. *Zhongpian Xiaoshuo Xuankan* (《中篇小说选刊》) 1994(6), including (1), (3), and (7); 1997(4), including (13);
16. *Zhongshan* (《钟山》) 1983(4), including (10).

Bibliography

[1] ZHANG Zhigong (张志公) (Ed.) *Chinese Knowledge* (《汉语知识》). People's Education Press, 1979.

Note: In traditional Chinese culture, old age symbolizes rich knowledge and life experience; hence, a person's last name followed by "lao" (old) is an honorific title.

7 Varieties of *"yī p, jiù q"*

This chapter deals with four varieties of *"yī p, jiù q"*:

"gāng yī p, jiù q"
"cóng yī p, jiù q"
"zhème yī p, jiù q"
"zhǐyào yī p, jiù q"

As can be seen, these varieties each include a functional word that precedes *yī*, such as *gāng* ('just'), *cóng* ('since'), *zhème* ('so'), and *zhǐyào* ('so long as').

If *"yī p, jiù q"* is regarded as a simple form, the four forms mentioned earlier can be considered compound forms.

In some cases, *"yī...jiù..."* only indicates a successive relationship, while in other cases, it can imply a conditional or causal relationship as well. More details are presented in Chapter 2, Volume IV. Whatever the situation is, the simple form of *"yī p, jiù q"* indicates the primary relationship of successiveness, that is, one action following the other closely, whereas the compound forms can manifest a successive relationship as well as some other relationships, such as point in time, duration of time, modality, condition, and so on.

In some cases, the subject is absent in sentences in the form of *"yī p, jiù q,"* although usually it is present. Therefore, if S stands for the subject, the possible forms are "S *yī p, jiù q*"; "*yī p*, S *jiù q*"; "S_1 *yī p*, S_2 *jiù q*"; and so on. In this chapter, *"yī p, jiù q"* is used to refer to all the previously mentioned forms regardless of whether the subject is present or not.

In this chapter, sentences in the form of *"yī p, jiù q"* are limited to those with the cooccurrence of *yī* and *jiù*. In some sentences, *biàn* is used instead of *jiù*. In these forms, *biàn* and *jiù* are treated equally.

This chapter is based on the present author's article published in *Studies of the Chinese Language*. Due to space constraints, the sources of the examples in the article were omitted and cannot be recovered. All the examples with the sources provided are supplemented ones.

7.1 "gāng yī p, jiù q"

7.1.1 Occurrence of p immediately followed by the occurrence of q

The correlative conjunction "yī . . . jiù . . ." in "gāng yī p, jiù q" indicates that as soon as *p* occurs *q* takes place. The immediacy is further enhanced by the word *gāng*. Just as Professor LV Shuxiang put, "the gap between the two instants is too small to allow in even a hair."[1] The following are three examples:

(1) 刚一搭话，刘大头就哭起来，……
    Gāng   **yī . . . jiù . . .**   dāhuà,   Liú dàtóu   **jiù**   kū-qǐlái,. . .
    just   as soon as   respond LIU big head   begin to cry
    {No sooner had Big Head LIU responded than he started to cry . . . }

(2) 老队长真敏捷，刚一沾地，就顺势地一滚一翻，正好躲过车沟。
    Lǎo duìzhǎng   zhēn   mǐnjié,   **gāng**   **yī . . . jiù . . .**   zhāndì,   **jiù**
    old captain   really agile   just   touch the ground
    shùnshì
    de   yīgǔn-yīfān,   zhènghǎo   duǒ-guò   chēgōu.
    take advantage of an opportunity   SP   roll and turn   just right   avoid   groove
    {The old captain was so agile that no sooner had he fallen to the ground than he rolled and turned in the right direction to avoid the groove.}

(3) 田福堂的这个宝贝儿子刚一进城，就把干部子弟的派势都学会了。
    Tián Fútáng   de   zhè gè   bǎobèi   érzi   **gāng**   **yī . . . jiù . . .**   jìnchéng,   **jiù**
    TIAN Futang   SP   this CL precious son   just   as soon as   go into town
    bǎ   gànbu zǐdì   de   pàishì   dōu   xué-huì-le.
    BA   cadres' child   SP   manner   all   learn-PEF
    {No sooner had TIAN Futang's precious son gone to town than he learned the manner of the cadres' children.}

The presence of *gāng* before *yī* in the anterior clause highlights the starting time of the action in the posterior clause, which can be illustrated by the following example:

(4) 讨论会一结束，人们刚一走，庄文伊就克制不住他的激烈情绪了……
    Tǎolùnhuì   **yī . . . jiù . . .**   jiéshù,   rén-men   **gāng**   **yī . . . jiù . . .**   zǒu,
    seminar   as soon as   finish   person-PL just   as soon as   leave
    Zhuāng Wényī   **jiù**   kèzhì bù zhù   tā   de   jīliè   qíngxù   le . . .
    ZHUANG Wenyi   cannot restrain he   SP   intense emotion MP
    {After the seminar, no sooner had the people left than ZHUANG Wenyi lost control of his intense emotion . . . }

In this example, it is unlikely that ZHUANG Wenyi lost control of his emotion before the people left, therefore although the first two clauses are both introduced by *yī*, *gāng* is only present before *yī* in the second clause, which emphasizes that ZHUANG Wenyi lost control of his emotion as soon as people started to leave rather than as soon as the seminar ended. For this reason, *gāng* should not be present before *yī* in the first clause.

7.1.2 Indication of one-off realis actions

In general, the action in a sentence in the form of "*gāng yī p, jiù q*" is one-off. As soon as *p* took place, *q* occurred, i.e.,

> At a certain time, *gāng yī p, jiù q*.

However, if the same action occurs repeatedly under the same circumstances, then the occurrences are a normal phenomenon, that is,

> At Time A, *gāng yī p, jiù q*.
> + At Time B, *gāng yī p, jiù q*.
> + At Time C, *gāng yī p, jiù q*.
> = *Měiměi* ('each time') *gāng yī p, jiù q*.

In other words, in some cases, the actions in "*gāng yī p, jiù q*" can be recurrent ones. In these cases, *měi* ('every') is usually present, as in the following example:

(5) 每天清晨，溯源阁刚一开门，便会迎来不少顾客。
 Měi   tiān   qīngchén,   Sùyuángé   gāng   yī . . . biàn . . . kāimén,   biàn   huì
 every day   early morning Suyuange   just   as soon as   open   will
 yíng-lái   bùshǎo   gùkè.
 receive   many   customer
 {Every day as soon as Suyuange opens early in the morning it receives lots of customers.}

Sentences like (5) make a generalization based on the recurrent situation; therefore, although the generalization is about realis actions, it is also a prediction of the future—the same actions will continue to occur.

7.1.3 Synonyms of gāng in "gāng yī p, jiù q"

Synonyms of *gāng* in "*gāng yī p, jiù q*" include *gānggāng* and *cáigāng*. The forms "*gānggāng yī p, jiù q*" and "*cáigāng yī p, jiù q*" usually indicate that the actions are one-offs and realis, as in the following two examples:

(6) 汽车刚刚一到，他就来找我，带来师部曾参谋的信和一把小刀。
 Qìchē   gānggāng   yī . . . jiù . . .   dào,   tā   jiù   lái   zhǎo   wǒ,   dài-lái
 vehicle just   as soon as   arrive   he   come look for me   bring

Varieties of "yī p, jiù q"   155

shībù   Zēng cānmou   de   xìn   hé   yī bǎ   xiǎodāo.
division headquarters ZENG staff officer SP letter and a CL small knife
{No sooner had the car arrived than he came to me to give me a letter and a small knife from Staff Officer ZENG at the Division Headquarters.}

(7) 可是，他才刚一动脚，丫丫的祖父就喊了一声："你等等！"
Kěshì,   tā   cáigāng yī ... jiù ... dòngjiǎo,   Yāyā de zǔfù   jiù
however he just   as soon as   start to leave   Yaya SP paternal grandfather
hǎn-le   yī shēng   "Nǐ   děng-děng!"
yell-PEF a   CL   you   wait a moment
{However, hardly had he started to leave than Yaya's grandfather yelled, "Wait a second!"}

The word *gāngcái* or *fāngcái* means "only a moment ago"; therefore, *gāngcái* differs from *gāng* in meaning. The presence of *gāngcái* before *yī* in the anterior clause does not indicate the starting time of the action in the posterior clause, as in the following example:

(8) 我刚才一推门，就听见有人仰在椅背上一边理牌一边拉着调儿说："咱们这辈子就算彻底交代啰！" 是吧？
Wǒ **gāngcái** yī...jiù... tuī mén, jiù tīngjiàn yǒu rén yǎng zài
I   just now as soon as push door hear there be person lean back at
yǐbèi-shàng   yībiān ... yībiān ...   lǐpái   yībiān   lā-zhe
on the back of chair meanwhile   sort playing cards   stretch-PRG
diàor shuō: "Zán-men zhè bèizi jiù suàn chèdǐ jiāodài luo!" Shì ba?
voice say   we   this life just count thorough finish MP right MP
{Just now, as soon as I pushed the door open, I saw someone leaning back in a chair. While sorting his playing cards, he said in a stretched voice and strange tone, "That's the very end of our personal life!" Right?}

However, if *gāngcái* precedes the subject, *gāng* can be present as follows:

(9) 刚才，我刚一推门，就听见……
Gāngcái, wǒ gāng yī ... jiù ... tuī   mén, jiù tīngjiàn ...
just now   I   just   as soon as   push door   hear
{Just now, as soon as I pushed the door open, I heard ... }

7.1.4 Adverbs and le *in the posterior clause*

In sentences in the form of "*gāng yī p, jiù q*," the posterior clauses often include such adverbs as *lìjí* ('immediately') and *cùrán* ('suddenly') and the particle *le*. If *le* is absent, it can often be added. Moreover, *le* can occur at the end of or in the middle of the clause. The "*gāng yī ... jiù lìjí ... le*" sentence is a distinctive form emphasizing a point in time. The following are three examples:

(10) ......八个小时才下台，刚一摘口罩就（立即）晕倒了。
...Bā gè xiǎoshí cái xià tái, **gāng yī...jiù**... zhāi
eight CL hour late leave operating table just as soon as remove
kǒuzhào jiù (**lìjí**) yūn-dǎo-le.
mask immediately faint-PEF
{...The operation lasted as long as eight hours, and no sooner had (the surgeon) left the operating table and removed his mask than he fainted.}

(11) 方案刚一批下，县广播站便（立即）以头条新闻进行了报道。
Fāng'àn **gāng yī...biàn**... pī-xià, xiàn guǎngbōzhàn **biàn**
scheme just as soon as approve county broadcasting station
(**lìjí**) yǐ tóutiáo xīnwén jìnxíng-le bàodào.
immediately as top story do-PEF report
{No sooner had the scheme been approved than the county radio station reported it as the top story.}

(12) 两人的眼锋刚刚一碰，便像受惊的黄羊，猝然分开（了）。
Liǎng rén de yǎnfēng **gānggāng yī...biàn**... pèng, biàn xiàng
two person SP eyes just as soon as meet be like
shòujīng de huángyáng, **cùrán** fēnkāi-(le).
be frightened SP Mongolian gazelle suddenly separate-PEF
{No sooner had the eyes of the two people met than they went away like frightened Mongolian gazelles.}

In "*gāng yī... jiù lìjí... le*" sentences, the adverb *yǐjīng* can occur in place of *lìjí*, as in the following example:

(13) 那一小列队伍在远方的田埂上刚一出现，申丝的心就已经狂跳起来了。
Nà yī xiǎo liè duìwǔ zài yuǎnfāng de tiángěng-shàng **gāng**
that one small CL line of people in distant place SP on ridge in fields just
yī...jiù... chūxiàn, Shēn Sī de xīn jiù **yǐjīng** kuáng tiào-qǐlái-le.
as soon as appear SHEN Si SP heart already wild begin to beat-PEF
{No sooner had the small group of people appeared on the ridge in the fields in the distance than SHEN Si's heart began to beat wildly.}

What "*gāng yī... jiù yǐjīng... le*" sentences emphasize is that the action stated in the posterior *q* has already occurred before the situation stated in the anterior clause recurs and develops. In other words, those sentences emphasize that as soon as the situation in *p* occurs, the action in *q* starts. In this sense, *yǐjīng* and *lìjí* are similar in meaning. However, if the situation in *p* does not recur or develop, *lìjí* can occur in *q*, but *yǐjīng* cannot. Compare the following examples:

(14) a 任命刚一宣布，就立即有人巴结送礼了。
Rènmìng **gāng yī...jiù**... xuānbù, jiù **lìjí** yǒu rén
appointment just as soon as announce immediately there be person

bājie   sònglǐ-le.
fawn on   give a present-PEF
{No sooner had the appointment been announced than some people fawned over and gave presents (to the appointee).}

b 任命刚一宣布，就已经有人巴结送礼了。
Rènmìng   gāng yī   jiù   xuānbù,   jiù yǐjīng   yǒu   rén   bājie
appointment just as soon as   announce already there be person fawn on

sònglǐ-le.
give a present-PEF
{No sooner had the appointment been announced than some people fawned over and gave presents (to the appointee).}

(15) a 药刚一喝下，就立即吐了出来。
Yào   gāng   yī   jiù   hē-xià,   jiù   lìjí   tù-le-chūlái.
medicine just   as soon as drink   immediately   vomit up-PEF
{No sooner had the liquid medicine been taken than it was vomited up.}

*b 药刚一喝下，就已经吐了出来。
Yào   gāng   yī   jiù   hē-xià,   jiù   yǐjīng   tù-le-chūlái.
medicine just   as soon as drink   already   vomit up-PEF

7.1.5 *Comparisons among three forms in syntactic structure*

In syntactic structure, "*gāng yī p, jiù q*" is similar to "*yī p, jiù q*" but different from "*gāng p, jiù q*."

In general, "*gāng yī p, jiù q*" can be rewritten as "*yī p, jiù q*" or "*gāng p, jiù q*" with the meaning remaining roughly the same. For example, (16a) can be rewritten as (16b) or (16c).

(16) a 刚一开门，柜台前就出现了一长队人。
Gāng yī   jiù   kāimén, guìtái-qián   jiù   chūxiàn-le   yī   cháng
just   as soon as   open   in front of counter   appear-PEF   one   long
duì   rén.
line   person
{No sooner had (the store) opened than there appeared a long line of people in front of the counter.}

→b 一开门，柜台前就出现了一长队人。
Yī   jiù   kāimén, guìtái-qián   jiù   chūxiàn-le   yī   cháng duì   rén.
as soon as   open   in front of counter   appear-PEF   one long   line person
{There appeared a long line of people in front of the counter as soon as (the store) opened.}

→c 刚开门，柜台前就出现了一长队人。

Gāng kāimén, guìtái-qián   jiù   chūxiàn-le yī cháng duì rén.
just open   in front of counter early appear-PEF one long line person
{There appeared a long line of people in front of the counter soon after (the store) opened.}

However, in sentences in the form of "*gāng p, jiù q*," the anterior clause can include a complement showing time duration, such as *bùjiǔ* ('a short while') and *jǐtiān* ('a few days'), or a complement indicating distance, such as *bùyuǎn* ('a short distance') and *jǐbù* ('a few steps'). On the contrary, such complements cannot enter sentences in the form of "*gāng yī p, jiù q*" or "*yī p, jiù q*." Compare the following examples:

(17) a 刚开门，柜台前就……

Gāng . . . jiù . . .   kāimén,   guìtái-qián   jiù . . .
as soon as   open   in front of counter
{Soon after (the store) opened . . . in front of the counter.}

→b 刚开门不久，柜台前就……

Gāng . . . jiù . . .   kāimén   bùjiǔ,   guìtái-qián   jiù . . .
as soon as   open   a short while in front of counter
{Shortly after (the store) opened . . . in front of the counter.}

c 刚开门几分钟，柜台前就……

Gāng . . . jiù . . .   kāimén   jǐ   fēnzhōng,   guìtái-qián   jiù . . .
as soon as   open   a few minute   in front of counter
{Only a few minutes after (the store) opened . . . in front of the counter.}

(18) a 一开门，柜台前就……

Yī . . . jiù . . .   kāimén,   guìtái-qián   jiù . . .
as soon as   open   in front of counter
{As soon as (the store) opened . . . in front of the counter.}

→*b 一开门不久，柜台前就……

Yī . . . jiù . . .   kāimén   bùjiǔ,   guìtái-qián   jiù . . .
as soon as   open   a short while in front of counter

*c 一开门几分钟，柜台前就……

Yī . . . jiù . . .   kāimén   jǐ   fēnzhōng,   guìtái-qián   jiù . . .
as soon as   open   a few minute   in front of counter

(19) a 刚一开门，柜台前就……

Gāng   yī . . . jiù . . .   kāimén,   guìtái-qián   jiù . . .
just   as soon as   open   in front of counter
{No sooner had (the store) opened than . . . in front of the counter.}

Varieties of "yī p, jiù q" 159

→*b 刚一开门不久，柜台前就 ……
Gāng yī ...jiù... kāimén bùjiǔ, guìtái-qián jiù...
just as soon as open a short while in front of counter

*c 刚一开门几分钟，柜台前就 ……
Gāng yī ...jiù... kāimén jǐ fēnzhōng, guìtái-qián jiù...
just as soon as open a few minute in front of counter

Compare more examples:

(20) a 刚走出校门，他就发现有人盯梢。
Gāng ...jiù... zǒu-chū xiàomén, tā jiù fāxiàn yǒu rén dīngshāo.
as soon as walk out school gate he find there be person shadow
{He found someone shadowing him soon after he walked out the school gate.}

→b 刚走出校门不远，他就发现有人盯梢。
Gāng ...jiù... zǒu-chū xiàomén bù yuǎn, tā jiù fāxiàn yǒu
as soon as walk out school gate NEG far he find there be
rén dīngshāo.
person shadow
{He had not gone far from the school gate when he noticed someone shadowing him.}

→c 刚走出校门几十步，他就发现有人盯梢。
Gāng ...jiù... zǒu-chū xiàomén jǐshí bù, tā jiù fāxiàn yǒu
as soon as walk out school gate a few tens step he find there be
rén dīngshāo.
person shadow
{He had just taken a few dozen steps from the school gate when he noticed someone shadowing him.}

(21) a 一走出校门，他就发现有人盯梢。
Yī ...jiù... zǒu-chū xiàomén, tā jiù fāxiàn yǒu rén dīngshāo.
as soon as walk out school gate he find there be person shadow
{As soon as he walked out the school gate, he found someone shadowing him.}

→*b 一走出校门不远，他就发现有人盯梢。
Yī ...jiù... zǒu-chū xiàomén bù yuǎn, tā jiù fāxiàn yǒu rén
as soon as walk out school gate NEG far he find there be person
dīngshāo.
shadow

*c 一走出校门几十步，他就发现有人盯梢。
Yī ...jiù... zǒu-chū xiàomén jǐshí bù, tā jiù fāxiàn yǒu rén dīngshāo.
as soon as walk out school gate dozens step he find there be person shadow

(22) a 刚一走出校门，他就发现有人盯梢。

Gāng yī jiù zǒu-chū xiàomén, tā jiù fāxiàn yǒu rén dīngshāo.
just as soon as walk out school gate he find there be person shadow
{No sooner had he walked out the school gate than he found someone shadowing him.}

→*b 刚一走出校门不远，他就发现有人盯梢。

Gāng yī jiù zǒu-chū xiàomén bù yuǎn, tā jiù fāxiàn yǒu rén dīngshāo.
just as soon as walk out school gate NEG far he find there be person shadow

→*c 刚一走出校门几十步，他就发现有人盯梢。

Gāng yī jiù zǒu-chū xiàomén jǐshí bù, tā jiù fāxiàn yǒu rén dīngshāo.
just as soon as walk out school gate a few tens step he find there be person shadow

Some sentences in the form of "*gāng yī p, jiù q*" can be rewritten as "*yī p, jiù q*" but not as "*gāng p, jiù q*," whereas other sentences in the form of "*gāng yī p, jiù q*" can be rewritten as "*gāng p, jiù q*" but not "*yī p, jiù q*." The following are two examples:

(23) 他手刚一抓，这团子就被他捏成了一把碎渣子。

Tā shǒu **gāng yī jiù** zhuā, zhè tuánzi jiù bèi tā niē-chéng-le yī bǎ suì zhāzi.
he hand just as soon as take this ball PASSIVE him crush-PEF one handful broken crumbs
{No sooner had he taken the (rice bran and vegetable) ball than it broke into a handful of crumbs.}

(24) 没想到，他们刚一回去，老队长就被揪了出来。

Méi xiǎng-dào, tā-men **gāng yī jiù** huíqu, lǎo duìzhǎng jiù bèi jiū-le-chūlái.
NEG expect they just as soon as go back old captain PASSIVE pick out-PEF
{Unexpectedly, no sooner had they gone back than the old captain was picked out.}

In (23), "*yī p*" has the meaning of "*p yī xià*", and the action in the anterior clause acts as the cause of the action in the posterior clause. In other words, because "*gāng yī zhuā*" means "*gāng zhuā yī xià*", the anterior clause can be writtern as "*Tā shǒu yī zhuā . . .*" but not as "*Tā shǒu gāng zhuā . . .*" In (24), however, there is no causality between the two actions; the occurrences of the actions are only coincidentally close in time. For this reason, the anterior clause in (24) can be rewritten as "... *gāng huíqu*" but not as "... *yī huíqu*."

Even those sentences in the form of "*gāng yī p, jiù q*," where there is no causality between the actions exclude any complements denoting time duration or distance, sentences in the form of "*gāng p, jiù q*" can include such complements. Compare the following examples:

(25) a 他们刚回去，老队长就被揪了出来。
Tā-men gāng ...jiù... huíqu, lǎo duìzhǎng jiù bèi jiū-le-chūlái.
they   as soon as go back   old captain   PASSIVE pick out-PEF
{The old captain (was picked out) soon after they went back.}

→b 他们刚回去不久/半个月，老队长就……
Tā-men gāng ...jiù... huíqu bùjiǔ/ bàn gè yuè, lǎo duìzhǎng jiù...
then   as soon as go back a short while half CL month old captain early
{Shortly/only half a month after they went back, the old captain ...}

(26) a 他们刚一回去，老队长就被揪了出来。
Tā-men gāng yī ...jiù... huíqu, lǎo duìzhǎng jiù bèi jiū-le-chūlái.
they just   as soon as go back old captain   PASSIVE pick out-PEF
{No sooner had they gone back than the old captain was picked out.}

→*b 他们刚一回去不久/半个月，老队长就……
Tā-men gāng yī ...jiù... huíqu bùjiǔ/ bàn gè yuè, lǎo duìzhǎng jiù...
they just   as soon as go back a short while half CL month old captain

7.2 "*cóng yī p, jiù q*"

7.2.1 Continuation of q *since the occurrence of* p

Sentences in the form of "*cóng yī p, jiù q*" indicate that the action stated in the posterior clause has continued since the action in the anterior clause occurred. Indicating the starting point of the continuation, "*cóng yī p*" can include *qǐ* ('start'), that is, "*cóng yī p qǐ*." It is not clear when exactly the action in the posterior clause ends, and besides, words defining the ending point of the continuation cannot occur. However, it is known that till "now" or "the time of speaking" the action is still in progress and that it may continue. The following are two examples:

(27) 从一见面，她就喜欢这个叔叔。
Cóng yī ...jiù... jiànmiàn, tā jiù xǐhuān zhè gè shūshu.
since   as soon as meet   she like   this CL uncle
{She has been fond of this uncle ever since she first met him.}

(28) 好像从一生下来，我就想当个歌手，可总是当不上。
 Hǎoxiàng cóng yī jiù shēng-xiàlái, wǒ jiù xiǎng dāng gè gēshǒu,
 as if   since as soon as be born   I   want to be CL singer
 kě   zǒngshì dāng bù shàng.
 but always   cannot be
 {It seems that I've always wanted to be a singer since I was born, but I haven't been able to.}

In (27) and (28), the word *qǐ* can be added and placed at the end of the first clause respectively. The following example is a sentence with the word *qǐ*:

(29) 金秋从一踏进门起，便做东忙西地巴结干活。
 Jīnqiū cóng...qǐ yī biàn... tà-jìn mén qǐ, biàn
 Jinqiu since   as soon as step into door
 zuòdōng-mángxī de bājie gànhuó.
 busy oneself with chores SP diligent work
 {Jinqiu has been busying herself with all the chores since she stepped into the house.}

Besides, *cóng* and *yī* can be separated from each other by some syntactic constituents, for instance, the subject, as in the following two examples:

(30) 从她一踏上城市的街道，就觉得自己好像失去了根底，……
 Cóng tā yī jiù... tà-shàng chéngshì de jiēdào, jiù juéde zìjǐ
 since she as soon as step on   city   SP street   feel oneself
 hǎoxiàng shīqù-le gēndǐ,...
 as if   lose-PEF roots
 {She has had the feeling of having lost her roots ever since she set foot on the city streets.}

(31) 爹！从我一出生，您就教导我：尽忠报国。
 Diē! Cóng wǒ yī jiù... chūshēng, nín jiù jiàodǎo wǒ:
 dad since I as soon as be born   you   teach   me
 Jìnzhōng-bàoguó.
 serve one's country loyally
 {Dad! Since I was born, you have been teaching me to serve our country faithfully.}

Since "*cóng yī p, jiù q*" emphasizes that the action has continued up to now, it is quite different from "*gāng yī p, jiù q*" in meaning. Compare the following two examples:

(32) a 十年前参军。刚一参军，就当班长！
 Shí nián qián cānjūn. Gāng yī jiù... cānjūn, jiù dāng bānzhǎng!
 ten year before join the army just as soon as join the army be squad leader
 {(He) joined the army ten years ago. No sooner had (he) joined the army than (he) became a squad leader!}

Varieties of "yī p, jiù q" 163

b 十年前参军。从一参军，就当班长！
Shí nián qián cānjūn. Cóng yī ... jiù ... cānjūn, jiù dāng bānzhǎng!
ten year before join the army since as soon as join the army be squad leader
{(He) joined the army ten years ago. Ever since (he) joined the army, (he) has been a squad leader!}

With the word *gāng* emphasizing earliness, (32a) implies that "he" was outstanding as he became a squad leader as early as he joined the army. On the contrary, with the word *cóng* emphasizing continuation, (32b) indicates that "he" is mediocre as he has remained as a squad leader ever since he joined the army.

7.2.2 Continuability of the action in posterior clause

The form "*cóng yī p, jiù q*" indicates that the action in the posterior clause is realis and continuable. If the action in the posterior clause is not continuable, the sentence cannot be in the form of "*cóng yī p, jiù q*." Compare the following examples:

(33) a 从一上车，他就闭目养神。
Cóng yī ... jiù ... shàngchē, tā jiù bìmù-yǎngshén.
since as soon as get on the bus he refresh oneself by closing the eyes
{Since he got on the bus, he has been resting with his eyes closed.}

*b 从一上车，他就转身跳下。
Cóng yī ... jiù ... shàngchē, tā jiù zhuǎnshēn tiào-xià.
since as soon as get on the bus he turn around jump off

*c 从一上车，他就瞟我一眼。
Cóng yī ... jiù ... shàngchē, tā jiù piǎo wǒ yī yǎn.
since as soon as get on the bus he glance me one CL

Among these three sentences, (33a) is well formed, but (33b) and (33c) are ill formed because in (33a) the action *bìmù-yǎngshén* ('resting with his eyes closed') is continuable, while the action "*zhuǎnshēn tiào-xià*" ('turning around and jumping off') in (33b) and the action "*piǎo wǒ yī yǎn*" ('darting a glance at me') in (33c) are not continuable.

Unlike "*cóng yī p, jiù q*," which highlights the continuation of the action, "*gāng yī p, jiù q*" does not require the action to be continuable because it emphasizes the starting time of the action. All the following three examples are well formed:

(34) a 刚一上车，他就闭目养神。
Gāng yī ... jiù ... shàngchē, tā jiù bìmù-yǎngshén.
just as soon as get on the bus he refresh one's spirit by closing one's eyes
{As soon as he got on the bus, he closed his eyes and rested.}

b 刚一上车，他就转身跳下。

Gāng yī... jiù... shàngchē, tā jiù zhuǎnshēn tiào-xià.
just as soon as get on the bus he turn around jump off
{No sooner had he gotten on the bus than he turned around and jumped off (the bus).}

c 刚一上车，他就瞟我一眼。

Gāng yī... jiù... shàngchē, tā jiù piǎo wǒ yī yǎn.
just as soon as get on the bus he glance me one CL
{The moment he got on the bus, he darted a glance at me.}

7.2.3 *cóng* vs. *zìcóng*

In some sentences in the form of "*cóng yī p, jiù q*", *cóng* can be replaced by *zìcóng* ('ever since'), which indicates a relatively long duration of the action stated in the posterior clause, as in the following two examples:

(35) 自从一戴上右派帽子，雷治邦就沉默寡言了。

Zìcóng *yī... jiù...* dài-shàng yòupài màozi, Léi Zhìbāng *jiù*
ever since as soon as wear rightist hat LEI Zhibang
chénmò-guǎyán le.
taciturn MP
{LEI Zhibang has been taciturn ever since he was labeled as a rightist.}

(36) 自从一进了省城踏进表姑家的门，葛金秋就觉得自己变得畏畏缩缩而又十分迟呆。

Zìcóng *yī... jiù...* jìn-le shěngchéng tà-jìn biǎogū
ever since as soon as enter-PEF provincial capital step into cousin
jiā de mén, Gě Jīnqiū *jiù* juéde zìjǐ biàn de wèiwèi-suōsuō
house SP door GE Jinqiu feel oneself become SP be timid
ér yòu shífēn chídāi.
and also very slow
{GE Jinqiu has had the feeling that she became timid and slow ever since she came to the provincial capital and stepped into her cousin's house.}

In cases in which an action lasts for a long time, either *zìcóng or cóng* can be used, although there are some minor differences between the two words in function. However, if the duration is short, only *cóng* can be used. Compare the following two examples:

(37) a 从一回家，他就抚育弟妹苦挣扎。

Cóng *yī... jiù...* huíjiā, tā jiù fǔyù dìmèi kǔ zhēngzhá.
since as soon as return home he nurture younger sibling hard struggle
{He has struggled to nurture his younger siblings since he returned home.}

b 自从一回家，他就抚育弟妹苦争扎。
Zìcóng yī ... jiù ... huíjiā, tā jiù fǔyù dìmèi kǔ zhēngzhá.
ever since as soon as return home he nurture younger sibling hard struggle
{He has struggled to nurture his younger siblings ever since he returned home.}

In (37), either zìcóng or cóng can be used, for his struggling to nurture his siblings might have lasted for a few years, which is quite a long time. Compared with cóng, zìcóng is emphatic about the long duration. Compare the following examples:

(38) a 从一回家，他就大声叫喊要吃饭。
Cóng yī ... jiù ... huíjiā, tā jiù dàshēng jiàohǎn yào chīfàn.
since as soon as return home he loud voice yell want to eat
{Since he got home, he has been shouting for food.}

*b 自从一回家，他就大声叫喊要吃饭。
Zìcóng yī ... jiù ... huíjiā, tā jiù dàshēng jiàohǎn yào chīfàn.
ever since as soon as return home he loud voice yell want to eat

It is unlikely for anyone to have shouted for food for more than a few hours; therefore, (38a) is appropriate, but (38b) is not.

Synonyms of *cóng* and *zìcóng* include *dǎ*, *dǎcóng*, and *cóngdǎ*, which are more colloquial. The following are two examples:

(39) 打我一工作起，就一个心眼干、干，可到头儿落着个啥？
Dǎ ... qǐ wǒ yī ... jiù ... gōngzuò qǐ, jiù yī gè xīnyǎn gàn, gàn,
since I as soon as work one CL intention do do
kě dàotóur lào-zhe gè shá?
however in the end get-PRG CL what
{Since I started to work, I've been putting my heart and soul into the work, but what have I gotten in the end?}

(40) 从打代表团脚后跟一落地，就涌来大批各界人物，……
Cóngdǎ dàibiǎotuán jiǎohòugēn yī ... jiù ... luòdì, jiù yǒng-lái dà-pī
since delegation heel as soon as land pour in a large number of
gè jiè rénwù, ...
every field people
{Since the delegation landed, a large number of people from all circles have poured in ...}

7.2.4 Negative form of "cóng yī p, jiù q"

In "*cóng yī p, jiù q*," the anterior clause indicates that what is stated in *q* has always been the case since the occurrence of *p*. To negate the posterior clause, "*(yīzhí)méi ... guò*" ('never been the case since ...') can be used.

The "*cóng yī . . . jiù yīzhí . . .*" sentence and the "*cóng yī . . . jiù méi . . . guò*" sentence can be regarded as two distinctive forms that emphasize the duration of an action. For example:

(41) a 从一上车，他就一直坐着。
        Cóng yī . . . jiù . . . shàngchē, tā jiù yīzhí zuò-zhe.
        since as soon as get on the bus he all the time sit-PRG
        {He has been sitting all the time since he got on the bus.}

    →b 从一上车，他就没走动过。
        Cóng yī . . . jiù . . . shàngchē, tā jiù méi zǒudòng-guò.
        since as soon as get on the bus he NEG move-EXP
        {He hasn't moved since he got on the bus.}

(42) a 从一见面，我们就一直争吵。
        Cóng yī . . . jiù . . . jiànmiàn, wǒ-men jiù yīzhí zhēngchǎo.
        since as soon as meet we all the time argue
        {We have been arguing all the time since we met.}

    →b 从一见面，我们的争吵就没停止过。
        Cóng yī . . . jiù . . . jiànmiàn, wǒ-men de zhēngchǎo jiù méi tíngzhǐ-guò.
        since as soon as meet we argue NEG stop-EXP
        {We have never stopped arguing since we met.}

The following are two more examples:

(43) ……这女的从一上山来，蒙住的脸，就一直朝着那个湖南兵。
        . . . *Zhè nǚ-de **cóng yī . . . jiù . . .** shàngshān-lái, méng-zhù de liǎn, jiù*
        this woman since as soon as come up the hill cover SP face

        yīzhí cháo-zhe nà gè Húnán bīng.
        all the time face-PRG that CL Hunanese soldier
        {The woman's masked face has been facing the Hunanese soldier since she came up the hill.}

(44) 我对不起你。从你一过门，我就没对你笑过。
        *Wǒ duìbùqǐ nǐ. **Cóng** nǐ *yī . . . jiù . . .* guòmén,*
        I feel sorry you since you as soon as move into the husband's household upon marriage

        wǒ jiù méi duì nǐ xiào-guò.
        I NEG at you smile-EXP
        {I apologize. I have never smiled at you since you married into my family.}

Moreover, either the "*cóng yī . . . jiù yīzhí . . .*" sentence or the "*cóng yī . . . jiù méi . . . guò*" sentence emphasizes that the action/situation has always been consistent, but the affirmative and negative forms can carry different tones, that is, commendatory or depreciatory. For example:

(45) a 从一参军，就当班长。
   Cóng   yī ... jiù ...   cānjūn,   jiù   dāng   bānzhǎng.
   since   as soon as   join the army be   squad leader
   {(He) has been a squad leader since (he) joined the army.}

   b 从一参军，就没当过大头兵。
   Cóng   yī ... jiù ...   cānjūn,   jiù   méi   dāng-guò   dàtóubīng.
   since   as soon as   join the army   NEG   be-EXP   private
   {(He) has never been a private since (he) joined the army.}

Between the two sentences, (45a) has the depreciatory implication that someone being a squad leader all the time is incapable, while (45b) implies that someone who has never been a private is capable.

Besides, if the posterior clause is affirmative in form, *kāishǐ* ('start') can be present in the place where *yīzhí* would occur, or *kāishǐ* (*le*) can simply act as the predicate of the posterior clause. Even so, the sentence still means that the action/situation stated in the posterior clause has always been consistent. For example:

(46) 从一当上干部，他就开始追求享受了。
   Cóng   yī ... jiù ...   dāng-shàng   gànbu, tā   jiù   kāishǐ   zhuīqiú   xiǎngshòu   le.
   since   as soon as   be   cadre   he   start pursue   enjoyment MP
   {His pursuit of pleasure began the moment he became a cadre.}

The following is an example:

(47) 自从婚礼一结束，他的不幸就开始了。结婚虽然已经三个月，但他还是等于一个光棍。
   Zìcóng   hūnlǐ   yī ... jiù ...   jiéshù, tā de bùxìng   jiù   kāishǐ-le. Jiéhūn
   ever since wedding as soon as   end   he SP misfortune start-PEF   get married
   suīrán   yǐjīng   sān   gè   yuè,   dàn tā háishì   děngyú   yī   gè   guānggùn.
   though   already three CL   month but he still   equal   one CL   bachelor
   {His misfortune began the moment his wedding ended. Though he has been married for three months, he is no different from a bachelor.}

Both examples indicate that the action/situation stated in the posterior clause has been consistent since it started and will continue: "pursuing pleasure" in (46) and "misfortune" in (47).

7.2.5 Differences between "cóng yī p, jiù q" and "cóng p, jiù q" in structure

In terms of syntactic structure, there are differences between the two forms of "*cóng yī p, jiù q*" and "*cóng p, jiù q*."

First, the sentences in the form of "*cóng yī p, jiù q*" can all be rewritten as "*yī p, jiù q*," but some of them cannot be rewritten as "*cóng p, jiù q*." The following is an example:

168　*Varieties of "yī p, jiù q"*

(48) 从一进门，他就发现这还是独身女子的宿舍。
　　Cóng yī......jiù......jìnmén,　　tā jiù fāxiàn zhè háishì dúshēn nǚzǐ　de sùshè.
　　since as soon as　enter the room he　find　this still　single　woman SP dormitory
　　{He discovered that this was also a dormitory room for single women the moment he entered the room.}

In the above example, "*cóng yī jìnmén*" ('from the moment he entered the room') can be rewritten as "*yī jìnmén*" ('as soon as [he] entered the room') but not as **cóng jìnmén* ('*from entering the room').

Second, some postpositional elements, such as *hòu* ('after'), *yǐhòu* ('later'), and *yǐlái* ('since') cannot occur in sentences in the form of "*cóng yī p, jiù q*" but can be present in "*cóng p, jiù q*" as in (49). However, if (49) is to be rewritten as "*cóng yī p, jiù q*," it will be (50), where the propositional word *hòu* is removed.

(49) 从堂吉诃德被俘后，我就想借此寻找他的踪迹。
　　Cóng Tángjíhēdé bèi　　fú　　hòu, wǒ jiù　xiǎng jiè cǐ　xúnzhǎo tā
　　since Don Quixote PASSIVE capture after I　early want use this look for he
　　de　zōngjì.
　　SP　trace
　　{Ever since Don Quixote was captured, I have sought to trace him.}

(50) 从堂吉诃德一被俘，我就想借此寻找他的踪迹。
　　Cóng Tángjíhēdé yī......jiù......bèi　　fú,　　wǒ jiù xiǎng jiè cǐ　xúnzhǎo
　　since Don Quixote as soon as　PASSIVE capture I　　want use this look for
　　tā de　zōngjì.
　　he SP　trace
　　{Ever since Don Quixote was captured, I have sought to trace him.}

7.3 "*zhème yī p, jiù q*"

7.3.1 *Reference to a specific situation with* zhème

Sentences in the form of "*zhème yī p, jiù q*" emphasize that the action stated in the posterior clause occurs in a specific situation summarized and referred to by *zhème*. The situation is usually stated in the preceding context. The following are two examples:

(51) （可是我又总这样想，……）这么一想，我的气就消了。
　　(Kěshì wǒ yòu　　zǒng　zhèyàng xiǎng,...) Zhème yī......jiù......
　　however I　on the contrary always such　think　so　as soon as
　　xiǎng, wǒ de qì　jiù xiāo-le.
　　think　I　SP anger　disappear-PEF
　　{[But on the other hand, I always think that . . .] Every time I think that way, my anger will drain from me right away.}

(52) （黑妹在一旁话中有话地说：……）小韦无可奈何地一笑，
说："这么一讲，我就只好不走了。"
(Hēimèi   zài   yīpáng   huàzhōng-yǒuhuà   de   shuō: ...)   Xiǎowěi
dark skinned girl on   side   have implications   SP   say   Xiaowei
wúkě-nàihé   de   yī   xiào, shuō: "**Zhème** *yī*   *jiù*   jiǎng, wǒ   *jiù*
have no alternative SP   once smile say   so   as soon as   say   I
zhǐhǎo   bù   zǒu   le."
have to   NEG   leave   MP
{[On the side, the dark-skinned girl, said, in a tone of voice suggesting something
. . .] With a helpless smile, Xiaowei said, "Since you have said that, I'll have no
choice but to stay."}

What "I" in (51) really think and what Xiaowei in (52) says are mentioned in
the preceding context. Ellipsis dots are used because the original texts are too
long.

In some cases, there is no antecedent sentence before the sentence in the form
of "*zhème yī p, jiù q*." The circumstance denoted by *zhème* can be shown by a
certain act, for instance, gestures, as in the following example:

(53) 有些事情看起来是不沾边，用你两只手这么一摆弄，像捏饺子皮一样，
也就沾到一块去了。
Yǒuxiē shìqing kàn qǐlái shì   bù   zhānbiān, yòng nǐ   liǎng zhī shǒu **zhème**
some   matter   seem   COP NEG be related by your two   CL hand so
yī   *jiù*   bǎinòng,   xiàng   *yīyàng*,   niē   jiǎozipí   yīyàng,
as soon as   fiddle with   be like   press dumpling wrapper
yě   *jiù*   zhān-dào-yīkuài-qù-le.
also   stick together-PEF
{Some matters are seemingly unrelated to one another, but as soon as you have
fiddled with them, like pressing dumpling wrappers, they are now connected.}

7.3.2 Focus of "*zhème yī p*"

In sentences in the form of "*zhème yī p, jiù q*," "*zhème yī p*" emphasizes the summarized situation in which *q* occurs but not the starting time or the duration of *q*.

The most generalized form of "*zhème yī p*" is "*zhème yī lái*," in which *lái* has no concrete meaning even though it is a verb. For example, "*zhème yī xiǎng*" in (51) and "*zhème yī jiǎng*" in (52) can be both rewritten as "*zhème yī lái*". The following are three examples:

(54) （她学着捣蛋了……）这么一调皮，不知怎么，就有许多同学和她交上
了朋友，和她一起捣蛋。
(Tā   xué-zhe   dǎodàn-le...)   **Zhème** *yī*   *jiù*   tiáopí,   bù zhī zěnme,
she   learn-PRG   be naughty-PEF   such   as soon as   be naughty   somehow
jiù   yǒu   xǔduō   tóngxué   hé   tā   jiāo-shàng-le péngyǒu,   hé   tā
        there be   many   schoolmate with her   make friends-PEF   with her

170   *Varieties of "yī p, jiù q"*

    yīqǐ   dǎodàn.
    together be naughty
    {[She has learned to be mischievous . . .] As she has become so naughty, somehow, many of her classmates have become her friends and made mischief together.}

(55) （这两件事加起来，李书记就给我扣了帽子，……）这么<u>一</u>分析批判，<u>就</u>把我到手的房子批判走了。
    Zhè liǎng jiàn shì   jiā-qǐlái, Lǐ shūjì   jiù gěi wǒ kòu-le   màozi, . . .)
    these two CL matter add up LI secretary just on me put-PEF hat
    Zhème yī   . . . jiù . . . *fēnxī   pīpàn, <u>jiù</u> bǎ wǒ dàoshǒu   de*
    so   as soon as analyze criticize BA me be in one's possession SP
    fángzi pīpàn   zǒu-le.
    house   criticize go-PEF
    {[After linking those two matters, Secretary LI put a label on me . . .] Right after I was analyzed and criticized like that, I lost the house that I had gotten.}

(56) ……这么<u>一</u>收拾，峰峰<u>就</u>焕然一新了……
    . . . ***Zhème yī . . . jiù*** . . . *shōushi, Fēngfēng <u>jiù</u> huànrán-yīxīn-le . . .*
    such   as soon as clean up Fengfeng   take on a new look-PEF
    { . . . With such a cleanup, Fengfeng has taken on a new look . . . }

Among the three examples, "*zhème yī tiáopí*" in (54), "*zhème yī fēnxī pīpàn*" in (55), and "*zhème yī shōushí*" in (56) can all be replaced by "*zhème yī lái.*" In actual language use, "*zhème yī lái, jiù . . .*" is commonly used. The following are two more examples:

(57) （事有凑巧，……）这么<u>一</u>来，他<u>便</u>更有些惶惶然了。
    *(Shìyǒucòuqiǎo, . . .)   **Zhème yī . . . <u>biàn</u>**. . . lái, tā <u>biàn</u> gèng*
    something happened by coincidence so   as soon as   he   more
    yǒuxiē huánghuángrán-le.
    slightly frightened and restless-PEF
    {[It happened by coincidence . . .] And as a result of this, he was more frightened and restless.}

(58) （这你们难道想不到？……）这么<u>一</u>来，歌舞团<u>就</u>更成了无源之水了。
    *(Zhè nǐ-men nándào xiǎng bù dào? . . .) **Zhème yī . . . jiù** . . . lái,*
    this   you-PL surely not cannot foresee   such   as soon as
    gēwǔtuán   <u>jiù</u> gèng chéng-le   wúyuánzhīshuǐ   le.
    singing and dancing troupe   more become-PEF water without source MP
    {[Can't you think of that? . . .] In this way, the singing and dancing troupe has even less to be based on.}

In general, the highly generalized form of "*zhème yī lái*" is subjectless. Compare the following two examples:

(59) a 这么一忙，我就很少跟他通信了。
Zhème yī *jiù* máng, wǒ jiù hěnshǎo gēn tā tōngxìn le.
such as soon as busy I seldom with him correspond MP
{I have rarely corresponded with him since I became busy.}

b 我这么一忙，就很少跟他通信了。
Wǒ zhème yī *jiù* máng, jiù hěnshǎo gēn tā tōngxìn le.
I such as soon as busy seldom with him correspond MP
{I have rarely corresponded with him since I became busy.}

Between the two examples, (59a) can be rewritten as "*zhème yī lái, wǒ jiù . . .*", whereas (59b) cannot be rewritten as "*wǒ zhème yī lái, jiù . . .*." The following is an example:

(60) 气氛这么一变，边晓玲就觉得太扫兴。
Qìfēn **zhème yī** *jiù* biàn, Biān Xiǎolíng *jiù* juéde tài sǎoxìng.
atmosphere such as soon as change BIAN Xiaoling feel too disappointed
{BIAN Xiaoling felt very disappointed as soon as such a change of atmosphere occurred.}

In the above example, "*zhème yī biàn*" cannot be rewritten as "*zhème yī lái.*"

In some cases, a subject can occur and precede "*zhème yī lái.*" in which *lái* is a highly abstract summary of the situation in the preceding context and needs to be stressed phonetically. Moreover, *lái* carries the meaning of messing things up or being unreasonably troublesome. Compare the following examples:

(61) a 他这么一闹，会就没法开下去了。
Tā zhème yī *jiù* nào, huì jiù méifǎ kāi-xiàqu le.
He such as soon as make trouble meeting be impossible continue MP
{The meeting can't continue since he has made trouble like this.}

→b 他这么一来，会就没法开下去了。
Tā zhème yī *jiù* lái, huì jiù méifǎ kāi-xiàqu le.
he such as soon as behave meeting be impossible continue MP
{The meeting can't continue because of such behavior of his.}

The following is an example:

(62) 他冲我一乐："过年了，哪那么多事。来两嗓子，我给你拉胡。"他这么一说，学生们就一齐拍手。
Tā chòng wǒ yī lè: "Guònián-le, nǎ nàme duō
he toward me once smile new year come-PEF definitely not so much
shì. Lái liǎng sǎngzi, wǒ gěi nǐ lāhú." Tā **zhème yī** *jiù*
consideration give two CL I for you play huqin he so as soon as
shuō, xuéshēng-men *jiù* yīqí pāishǒu.
say student-PL together applaud

{He smiled at me and said, "With New Year just around the corner, there is no need to have too much consideration. Sing a couple of lines, and I will accompany you on the *huqin*." As soon as he said this, the students all clapped.}

In this example, "*shuō*" cannot be rewritten as "*lái*." If it was "*la*", the word *lái* would be stressed and mean creating a disturbance, but this is not what *shuō* means.

7.3.3 Causality between p and q

The situation emphasized by "*zhème yī p, jiù q*" is often realis, and causality exists between *p* and *q*; that is, the situation stated in the anterior clause causes the event stated in the posterior clause. In other words, "*zhème yī p, jiù q*" equals "*yīnwèi/ yóuyú zhème yī p, jiù q*." The following are three examples:

(63) （算了算了，…… 大姐你情愿背那丑名声就自家背去，…… ）这么一赌气，以后妹麦<u>就</u>再也不管大姐的事了。

(Suàn-le suàn-le, ...dàjiě nǐ qíngyuàn bēi nà chǒu míngshēng
forget it forget it eldest sister you be willing carry that shameful reputation
jiù zìjiā bēi qu. ...) **Zhème** <u>yī</u> ... <u>jiù</u> ... dǔqì, yǐhòu Mèimài
just oneself carry go so as soon as be in a fit of pique after Meimai
<u>jiù</u> zài yě bù guǎn dàjiě de shì le.
not ever again care eldest sister SP business MP

{[Forget it, forget it . . . big sister, if you are willing to bear that shameful reputation, then keep it to yourself . . .] As Maimei said this in a fit of pique, she no longer cared about her big sister's business.}

(64) （老校长拉着儿子的手说：…… ）老父亲这么一吩咐，他<u>就</u>变了态度，又是给律师们递烟，又是请律师们喝工夫茶。

(Lǎo xiàozhǎng lā-zhe érzi de shǒu shuō: ...) Lǎo fùqin **zhème** <u>yī</u> ... <u>jiù</u> ...
old principal take-PRG son SP hand say old father such as soon as
fēnfù, tā <u>jiù</u> biàn-le tàidù, yòushì ... yòushì gěi lǜshī-men dì yān,
tell he change-PEF attitude both . . . and . . . to lawyer-PL pass cigarette
yòushì qǐng lǜshī-men hē gōngfuchá.
invite lawyer-PL drink Gongfu tea

{[The old principal took his son's hand and said . . .] As his old father (the old principal) had told him to do so, he changed his attitude and offered cigarettes and Gongfu tea to the lawyers.}

(65) 陈宝明这么一不言声，其他人也<u>就</u>猜出个七八分。

Chén Bǎomíng **zhème** <u>yī</u> ... <u>jiù</u> ... bù yánshēng, qítā rén yě <u>jiù</u>
CHEN Baoming so as soon as NEG speak other people indeed
cāi-chū gè qībā fēn.
guess correctly CL seven or eight one tenth

{As CHEN Baoming became silent, the others then guessed 70% or 80% correctly.}

Among the three examples, *yīnwèi* ('because') can be added and placed before *zhème* in (63), and *yóuyú* ('because') can be added and placed before the subject in (64) and (65), respectively.

In sentences in the form of "*zhème yī p, jiù q*," "*jiù q*"—indicating the result—can be worded as "*kě jiù p le*" ('really *p*') in some cases. In "*kě jiù p le*," *kě* is a modal adverb, which emphasizes the decisive influence on the result by the cause with a touch of exaggeration. The following are two examples:

(66) 他仔细这么一看呀，可就禁不住高兴得心花怒放了。
Tā zǐxì **zhème** <u>yī</u> ... <u>jiù</u> ... *kàn ya, kě* <u>jiù</u> *jīn bù zhù gāoxìng*
he carefully such as soon as look MP really cannot help happy
de xīnhuā-nùfàng le.
SP wild with joy MP
{He couldn't help but go wild with joy as soon as he had a careful look.}

(67) （我提醒他，……）可是，这么一来，我可就引火烧身了。
(Wǒ tíxǐng tā, ...) Kěshì, **zhème** <u>yī</u> ... <u>jiù</u> ... *lái, wǒ kě* <u>jiù</u>
I remind him however so as soon as I really
yǐnhuǒ-shāoshēn le.
ask for trouble MP
{[I reminded him ...] But, by so doing, I was asking for trouble.}

In some cases, besides emphasizing a specific situation, "*zhème yī p, jiù q*" can also infer an irrealis result. That is to say, "*zhème yī p*" is the basis for the inference "*jiù q*." The following is an example:

(68) 要不是早年练过武艺，有身好骨头，这么一折腾，没准就归了西。
Yào bù shì zǎonián liàn-guò wǔyì, yǒu shēn hǎo gǔtou, **zhème**
if not early years practice-EXP martial art have CL good bone so
yī ... <u>jiù</u> ... *zhēteng, méizhǔn* <u>jiù</u> *guīxī-le xī.*
as soon as suffer maybe die-MP
{If he had not practiced martial arts in his early years and is in good shape, he might have died after such an upheaval.}

7.3.4 Synonyms of *zhème* in "*zhème yī p, jiù q*"

In sentences in the form of "*zhème yī p, jiù q*," *zhème* can be replaced by its synonym, for instance, *zhèyàng, nàme*, or *zhè*.

In the following three examples, *zhèyàng* is used as a synonym of *zhème*.

(69) 这样一想，就觉得还是隐忍为上。
Zhèyàng <u>yī</u> ... <u>jiù</u> ... *xiǎng, jiù juéde háishi yǐnrěn wéi shàng.*
so as soon as think feel had better quietly endure COP Best
{Thinking that way, (someone) realized that endurance would be the best strategy.}

(70) 这办法当然好嘛！这样一搞，就肯定没耍奸溜滑的人了。

Zhè bànfǎ   dāngrán hǎo ma! **Zhèyàng** *yī* . . . *jiù* . . . gǎo, jiù kěndìng méi
this method certainly good MP   so   as soon as   do   surely there not be
shuǎjiān-liūhuá   de rén   le.
cheat   SP person MP
{This is of course a good idea! This way, no one will be able to cheat.}

(71) 大概是出于对知识的实用主义观点吧，郝师傅把两个光头孩子领来了，除了免费剃头还请我为他们辅导小学算术。这样一来，就多少有点交情了。

Dàgài   shì chūyú   duì zhīshi de shíyòngzhǔyì guāndiǎn   ba,
probably COP come from about knowledge SP pragmatism   point of view MP
Hǎo shīfu   bǎ liǎng gè guāngtóu háizi lǐng-lái-le, chúle   miǎnfèi
HAO master BA two   CL shaved head child bring-PEF besides not charge
tìtóu   hái qǐng wǒ wèi tā-men fǔdǎo xiǎoxué   suànshù.
shave the head also ask me for them tutor elementary school arithmetic
Zhèyàng *yī* . . . *jiù* . . . lái, jiù duōshǎo yǒu diǎn jiāoqing le.
so   as soon as   more or less have some friendship MP
{Presumably from a pragmatic point of view of knowledge, Master HAO brought in his two kids with a shaved head. In addition to (asking someone else to give his kids) free haircuts, he also asked me to tutor them in elementary school arithmetic. We have sort of become friends after we did those things.}

In some cases, *nàme* is used to indicate a past event, as in the following two examples:

(72) 所以，女娲走后，果然州河涨水，那两个泥人就变成了有血有肉的人，那么一配合，就儿孙孙全生下来了。

Suǒyǐ, nǚwā   zǒu hòu, guǒrán Zhōuhé
therefore Nvwa (a goddess in Chinese mythology) leave after as expected Zhou River
zhǎngshuǐ, nà liǎng gè nírén   jiù biànchéng-le yǒuxiě-yǒuròu
water rises that two CL clay figurine then become-PEF have flesh and blood
de rén, **nàme** *yī* . . . *jiù* . . . pèihé, jiù érér-sūnsūn quán shēng-xiàlái-le.
SP person so   as soon as   unite   descendant   all be born-PEF
{Therefore, after Nvwa left, as expected, the water in the Zhou River rose, and then the two clay figurines became flesh-and-blood people. After (the two of them) were united that way, their children and grandchildren were all born.}

(73) 你今天在台子上那么成功的一表演，得！好多人便向我打听你的情况，……

Nǐ jīntiān zài táizi-shàng **nàme** chénggōng de *yī* . . . *biàn* . . . biǎoyǎn, dé!
you today at on stage   such   successful SP as soon as   perform see
Hǎoduō rén **biàn** xiàng wǒ dǎtīng nǐ de qíngkuàng, . . .
many person to   me   inquire you SP information
{You see, so many people have asked me about you . . . as soon as you gave such a successful performance on stage today.}

Moreover, *zhè* can be also used as a synonym of *zhème*, that is, "*zhè yīlái*." The following are two examples:

(74) （只是这婚配，有点"冲喜"的味道，……）这一结婚，就给天明拴上了已婚的徽号，……
(Zhǐshì zhè hūnpèi, yǒu diǎn
only this marry there be a little
"chōngxǐ" *de*
save someone's life with a wedding in the hope that the joyous occasion will SP
ward off the illness
wèidào,...) Zhè yī jiù jiéhūn, jiù gěi Tiānmíng shuān-shàng-le yǐhūn de
taste so as soon as marry give Tianming put-PEF married SP
huīhào,...
sign
{[But this marriage has a bit of the taste of "curing illness" . . .] Such a wedding has put a "married" badge on Tianming.}

(75) （如今大空死了，说是畏罪自杀，……）大空这一死，金狗我看也就活不了多久了！
(Rújīn Dàkōng sǐ-le, shuō shì wèizuì-zìshā,...)
now Dakong die-PEF say COP commit suicide to escape punishment
Dàkōng zhè yī jiù sǐ, Jīn'gǒu wǒ kàn yě jiù huó bù liǎo
Dakong so as soon as die Jin'gou I see also cannot live
duō jiǔ le!
much long (time) MP
{[Now Dakong is dead, and it is said that he committed suicide to escape punishment . . .] With Dakong's death, I don't think Jin'gou can survive long!}

7.4 "zhǐyào yī p, jiù q"

7.4.1 p as a condition for q

Sentences in the form of "*zhǐyào yī p, jiù q*" emphasize that the anterior clause acts as the condition for the posterior clause.

There are two types of conditions: hypothetical prediction and factual conclusion. The former is a prediction about what will happen, although it has never happened before. The latter is a conclusion of the recurrent connections between the actions in the two clauses. The following are two examples, between which the former indicates a hypothetical prediction, and the latter indicates a factual conclusion based on facts.

(76) 我们只要一倒手，……几十万票子就哗哗淌来了，……
Wǒ-men zhǐyào yī jiù dǎoshǒu,... jǐshí-wàn piàozi
we so long as as soon as change hands hundreds of thousands of money
jiù huā-huā tǎng-lái le,...
gush pour in MP
{Once we resell (it) . . . hundreds of thousands (of *yuan*) will pour into our pockets . . . }

176 *Varieties of "yī p, jiù q"*

(77) 时至今日，只要一想到那晚上的事，他的心就发颤……
Shízhìjīnrì, **zhǐyào** <u>yī</u>...<u>jiù</u>... xiǎng-dào nà wǎnshàng de shì, tā de
to this day so long as as soon as think of that night SP matter he SP
xīn   <u>jiù</u> fāchàn...
heart   tremble
{Even to this day, his heart will tremble as soon as he thinks of what happened that night...}

Moreover, in sentences in the form of "*zhǐyào yī p, jiù q,*" *zhǐyào* and *yī* can be separated by the subject or some other syntactic constituents, as in the following two examples:

(78) 只要这几家人一搬迁，就准备立即炸山。
Zhǐyào zhè   jǐ   jiā   rén   <u>yī</u>...<u>jiù</u>... bānqiān, jiù zhǔnbèi
so long as this several household person as soon as evacuate   plan
lìjí   zhà   shān.
immediately blast mountain
{Once these households have been evacuated, the mountain will be blasted.}

(79) 只要她一出去，一宿就没有响动了。
Zhǐyào   tā   <u>yī</u>...<u>jiù</u>... chūqu, yī   xiǔ   <u>jiù</u> méiyǒu
so long as she as soon as go out whole night   there not be
xiǎngdòng   le.
sound and movement MP
{As long as she was not in, there was no sound for the whole night.}

In some sentences in the form of "*zhǐyào yī p, jiù q,*" some inferential words, such as *néng* ('can'), *huì* ('will'), *yào* ('will'), and so on, can occur in "*jiù q.*" The following are two examples:

(80) ……恍惚她并没有走，还在我身边，只要一低头，就能瞧见她。
...Huǎnghū   tā   bìng   méiyǒu zǒu,   hái   zài   wǒ
in a trance she   on the contrary NEG leave still at   my
shēnbiān,   **zhǐyào**   <u>yī</u>...<u>jiù</u>... dītóu,   <u>jiù</u> néng
a place next to someone so long as as soon as lower the head   can
qiáojiàn tā.
see   her
{...I felt in a trance that she had not gone but was still by my side, and that once I looked down, I could see her.}

(81) 从那以后，只要一听到他柔和和深沉的声音，她就要检查检查自己的门窗是不是关严了……。
Cóng   nà   yǐhòu, **zhǐyào**   <u>yī</u>...<u>jiù</u>... tīng-dào tā róuhé hé shēnchén de
from   that after so long as as soon as hear   his soft and deep SP
shēngyīn,   tā   <u>jiù</u> yào   jiǎnchá-jiǎnchá zìjǐ   de   mén chuāng
voice   she   will check-REDP   oneself SP   door windows

shì bù shì   guān-yán-le . . .
whether   close tightly-PEF
{From then on, whenever she heard his soft and deep voice, she would check to see whether her door and windows had been closed tightly . . . }

7.4.2 Replacement of zhǐyào in "zhǐyào yī p, jiù q" indicating a hypothetical prediction

If a sentence in the form of "*zhǐyào yī p, jiù q*" indicates a hypothetical prediction, *zhǐyào* can be replaced by *rúguǒ* ('if') but cannot be replaced by *měidāng/měiféng* ('every time'). The following are two examples, in which *zhǐyào* can be replaced by *rúguǒ* but not *měidāng/měiféng*:

(82) 那俩娃娃，手持柳条鞭，猪倌似的，在我们左左右右盯住，好像<u>只要一</u>不如意，<u>就</u>准备再猛抽一气。
Nà   liǎ   wáwa, shǒu chí   liǔtiáo biān,   zhūguān   shìde,   zài
that two   child hand hold willow stick whip swineherd as if   at
wǒ-men zuǒzuǒ-yòuyòu dīng-zhù,   hǎoxiàng   **zhǐyào**
our   side   keep a close watch as if   so long as
<u>yī</u> . . . <u>jiù</u> . . . bù   rúyì,   jiù   zhǔnbèi zài   měng chōu yī   qì.
as soon as   NEG be not as one wishes   plan   again violent whip one CL
{The two children, with wicker whips in their hands, were watching us closely like swineherds, as if they were going to lash out again once they were unhappy.}

(83) 主任，让我们暂时上白班吧，<u>只要一</u>抓住流氓，我们<u>就</u>恢复倒班。
Zhǔrèn,   ràng   wǒ-men zànshí   shàng báibān ba, **zhǐyào**   <u>yī</u> . . . <u>jiù</u>
director   allow us   temporarily   take day shift MP so long as   as soon as
zhuā-zhù   liúmáng,   wǒ-men   <u>jiù</u>   huīfù   dǎobān.
catch   hooligan   we   resume   shift
{Director, please allow us to take the day shift for the time being, and we'll resume shifts once we have caught the hooligans.}

In (82), "as long as they were unhappy" can be rewritten as "if they were unhappy" but not as "every time they were unhappy," and in (83), "as long as the hooligans were caught" can be rewritten as "if the hooligans were caught" but not as "every time the hooligans were caught." Therefore, *zhǐyào* in (82) and (83) can be replaced by *rúguǒ* but not by *měidāng*.

In actual language use, there are sentences in the form of "*rúguǒ yī p, jiù q*," in which *rúguǒ* can be substituted by *zhǐyào*. The following are two examples:

(84) <u>如果</u>德国人一出现疏忽，<u>就</u>会立即给这些前锋钻空子，……
Rúguǒ Déguórén <u>yī</u> . . . <u>jiù</u>   chūxiàn shūhū,   jiù   huì   lìjí
if   German   as soon as   appear   be careless will   immediately
gěi   zhèxiē   qiánfēng   zuān kòngzi, . . .
PASSIVE   these   striker   take advantage
{Once the Germans are careless, these strikers will immediately take advantage of their mistake.}

178 *Varieties of "yī p, jiù q"*

(85) 同志们，我们的任务是艰巨的，我们推车时，如果<u>一</u>不小心，<u>就</u>会掉下去。
Tóngzhì-men, wǒ-men de rènwù shì jiānjù de, wǒ-men tuī chē
comrade-PL we SP task COP arduous MP we push cart
shí, **rúguǒ** <u>yī</u> ... <u>jiù</u> ... bù xiǎoxīn, <u>jiù</u> huì diào-xiàqù.
time if as soon as NEG be careful will fall off
{Comrades, our task is arduous. If we are not careful when "pushing the carts", we will "fall off (the cliff)".}

In the above two examples, *rúguǒ* can be replaced by *zhǐyào*.

It should be noted that *zhǐyào* indicates that a hypothetical situation is regarded as a specific condition. If only a hypothesis is needed to act as the ground for the inferential result, *rúguǒ* is more appropriate than *zhǐyào*, as in the following example:

(86) 如果<u>一</u>败，事情<u>就</u>将成定局，为父的纵然三头六臂，也无回天之力了。
Rúguǒ <u>yī</u> ... <u>jiù</u> ... bài, shìqing <u>jiù</u> jiāng chéng dìngjú, wéifù de
if as soon as fail matter will become foregone conclusion father
zòngrán sāntóu-liùbì, yě wú huítiān-zhīlì
even if three heads and six arms still not have power to save a desperate situation
le.
MP
{If it fails, the outcome will be a foregone conclusion. Dad wouldn't be able to reverse the defeat even if I were a superman.}

Obviously, the speaker of (86) puts emphasis on the prediction of the outcome rather than the condition for the outcome.

7.4.3 Replacement of *zhǐyào* in *"zhǐyào yī p, jiù q"* indicating a factual conclusion

If a sentence in the form of *"zhǐyào yī p, jiù q"* indicates a conclusion based on facts, *zhǐyào* can be replaced by *měidāng/měiféng*, as in the following three examples:

(87) 我们移民队走到哪里，歌就唱到哪里。只要我们<u>一</u>唱，男男女女、老老少少<u>就</u>立时把我们围起来。听着听着，他们的嘴也动起来，像是早就会唱这支歌，又像是早就想唱这支歌。
Wǒ-men yímíndùi zǒu-dào nǎlǐ, gē jiù chàng dào nǎlǐ.
we relocatee group travel to anywhere song then sing arrive anywhere
Zhǐyào wǒ-men <u>yī</u> ... <u>jiù</u> ... chàng, nánnán-nǚnǚ, lǎolǎo-shàoshào <u>jiù</u>
so long as we as soon as sing men and women old and young
lìshí bǎ wǒ-men wéi-qǐlái. Tīng-zhe tīng-zhe, tā-men de zuǐ yě
immediately BA us surround listen-PRG listen-PRG they SP lips also
dòng-qǐlái, xiàng shì zǎo jiù huì chàng zhè zhī gē, yòu xiàng shì zǎo
start to move as if COP early early can sing this CL song also as if COP early
jiù xiǎng chàng zhè zhī gē.
early want sing this CL song
{Wherever our relocatee group traveled to, we sang, and once we started to sing, people—men and women, old and young—would immediately surround us. As they were listening (to our songs), their lips also started to move, as if they knew

Varieties of "yī p, jiù q" 179

how to sing the songs a long time ago, and as if they had long wanted to sing them.}

(88) 有那么几天，她只要一闭上眼，立刻就能浮现火车上那几张幸灾乐祸的脸，还有那些不堪入耳的话。

Yǒu nàme jǐ tiān, tā **zhǐyào** yī...jiù... bì-shàng yǎn,
there be such several day she so long as as soon as close eye
likè jiù néng fúxiàn huǒchē-shàng nà jǐ zhāng
immediately can emerge on train that several CL
xìngzāi-lèhuò de liǎn, háiyǒu nàxiē
take pleasure in other people's misfortune SP face and those
bùkān-rù'ěr de huà.
intolerable to the ear SP words

{For a few days, once she closed her eyes, she could immediately recall the gloating look on those faces (she saw) on the train, as well as those unbearable words.}

(89) 可她只要一看到俊俊娃那双细长迷人的眼睛，就满心喜欢哩。

Kě tā **zhǐyào** yī...jiù... kàn-dào Jùnjùn wá nà shuāng
but she so long as as soon as see Junjun's child that pair
xìcháng mírén de yǎnjing, jiù mǎnxīn-xǐhuān li.
narrow and long charming SP eye filled with love MP

{But once she saw Junjun's child's long charming eyes, she would be filled of love.}

In actual language use, there are some sentences in the form of "*měidāng/měiféng yī p, jiù q*," in which *měidāng/měiféng* can be replaced by *zhǐyào*, as in the following two examples:

(90) 我所讨厌的破习惯就是每当第二节预备铃一响，大便就必在肛门附近挤压，大有非排不可之势，因此总得迟到几分钟。

Wǒ suǒ tǎoyàn de pò xíguàn jiù shì **měidāng** dì'èr jié yùbèilíng
I PAP hate SP bad habit just COP every time second class first bell
yī...jiù... xiǎng, dàbiàn jiù bì zài gāngmén fùjìn jǐyā, dà yǒu
as soon as ring feces inevitably at anus near squeeze great there be
fēi pái bù kě zhī shì, yīncǐ zǒng děi chídào jǐ fēnzhōng.
must be discharged SP potential therefore always need be late several minute

{The bad habit I hated was that every time the first bell for the second class went off, feces were inevitably squeezed near my anus and were determined to come out, so I was always a few minutes late (for class).}

(91) 时间长了，每逢怀西往旁边一蹲，老喇嘛就递给他一张小氆氇，……

Shíjiān cháng le, **měiféng** Huáixī wǎng pángbiān yī...jiù... dūn, lǎo lǎma
time long MP every time Huaixi on side as soon as squat old lama
jiù dì gěi tā yī zhāng xiǎo pǔlu,...
hand to him one piece small woolen fabric produced in Tibet for making blankets, garments, etc.

{After a long time, whenever Huaixi squatted next to him, the old lama would hand him a small pulu ... }

180 *Varieties of "yī p, jiù q"*

The word *měidāng* or *měiféng* emphasizes that something has happened so often that it has become a rule, and *zhǐyào* highlights a rule as a condition, therefore *zhǐyào* and *měidāng/měiféng* have something in common. There is also similarity between "*měiměi gāng yī p, jiù q*"—which has been mentioned in Section 7.1.2—and "*zhǐyào yī p, jiù q*"; therefore, *zhǐyào* can also be added, i.e., "*měiměi zhǐyào gāng yī p, jiù q*."

7.4.4 Replacement of zhǐyào in "zhǐyào yī p, jiù q" indicating a factual conclusion

If a sentence in the form of "*zhǐyào yī p, jiù q*" indicates a conclusion based on facts, *zhǐyào* can be replaced by *rúguǒ* in some cases, which can be accounted for in the following three aspects:

First, in some cases, although the event stated in the anterior clause with "*zhǐyào yī p, jiù q*" has occurred many times, it is just coincidental. In these cases, *zhǐyào* cannot be replaced by *rúguǒ*, as in the following example:

(92) a 只要一搬家，天就下雨。（真怪！）

Zhǐyào   yī ... jiù ...   bānjiā, tiān jiù   xiàyǔ.   (Zhēn guài!)
so long as   as soon as   move   sky   rain   really strange
{Every time we moved houses, it started to rain. [Strange!]}

*b 如果一搬家，天就下雨。（真怪！）

Rúguǒ   yī ... jiù ...   bānjiā, tiān jiù   xiàyǔ.   (Zhēn guài!)
if   as soon as   move   sky   rain   really strange

Second, in some cases, the event stated in the anterior clause of "*zhǐyào yī p, jiù q*" only reoccurs at a specific time, particularly at the time of speaking. In these cases, *zhǐyào* cannot be replaced by *rúguǒ*, as in the following example:

(93) a 看看，只要一下班，他的精神就来了。真不像话！

Kàn-kàn,   **zhǐyào**   yī ... jiù ...   xiàbān,   tā de jīngshen jiù lái le.
look-REDP so long as as soon as get off work he SP energy   come MP
Zhēn   bù   xiànghuà!
really NEG   reasonable
{Look, as soon as he has finished work, he is refreshed. What a shame!}

*b 看看，如果一下班，他的精神就来了。真不像话！

Kàn-kàn,   rúguǒ yī ... jiù ...   xiàbān,   tā de jīngshen jiù lái le.
see-REDP   if   as soon as   get off work he SP energy   come MP
Zhēn   bù   xiànghuà!
really NEG   reasonable

Third, the event stated in the anterior clause in some sentences in the form of "*zhǐyào yī p, jiù q*" is a general rule that summarizes the realis and predicts the irrealis. Only in these sentences can *rúguǒ* replace *zhǐyào*, as in the following examples:

(94) a 这一向，他只要一不顺心，就拿孩子出气！
Zhè yīxiàng,   tā **zhǐyào**   *yī*...*jiù*...   bù   shùnxīn, *jiù*   ná   háizi
this period of time he so long as as soon as   NEG satisfied   use child
chūqì!
vent one's anger
{Recently, whenever anything goes against his wishes, he will vent his anger on the child!}

→b 这一向，他如果一不顺心，就拿孩子出气！
Zhè yīxiàng,   tā rúguǒ yī...*jiù*... bù   shùnxīn, *jiù* ná háizi chūqì!
this period of time he if   as soon as   NEG satisfied   on child vent one's anger
{Recently, if anything goes against his wishes, he will vent his anger on the child!}

The following are two two examples:

(95) 他要是一上场，球场上就变成战场了，……
Tā **yàoshì**   *yī*...*jiù*...   shàngchǎng, qiúchǎng-shàng   *jiù*   biànchéng
he if   as soon as   go on court   on basketball court   become
zhànchǎng   le,...
battleground MP
{Once he goes on the basketball court, the court will become a battleground...}

(96) 水汉子们倘一歇憩，便要寻快活，嘴巴哗哗敞开了口，没遮没拦谈女人，相互拿老婆来开心。
Shuǐhànzi-men **tǎng** *yī*...*biàn*... xiēqì, *biàn* yào   xún   kuàihuo, zuǐba
boatman-PL   if   as soon as rest   will look for happy   mouth
huā-huā chǎngkāi-le kǒu,   méizhē-méilán tán   nǚrén, xiānghù   ná
noisy   open-PEF opening straightforward talk woman with each other use
lǎopo lái kāixīn.
wife   PAP happy
{Once the crew members take a rest, they will look for fun by bluntly talking about women and making fun of each other's wife.}

Both *yàoshì* in (95) and *tǎng* in (96) are synonyms of *rúguǒ*. Although (95) and (96) carry a hypothetical tone, they are similar to the ones that indicate a conclusion based on facts.

However, based on facts, it should be pointed out that "*zhǐyào yī p, jiù q*," indicating a conclusion, is still different from "*zhǐyào yī p, jiù q*," indicating a hypothetical inference, for *zhǐyào* in the former can be replaced by *měidāng* or *měiféng*, and by *rúguǒ*. For instance, *yàoshì* in (95) and *tǎng* in (96) can be replaced by *rúguǒ* and by *měidāng* or *měiféng*.

7.4.5 Correlation within "zhǐyào yī" and "jiù"

In sentences in the form of "*zhǐyào yī p, jiù q*," "*zhǐyào yī*" is a compound form, but both *zhǐyào* and *yī* correlate with *jiù*, as in the following example:

(97)   a 只要一有空，我就动笔修改。

Zhǐyào   yī   jiù ...   yǒukòng,   wǒ   jiù   dòngbǐ   xiūgǎi.
so long as as soon as   have time   I   start to write   revise
{I'll start to revise it once I have time.}

However, *yī*, by itself, correlates with *jiù*, so does *zhǐyào*, as in the following two examples:

b 一有空，我就动笔修改。

Yī ... jiù ...   yǒukòng,   wǒ   jiù   dòngbǐ   xiūgǎi.
as soon as   have time   I   start to write   revise
{As soon as I'm free, I'll start to revise it.}

c 只要有空，我就动笔修改。

Zhǐyào ... jiù ...   yǒukòng,   wǒ   jiù   dòngbǐ   xiūgǎi.
so long as   have time   I   start to write   revise
{As long as I'm free, I'll start to revise it.}

In sentences in the form of "*zhǐyào yī p₁, jiù q₁, yī p₂, jiù q₂*," the correlation between *yī* and *jiù* is more visible, as in the following example:

(98)   只要一听到他的声音，她就会心跳；一看见他的眼睛，她就会脸红。

Zhǐyào   yī ... jiù ...   tīngdào tā de shēngyīn, tā   jiù   huì   xīntiào;
so long as   as soon as   hear   he SP voice   she   will   heart beat fast

yī ... jiù ...   kànjiàn   tā   de   yǎnjing,   tā   jiù   huì   liǎnhóng.
as soon as   see   he   SP   eye   she   will   blush
{Whenever she heard his voice, her heart would beat fast, and whenever she saw his eyes, her face would blush.}

In sentences in the form of "*zhǐyào yī p₁, yī p₂, jiù q*," the correlation between *zhǐyào* and *jiù* is more visible, as in the following example:

(99)   现在，只要车一停，门一开，他俩便可以大步流星回家去。

Xiànzài,   **zhǐyào**   chē   yī ... biàn ...   tíng,   mén   yī ... biàn ...   kāi,
now   so long as   bus   as soon as   stop   door as soon as   open

tāliǎ   biàn   kěyǐ   dàbùliúxīng   huí   jiā   qù.
the two of them   can   with long strides   return   home   go
{Now, the two of them can walk back home with long strides so long as the bus stops and the door opens.}

Summary

First, some functional words, such as *gāng, cóng, zhème, zhǐyào*, and so on, can occur at the beginning of sentences in the form of "*yī p, jiù q*"; thus, four varieties are formed, that is, "*gāng yī p, jiù q*," emphasizing the starting time of *q*; "*cóng yī p, jiù q*," stressing the duration of *q*; "*zhème yī p, jiù q*," highlighting the specific situation for *q*; and "*zhǐyào yī p, jiù q*," underlining the condition for *q*. Compared with the simple form "*yī p, jiù q*," these compound forms not only indicate a successive relationship between *p* and *q* but also have different semantic emphases. For example:

(100) a 一接触，就感到这个人不简单。
    Yī . . . jiù . . . jiēchù,   jiù gǎndào zhè gè rén bù jiǎndān.
    as soon as come into contact feel this CL person NEG ordinary
    {(Someone) felt that this person wasn't ordinary as soon as they came into contact with him.}

→b 刚一接触，就感到这个人不简单。
    Gāng yī . . . jiù . . . jiēchù,   jiù gǎndào zhè gè rén bù jiǎndān.
    just as soon as come into contact feel this CL person NEG ordinary
    {(Someone) felt that this person wasn't ordinary upon their very first contact with him.}

→c 从一接触，就感到这个人不简单。
    Cóng yī . . . jiù . . . jiēchù,   jiù gǎndào zhè gè rén bù jiǎndān.
    since as soon as come into contact feel this CL person NEG ordinary
    {(Someone) has had the feeling that this person isn't ordinary since the first contact with him.}

→d 这么一接触，就感到这个人不简单。
    Zhème yī . . . jiù . . . jiēchù,   jiù gǎndào zhè gè rén bù jiǎndān.
    such as soon as come into contact feel this CL person NEG ordinary
    {(Someone) felt that this person was extraordinary as soon as they came into contact with him in such a way.}

→e 只要一接触，就感到这个人不简单。
    Zhǐyào yī . . . jiù . . . jiēchù,   jiù gǎndào zhè gè rén bù jiǎndān.
    so long as as soon as come into contact feel this CL person NEG ordinary
    {(Anyone) will feel that this person is extraordinary once they come into contact with him.}

If two functional words cooccur in sentences in the form of "*yī p, jiù q*," the sentence has two different semantic emphases, as in the following example:

(101) （他曾闪过卖基宅的念头。）刚这么一想，就收回去了……
(Tā céng shǎn-guò mài jīzhái de niàntou.) Gāng
he once suddenly occur-EXP sell residence base SP thought just
zhème yī jiù xiǎng, jiù shōu-huíqu-le…
such as soon as think take back-PEF
{[He once flirted with the idea of selling his residence base.] He gave up the idea the moment it occurred to him…}

An in-depth investigation into various compound forms can help to make clear their subtle differences among them and to enhance the understanding of sentences in the form of "*yī p, jiù q*."

Second, the use of functional words is subject to the logical basis of the sentence. A complex sentence in the form of "*yī p, jiù q*" can indicate multiple other relationships in addition to the successive relationship or only one or even no other relationships. Whether a functional word can be used, what functional word can be used, and whether functional words can cooccur all depend on whether there is a corresponding relationship within the sentence. Some sentences only allow the occurrence of some particular functional words, and other sentences do not allow the presence of any functional words mentioned in this chapter. The following are two examples:

(102) 我给咱做彩娥的工作！彩娥一同意，就把俊武家的缺口打开了！
Wǒ gěi zán zuò Cǎi'é de gōngzuò! Cǎi'é yī jiù tóngyì, jiù bǎ
I for us do Cai'e SP task Cai'e as soon as agree BA
Jùnwǔ jiā de quēkǒu dǎkāi le!
Junwu's house SP breakthrough open MP
{Let me persuade Cai'e! If Cai'e agrees, Junwu's house will no longer be an obstacle!}

(103) 一楼第一展厅陈列的是清代山水画的临摹画展。一踏进去，就有一派清逸、宁静、淡泊的山光水色。
Yīlóu dìyī zhǎntīng chénliè de shì qīngdài shānshuǐhuà
first floor first exhibition hall display SP COP Qing Dynasty landscape painting
de línmóhuà zhǎn. Yī jiù tà-jìnqù, jiù yǒu yī pài
SP exhibition of imitations paintings as soon as step in there be one CL
qīngyì, níngjìng, dànbó de shānguāng-shuǐsè.
fresh and refined peaceful light in color SP landscape of mountains and waters
{The First Exhibition Hall on the first floor displays an exhibition of imitations of Qing Dynasty landscape paintings. As soon as (visitors) step in, they will see fresh, tranquil, and light-colored mountains and waters.}

Example (102) can include *zhǐyào* or *rúguǒ* but not *gāng*, *cóng*, or *zhème*. However, none of these words can be present in (103).

Third, the use of functional words is subject to the pragmatic requirements of the particular sentence. Modern Chinese grammar has an important feature: particular functional words can be present or absent, but in general, they are absent unless absolutely necessary. In other words, they are present only when they are needed pragmatically. Between the following two examples, (104a) is a rewrite of (104b).

(104) a 一扬起脸，就被划了一刀。
Yī ... jiù ... yáng-qǐ   liǎn, jiù   bèi   huá-le   yī   dāo.
as soon as   raise   face   PASSIVE   cut   one   knife
{As soon as (someone) looked up, (they) got a knife cut in the face.}

→b 刚一扬起脸，就被划了一刀。
Gāng   yī ... jiù ... yáng-qǐ liǎn, jiù   bèi   huá-le   yī   dāo.
just   as soon as   raise   face   PASSIVE   cut   one   knife
{(Someone) got a knife cut in the face the moment (they) looked up.}

The presence of *gāng*, which emphasizes the starting point of the action, gives the reader the impression of the quickness of *q* in (104b). The following are another two examples, between which (105a) is a rewrite of (105b).

(105) a 厂子一投产，他就调来当了书记。
Chǎngzi yī ... jiù ... tóuchǎn,   tā jiù diào-lái dāng-le shūjì.
factory   as soon as   start production he transfer be-MP   secretary
{As soon as the factory started production, he was transferred from elsewhere to be the secretary.}

→b 自从厂子一投产，他就调来当了书记。
Zìcóng chǎngzi yī ... jiù ... tóuchǎn,   tā jiù diào-lái dāng-le shūjì.
since   factory as soon as   start production he transfer be-MP   secretary
{He has been the secretary of the factory ever since he was transferred from elsewhere when the factory started production.}

The presence of *zìcóng*, which emphasizes the duration, gives the reader the impression that the duration of *q* is very long in (105b).

In short, in actual language use, a specific word is added because the speaker feels the need to place a special emphasis on a nonbasic semantic relationship. The speaker's feeling is related to their mental activities at the moment.

Fourth, functional words that can be present in the form of "*yī p, jiù q*" are not limited to the ones discussed in this chapter. The following are some examples:

A: *shāo* + "*yī ... jiù ...*" → "*shāo yī p, jiù q*." The following are two examples:

(106) 稍一挣扎，它就从那双抖得发软的脚下穿走了。
Shāo   yī ... jiù ... zhēngzhá, tā jiù cóng nà shuāng dǒu   de
slightly as soon as   struggle   it from that pair   tremble SP
fāruǎn de   jiǎo-xià chuān-zǒu-le.
feel limp SP underfoot pass through-PEF
{With a little effort it slipped through the trembling feet.}

(107) …… 稍一动摇，就会使这次战役一败涂地。

… Shāo yī … jiù … dòngyáo, jiù huì shǐ zhè cì zhànyì
slightly as soon as waver will make this CL campaign
yībài-túdì.
suffer a devastating defeat
{ … (We) would completely lose the campaign once we wavered, even slightly.}

B: *dāng* + "*yī…jiù…*" → "*dāng yī p, jiù q.*" The following are two examples:

(108) …… 当她一抬头，便从他那黑汪的两眼中读懂了他文里的所有文字。

… Dāng tā yī … biàn … táitóu, biàn cóng tā nà hēiwāng de
when she as soon as look up from his that black and watery SP
liǎng yǎn zhōng dú-dǒng-le tā wén-lǐ de suǒyǒu wénzì.
two eye LOC understand-PEF his in article SP all word
{… As soon as she looked up, she understood everything he wrote from his black watery eyes.}

(109) 当她一走进教室，听班长发出"起立"的口令，耳畔就回荡起陶行知的一句名言……

Dāng tā yī … jiù … zǒu-jìn jiàoshì, tīng bānzhǎng fāchū "qǐlì" de
when she as soon as walk into classroom hear monitor give stand up SP
kǒulìng, ěr-pàn jiù huídàng-qǐ Táo Xíngzhī de yī jù míngyán …
instruction around ear reverberate TAO Xingzhi SP one CL well-known saying
{As soon as she walked into the classroom and heard the instruction of "stand up" from the monitor, a famous saying by TAO Xingzhi echoed in her ears …}

C: *děng* + "*yī…jiù…*" → "*děng yī p, jiù q.*" The following are two examples:

(110) 等论文答辩一结束，我就开始编写，写一本用比较的方法阐述的经济史。

Děng lùnwén dábiàn yī … jiù … jiéshù, wǒ jiù kāishǐ biānxiě, xiě yī běn
until thesis defend as soon as end I start compile write one book
yòng bǐjiào de fāngfǎ chǎnshù de jīngjìshǐ.
use Compare SP method elaborate SP economic history
{Once the thesis defense finishes, I will start to compile a book on economic history, described by means of a comparative approach.}

(111) 等这场风浪一过，就该轮到他回船队基地休假了。

Děng zhè chǎng fēnglàng yī … jiù … guò, jiù gāi
until this CL wind and wave as soon as be over be one's turn
lún-dào tā huí chuánduì jīdì xiūjià le.
be one's turn he return fleet base take a vacation MP
{It will be his turn to go back to the fleet base for a vacation once the storm is over.}

In conclusion, these compound forms have their special features that "*gāng yī p, jiù q*" and other forms discussed in this chapter do not have. More work needs to be done to give a full and detailed picture of these three forms.

Varieties of "yī p, jiù q" 187

NB Some examples in this chapter are cited from literary works, political essays, articles, and so on. The sources are listed as follows:

1. *A Report on a Disfigurement Case* (《一桩毁容案的报告》) by ZHU Chunlin, including Examples (83) and (104b);
2. *Baihuazhou* (《百花洲》) 1987(1), including (11) and (105b);
3. *Changjiang Literature* (《长江》) 1983(4), including (30); 1984(1), including (63); 1987(1), including (58) and (86);
4. *Changcheng* (《长城》) 1985(3), including (99);
5. *Changpian Xiaoshuo Xuankan* (《长篇小说专辑》) 1984(2), including (2);
6. *Chinese* for junior middle school students, Book 1, including (87);
7. *Chronicle of Bingwu (1966) and Dingwei (1967)* (《丙午丁未记事》) by YANG JIANG, including (49);
8. *Chunfeng* (《春风》) 1983(2), including (24) and (66); 1986(6), including (39);
9. *Dangdai* (《当代》) 1982(3), including (79); 1982(4), including (95); 1983(3), including (55); 1984(3), including (4) and (8); 1983(5), including (51); 1984(1), including (74); 1986(1), including (27) and (103); 1986(6), including (60) and (96);
10. *Fiction Monthly* (《小说月报》) 1982(2), including (29) and (36); 1985(8), including (28); 1997(5), including (71); 1997(6), including (88);
11. *Flower City* (《花城》) 1985(1), including (13); 1985(4), including (10), (48), and (77); 1989(1), including (64);
12. *Harvest* (《收获》) 1982(4), including (81); 1983(6), including (57) and (69); 1984(4), including (54); 1986(2), including (106) and (110); 1987(1), including (31), (72), and (75); 1988(4), including (101);
13. *Kunlun* (《昆仑》) 1986(1), including (53) and (76);
14. *Lotus* (《芙蓉》) 1984(2), including (52); 1985(2), including (109); 1987(1), including (68), (90), and (91);
15. *October* (《十月》) 1985(1), including (44);
16. *Old Stories in a Small City* (《小城旧事》) by TANG Jifu, including (62);
17. *People's Literature* (《人民文学》) 1982(3), including (16a); 1986(4), including (98);
18. *Popular Stories* (《大众小说》) 1987(1), including (40);
19. *Selected Stories* (《小说选刊》) 1985(8), including (5);
20. *The Dream of a Small City* (《小城的梦》) by TANG Jifu, including (82);
21. *The Ordinary World* (《平凡的世界》) by LU Yao (路遥), including (3), (23), (47), (70), (78), and (102);
22. *The Star* (《星星》) by ZHENG Yanying, including (108);
23. *Xiao Shuo Jia* (《小说家》) 1982(2), including (35); 1984(3), including (43); 1985(3), including (73) and (80);

24 *Zhongpian Xiaoshuo Xuankan* (《中篇小说选刊》) 1986(1), including (12); 1986(2), including (7); 1987(2), including (6) and (107); 1994(6), including (65); 1997(3), including (1), (56), and (89).

Bibliography

[1] LV Shuxiang(吕叔湘). *Sketches of Chinese Grammar* (《中国文法要略》). The Commercial Press, 1956.

Appendix
Notes on the special formats

Examples

1. There are two types of example sentences in this book: (1) sentences created by the author and (2) sentences cited from literary works, political essays, newspapers, textbooks, articles, and so on.
2. Examples are presented in a four-component format as follows:

   Line 1: original Chinese sentence
   Line 2: italicized pinyin symbols
   Line 3: English translation on a morpheme-by-morpheme basis
   Line 4: English translation of the entire sentence (included within curly brackets)

3. The words are segmented and labeled according to the *Modern Chinese Dictionary* (7th edition) and XING Fuyi's *Modern Chinese Grammar*. The meaning of each single word is based on the context of the sentence.
4. The sources of the examples are presented at the end of each chapter alphabetically. If more than one example is cited from the same source, they are presented chronologically. According to the original text, the sources of the citations of literary magazines contain such information as the magazine name in English and Chinese, the publishing year, the issue number, the number of the example in the chapter. For instance, "*October*（《十月》）1982(1), including (12)", which means that Example (12) in this chapter is cited from the First Issue of a Chinese literary magazine named *October*（《十月》）published in 1982. The sources of the citations from political essays, novels, newspapers, textbooks, articles, and so on just contain the information about the title/caption in English and Chinese, the author's name and the number of the example, for the publisher and publishing year are sporadically present in the original book. For instance, "*Other Tales of the Flying Fox*（《飞狐外传》）by JIN Yong (金庸), including (19)," which means Example (19) in this chapter is cited from a novel, whose title is translated into Other Tales of the Flying Fox from the original Chinese title 飞狐外传 in Chinese, written by JIN Yong.

5   To make the entire sentence translation easily understood, the translators add some information. The added information is supplemented (1) according to the source of the cited example, (2) according to the context of the example itself, and (3) for the sake of English grammar. The added information does no harm to the original sentence.
6   As mentioned earlier, the English translation of an entire sentence is included within curly brackets {}, in which the supplements in the original sentences contained in the example are included within the square brackets [], the author's supplements are included within angle brackets <>, and the translators' supplements are included within round brackets ().
7   The underlined words in the original examples are indicated by **bold** letters in pinyin.

Proper nouns

Proper nouns, including persons' names, place names, and institution names, are Romanized in standard Chinese Pinyin.

Upper-case letters are used in the spelling of a person's family name in pinyin, following the order of "surname + given name," as is conventional in Chinese.

Notation

The asterisk (*) (typically appearing before an example and its literal translations) indicates the ungrammaticality or unacceptability of the example.

The question mark (?) indicates that the grammaticality or acceptability of the expression is questionable.

The plus sign (+) indicates that the expression or construction exists.

The minus sign (−) indicates that the expression or construction does not exist.

Index

alternative complex sentence 117, 124, 125, 127, 128, 129, 130, 139, 141, 148, 150; alternative sentence 125, 128, 134
alternative relationship 127, 130
annotative sentence 32, 33, 34

"*bié shuō... lián—yě...*" sentence 84, 110, 111, 113, 114, 115
"*bùdàn... lián—yě...*" sentence 84, 96, 97, 98, 99, 104, 105, 106, 107
"*bùdàn p, érqiě q*" 84, 89, 115
"*bùshì p, jiùshì q*" 117, 125, 126, 127, 129, 130, 139, 140, 141, 142, 143, 144, 145, 150

"*cóng yī p, jiù q*" 152, 161, 162, 163, 164, 165, 167, 168, 183
contrastive causality 93
contrastive sentence 32, 34
coordinate complex sentence 1, 4, 5, 8, 12, 14, 18, 24, 35, 37; coordinate sentence 1, 26, 32, 33, 34
coordinate form 10, 22, 25, 32
coordinate marker 4
coordinate relationship 8, 12, 17, 20, 21, 24, 31, 34, 37, 89, 90, 91, 98, 106, 108
coordinate type in the broad sense i

downward (progression) 107, 108, 113, 115
downward progressive sentence 108, 115

"*gāng yī p, jiù q*" 152, 153, 155, 157, 158, 160, 161, 162, 163, 180, 183, 186

"*huòzhě p, huòzhě q*" 117, 119, 120, 125, 128, 129, 130, 139, 148, 149, 150

irrealis 71, 72, 120, 121, 127, 131, 133, 134, 150, 173, 181

"*jì p, yě q*" 1, 5, 7, 9, 34, 35
"*jì p, yòu q*" 1, 2, 3, 9, 13, 34, 35

"*lián—yě . . . biéshuō . . .*" sentence 84, 110, 113, 114, 115
linguistic form 1, 5, 10, 15, 18, 26, 65, 69, 84, 97, 100, 114, 117, 125
logic basis 3, 7, 12, 15, 20, 24, 25, 29, 30, 184

non-successive 81, 82

"*Ø p, yībiān q*" 37, 42, 58, 59, 60

"*p, jiēzhe q*" 65, 68, 69, 79
"*p, ránhòu q*" 65, 69, 71, 82
"*p, zhè cái q*" 79, 80, 82
progressive complex sentence 84, 86, 87, 115; progressive sentence 84, 86, 89, 91, 93, 98, 100, 105, 110
progressive marker 92

realis 71, 72, 122, 128, 131, 154, 163, 172, 180

"*shàngqiě p, hékuàng q*" 84, 100, 103, 105, 106, 107, 114, 115
successive complex sentence 65, 69, 77, 79, 81, 82; successive sentence 65, 82
successive form 82
successiveness 63, 65, 72, 73, 75, 77, 152
successive relationship 152, 183, 184

three-level progressive sentence 93, 94, 95

"*yàome p, yàome q*" 117, 130, 131, 132, 122, 139, 140, 140, 141, 143, 144, 145, 148, 149, 150
"*yě p, yě q*" 1, 15, 17, 34, 35

"*yībiān p, Ø q*" 37, 50, 58, 59
"*yībiān p, yībiān q*" 1, 18, 22, 24, 34, 35, 37, 43, 59, 61
"*yī fāngmiàn p, lìng yī fāngmiàn q*" 1, 25, 30, 31, 34, 35

"*yīmiàn p, yīmiàn q*" 1, 22, 24, 25, 31, 34, 35
"*yòu p, yòu q*" 1, 10, 12, 13, 17, 34, 35
"*zhème yī p, jiù q*" 152, 168, 169, 172, 183
"*zhǐyào yī p, jiù q*" 152, 175, 177, 178, 180

For Product Safety Concerns and Information please contact our EU representative GPSR@taylorandfrancis.com
Taylor & Francis Verlag GmbH, Kaufingerstraße 24, 80331 München, Germany